5/2000

THE
GREAT DANE

Model of Nobility

JILL SWEDLOW

 HOWELL BOOK HOUSE
NEW YORK

Howell Book House
1633 Broadway
New York, NY 10019-6785

Macmillan Publishing books may be purchased for business or sales promotional use.
For information please write: Special Markets Department, Macmillan Publishing
USA, 1633 Broadway, New York, NY 10019-6785.

MACMILLAN is a registered trademark of Macmillan, Inc.
Library of Congress Cataloging-in-Publication Data

    Swedlow, Jill, 1942–
        The Great Dane: Model of Nobility/Jill Swedlow.
           p.   cm.
        Includes bibliographical references (p. 211) and index.
        ISBN 0-87605-030-5
        1. Great Dane.   I. Title.
    SF429.G7S844   1998
    636.73—dc21   98–42647
                                     CIP

Manufactured in the United States of America

10 9 8 7 6 5 4 3 2 1

Cover and book design by George J. McKeon

Dedication

To Sandy Swedlow, whose love, encouragement and support has always been there for me.
And to Kathleen Twaits, my "other mother" and first mentor. She was dearly loved and is greatly missed.

(Diane Fleming)

Acknowledgments

Thank you to the following people who have, in some way, contributed to my knowledge and understanding of Great Danes and, by extension, to the production of this book.

Penny Twaits (Tallbrook Farms), a treasured friend who helped introduce me to the wonderful world of Great Danes.

The late Kathleen Twaits (Tallbrook Farms), my "other mother" and mentor, whom I loved and who is deeply missed.

Brucie Mitchell (von Raseac), with whom I've spent many long hours discussing breedings, both real and imaginary.

Lyn Richards, who was kind enough to lend her expertise on training, and who wrote the Obedience chapter.

Contents

Introduction

The intent of this book is to show what it's *really like* to share one's life with Great Danes, whether purely as companions or as the basis of an engrossing hobby. Although many Great Dane books exist, I've found very few that express the pros *and the cons* of owning the breed. Deciding to own, let alone breed and show, Great Danes is a decision never to be entered into without first being fully informed. I hope this book will fill this need.

As of this writing, I have loved, lived with, bred and shown Great Danes for over 25 years. Eighteen of my Danes have become champions, and others will do the same in the years ahead.

My first Dane was purchased as a pet. At the time, my opinion of "dog shows" was low. Of course, I had never even attended a dog show, but I had already decided that they were stupid (famous last thoughts)! Marge Siers, from whom I purchased Phoenix, my first Dane, had a friend who was looking for a room-mate. Her name was Penny Twaits. Marge said that since we were both crazy, we'd probably get along great. She was right.

Penny and I moved in together. At the time I had Phoenix and a German Shepherd named Aaron. Penny brought with her Ch. Tallbrook Farm's Taly Overcup, a daughter of the legendary Ch. Sham's Sacradotes and Ch. Thendara Henriette Keppen. Penny's mother was Kathleen Twaits, who with partner Jackie White, owned the well-known, highly successful Tallbrook Farms kennel. Under the circumstances, it didn't take long to change my opinion of dog shows! I couldn't wait to start showing Phoenix and coaxed

Penny into traveling two hours with me to my first match and handling for me.

My first show was the Great Dane Club of California's Specialty. I remember especially one dog who walked into the ring and gleamed like a jewel. He immediately caught my untrained eye and I fell in love. His name was Ch. Von Raseac's Great Caesar's Quote. I think that this was the moment that I knew I was hooked on showing and breeding Great Danes forevermore.

Phoenix lacked the necessary endowments to be a successful show dog, and I wanted to show, so the search began. My first attempt to find a show dog began with the classified section of *Dog World* magazine. I found an ad for a litter sired by a dog who was then the top winner in the United States. Naively, I assumed that the puppies would also grow to be top winners. Stupid me. I bought a bitch puppy from this litter and managed to do absolutely *everything* wrong! The breeders persuaded me to leave this pup with them until the upcoming Futurity, flying back to attend this show and then bring her home. She was just two weeks old when I bought her sight unseen. When I finally *did* get a couple pictures of her, I showed them to everyone I knew. They weren't terrible, but they weren't great either. I guess no one said so because I was already so committed to this purchase.

In any case, the puppy was five months old when I first laid eyes on her. I knew then that she was awful but immediately managed to sublimate the thought. Her social skills matched her confor-mation too. The breeders brought her into my house, and it was obvious she'd never even been indoors before; she was a nervous wreck. I wanted her to sleep in my room with me, but she was so unhappy that I finally took her back outdoors to her pen and doghouse so I could get some sleep. Naturally she did nothing at the Futurity.

When I arrived home with her and took her to her first match, *everyone* came over to see the daughter of the famous champion. I kind of won-dered why no one said anything about her. (To the uninitiated, this is the kindest way to express one's opinion of a really ugly dog.) Today I look at her pictures and the only redeeming quality I can find is that she had a very pretty head, if one could get past the headlight-yellow eyes! Her temperament was nothing to brag about, either. She'd lie under my chair at the matches and try to make a meal of any dog that walked by. It was not fun, to say the least.

Even so, I loved her and was devastated when my vet diagnosed a bad limp as possible bone can-cer. I knew that if I were the breeder, I'd want to know about it, so I called them and told them what we feared. The husband (who, incidentally, was also a veterinarian) had a cruelly sarcastic response to the bad news. "Oh well," he said, "you can always cut her leg off and breed her." As it turned out, it wasn't cancer. One night the bitch got out and was found dead the next morning, the victim of a hit-and-run driver. In spite of her numerous short-comings, my heart was nonetheless broken at her loss and the circumstances of it.

My real start was with the purchase of a bitch, Homewood Country Sunshine (Ch. Grenadilla's Bit'O Tallbrook ex Polldane's Fame of Bogart) from Barbara Hutton of Homewood Danes. Although a couple of her littermates finished their championships, Sunnie did not. She was big boned with a decent head; long, lovely neck; and excellent front, shoulder and topline. She had a good temperament and a good pedigree. On the strength of these assets, Barbara and I decided to breed her.

The first breeding and resultant whelping was perhaps the most stressful experience I'd ever had. On the morning the litter arrived, I got out of bed and immediately stepped barefoot on something that resembled the black skull of a crow with some black, stringy tissue attached to it. We later decided that these strange objects must be the remains of partially reabsorbed puppies. When the fully formed puppies finally began to appear, most were stillborn. Two dogs and a bitch survived. The bitch, Sunnyside Heather, was lovely and showed great promise, but she was not destined for the show ring.

From a repeat breeding came Ch. Sunnyside Daffodil, my first champion. I also kept (having taken her back from a home that couldn't keep her) Daffi's sister, Homewood Amber. Amber did some winning, but she hated the ring and so was retired. She and Daffi were both lovely and sound with excellent temperaments, who passed on their qualities to their offspring. Amber lived to age ten and Daffodil to nine.

In 1998 I was approved by the AKC to judge Great Danes. My hope is that by judging this wonderful breed, I can contribute more than I ever could within my limited breeding program. I am always interested in helping new Dane owners with any questions or problems they may have. Authoring this book, like judging, is a way to give back to a lifestyle that has given me so much.

CHAPTER 1

Are You Sure You Want a Great Dane?

There are many dog breeds from which to choose the one that is right for you. No breed is perfect for everyone and Great Danes are no exception. Just because someone thinks they want one is not reason enough to own one. In many cases, the beauty and size of this dog is its first attraction. I know it was for me. As a child I would admire a photo of a Dane with its forelegs resting on its owner's shoulders and its head towering over the owner's head in one of my dog books. I thought that it would really be fun to own such a huge dog. My parents, however, had other ideas, and since they paid the bills, they made the rules. Years later, when I was married, I finally had my first Dane, a rescue dog named Huey. At that time I wasn't really "into" dogs, and when we moved to California, Huey was placed with some good friends in Idaho.

A year later (1972) I purchased another Great Dane, Phoenix. He was a pick puppy from a bitch co-owned by Marge Siers of Bringold Great Danes. Herb and Marge Siers were veteran Great Dane breeders and Herb was a well-known handler. As I got to know Phoenix, I realized what a very special breed this was in terms of temperament. Calm, loving and silly, Phoenix made a Dane owner of me for life.

Sweet and wonderful as they are, Great Danes have their drawbacks, as do all breeds. First on the list is the normally short life span. Six to seven years is probably on the high end of average, although there certainly are many exceptions. My Kiwi was fortunate enough to celebrate her twelfth birthday on February 15, 1993. The following June, it was time to help her out of the pain of kidney failure. Her grandmother, Ch. Temple Dell's Sarah Davis, also lived to age twelve. Happily many of my Danes have reached ages eight, nine and ten. Longevity is inherited, and it pays to look for this when purchasing a puppy.

Since Danes don't usually live as long as dogs of smaller breeds, there must be some causes for their early deaths. Unfortunately it seems as though Great Danes have more than their share of health problems. (Health and diseases are considered in greater detail in chapter 6, "Keeping Your Great Dane Happy and Healthy.") Bloat, or gastric torsion, is probably one of the most common causes of death in Great Danes. Bloat does not usually occur in dogs under five years of age, but I co-bred a pup who had bloated and had surgery at less than five months! Fortunately, this is the exception.

Hypertrophic Osteodystrophy (HOD) is a disease that affects puppies, usually from around four to ten months, during the fastest period of growth. The cause is as yet unknown, and many vets don't even recognize it when presented. With early detection, treatment is usually successful.

Wobblers syndrome, or spondylolithesis, is a disease of the nervous system that causes the dog to have problems walking. There are several degrees of severity to this problem. Some dogs can live long lives with it; others must be euthanized at a young age.

Heart problems are quite common in the breed. Most heart problems do not affect the dog until age three or four or older. Some can be managed, some cannot.

Cancer is one of the most common causes of death in dogs, and Great Danes are possibly more prone to it than most—especially bone cancer (osteosarcoma). Fibrosarcoma and lymphosarcoma are also causes of death in Danes.

Many of the problems mentioned here are related to the extremely rapid growth that Danes experience. Stop and think that these dogs must achieve the equivalent growth in one year as a human adolescent experiences in eighteen! If anything small goes wrong with the metabolism or assimilation of nutrients during this very sensitive period, it's going to show up in the skeleton. Many of these problems can be managed or prevented with proper nutrition and all the elements for growth in the proper balance, effectively slowing the growth rate.

CAN YOU HANDLE THE "DEMOLITION FACTOR?"

"But we were only gone for an hour!" you exclaim as you take in the pile of fluff that used to be your sofa, or the shavings all over the floor that were once a chair. A teething Dane puppy can do a lot of damage in a short time. You must be prepared to prevent such disasters and to laugh them off when they do happen!

If you're the kind of person who must have an orderly house and a perfect yard, don't buy a Dane! Although most Danes are not destructive, when they do decide to taste the walls or munch on the stereo, those big mouths do BIG damage! If we could channel the digging power of a Great Dane, perhaps we could rent them to landscaping companies to plant entire gardens!

So, up to now all you've heard is negativity, and you're probably wondering why anyone would want a Great Dane if it can be so much trouble. There are very few books that will candidly detail the downside to the breed of interest. The fact is that *all* dog breeds have their own particular health/temperament problems. It's just difficult to find literature or people who will honestly show both sides of the coin.

Why do I own Danes? First and foremost, the joy and love they give more than makes up for the heartache of losing one. There is something wonderful about being able to barely get your arms around one of these big guys and hug them hard!

They're truly people dogs. They are house dogs who are happy to lie in front of the fire (or walk into it if they thought I needed them to do so) and be with those they love come what may. While that sounds like most breeds, there's more—lots more. Danes like to back up to people and rest their awesome rears in a selected lap. Danes can demonstrate their loving natures by just leaning against their human friends, rather than leaping and jumping and making a general nuisance of themselves. My Danes like to get a visitor between them and lean against the person until escape is impossible. Danes make great wall-to-wall carpets if there are enough of them. (With five, I've sometimes had trouble walking across the room). They are normally fearless guards; however, as soon as they know that an unfamiliar person is allowed in, the leaning game starts. Danes are very clean in the house. Most puppies can be housebroken in record time, some even before they've left for their new homes! Even with five adult Danes in my house, when they're all sleeping I hardly know they're around.

It's almost impossible to put into words what it's like to live with a Great Dane. These are just very special dogs and it would be necessary to experience Danes to understand. There's really no other way.

The beauty of these dogs is found in no other breed. When I watch my dogs gallop at full speed around my property up the back hill, ears alertly forward, heads held high, it simply takes my breath away. Then, in the next minute they're rolling on the grass inviting me to play with them or to scratch their huge chests. Some of mine "talk." They "sing" or chirrup like birds—usually while showing me their newest "stuffie." There truly is nothing like a Dane!

CHAPTER 2

The Great Dane's Ancestry

There is little doubt that Great Danes are an ancient breed. Evidence of Danelike dogs has been found among the excavations of ancient Assyrian artifacts. The Assyrian culture was advanced and active in trade with other countries. It is thought that perhaps their dogs were also included in some of the exported goods, as their likeness has also shown up in the artifacts of the ancient Romans and Greeks. There is a Grecian coin in the Royal Museum at Munich, which dates from the fifth century B.C. It depicts a likeness of a dog that greatly resembles the Great Dane of today.

The Mastiff, Greyhound and Irish Wolfhound have all been credited as more recent ancestors of the Great Dane as we know him today. The evidence for Greyhound ancestry is apparent in the merle coloration associated with the harlequin pattern seen in the breed today. According to Ernest Hart in his book *This Is the Great Dane* (Neptune City, NJ: IFH Publications, 1967).

> *. . . for the patchy dark-on-a-white-ground coloring of the harlequin variety, is a pattern derived from the Greyhound breeds through the Egyptian Greyhound, a direct descendent of the prototype dog, Canis Familiaris Leineri. The early Dane was also sometimes referred to as the "Tiger" dog, which again promoted controversy since some authorities claim the name was derived from the striped effect of brindling and others (particularly German breed historians) see the harlequin factor as the reason for the "Tiger" title.*

Because there was no "color code" in breeding in those days, there was a veritable rainbow of colors to be found in these dogs. Fawn and blue, blue, brindle and the classical black-and-white harlequin pattern abounded. The recessive blue color was widespread. There were interesting color patterns produced by a good deal of white, which was present in fawn and brindle as well as harlequin and black. This common extension of white led to German breeders disallowing the breeding of *harlequins,* or dogs with a predominance of white, to fawns or brindles so that the white was eventually bred out, with the exception of the occasional white mark on the chest or toes that we see today.

Germany is considered the most influential country behind the modern Great Dane, with England a close second. No one seems to know how this huge dog came to be called Great Dane, as there's no evidence he was ever popular in Denmark. In Germany he was known as *Deutsche Dogge.* The early German Danes were huge and coarse in appearance. More like the Mastiff than the present day Great Danes.

The early Great Dane was a large and powerful hunting hound, used as an effective war dog, guard and hunter of wild boar. The forests of Germany abounded with great numbers of wild boar, and large hunts were a common occurrence. Ears were cropped extremely short to prevent injury as the dog ran through heavy brush and to prevent damage from the razor-sharp tusks of the boar. Today the tradition of ear cropping continues in America and other countries where it isn't outlawed. The length has increased dramatically and gives a noble look to the head. However, it is *not* necessary to crop ears in order to show or otherwise enjoy a Dane.

In 1857, the first record of a Great Dane existing in the United States was when Mr. Francis

Butler shipped his harlequin named Prince from New York to London. Prince was shown in England, and a photo of him and his master appeared in the *Illustrated News.* Having seen this publication, Queen Victoria expressed an interest in seeing the dog.

The first time Great Danes were shown in the U.S. was in 1877 at the Philadelphia Grand National Show. They were then shown under the name of *Siberian,* or *Ulm dogs.* The Westminster Kennel Club offered a class for "Siberian" dogs in 1887.

The next notable show that included classes for Great Danes was held at the American Institute building in New York. Here the uncontrollable aggression of the breed was seen by all. Fights broke out both among the Danes and the other breeds in attendance. Because of this they were barred from further showing in this country. Seven years later, in 1888, they were once again allowed into an American show ring.

The Danes of the past *were* fierce and aggressive and had a temperament very different from the "gentle giant" we know today. The temperament of these early Danes, imported directly from Germany, was so aggressive as to be almost unmanageable. Their use as hunting dogs, war dogs and guard dogs required this type of temperament. It is a great tribute to the early American breeders to note the tremendous improvement in temperament within about 20 years of the first imports. This was achieved without losing the desired guarding behavior exhibited today by the modern Great Dane.

Today they are basically the most gentle of dogs. They should be devoted to their families and willing to accept into their homes anyone welcomed by their owners. In most cases this is the reality. However, the genes that cause the aggression and shyness do occasionally crop up. It is because of this that breeders must consistently select their breeding stock for *good* temperament. Keep this in mind when you begin your own search for a dog, whether for a pet or a breeding/show dog.

CHAPTER 3

Official Standard for the Great Dane

A breed Standard is like a blueprint. It is what the *Great Dane Club of America* (GDCA), the parent club for the breed in the United States, requires for a perfect specimen. Because there is no perfection in nature, breeders can only strive toward this goal. Occasionally a breeder produces a dog that comes *very* close, and if all goes well for such a dog, history accords it greatness. Only the GDCA has the authority to change the Great Dane Standard. When changes in the Standard *are* made, the action is only with the full authority of the parent club.

For anyone seriously interested in Great Danes, it is *imperative* for both the novice and the long-established enthusiast to fully comprehend the Standard and carry a mental picture of the perfect Great Dane. As a veteran or a budding fancier, you must study the Standard over and over. It is the *only* acceptable ideal of the breed toward which to strive, no matter what your own opinion of it or your own personal tastes may be.

A novice cannot expect to fully understand the breed Standard early in his association with the Dane, even if he has memorized it. Understanding what this blueprint for a Great Dane truly means takes many years of dedication and study. If you're new to the breed and just starting out with your first show puppy, ask the breeder from whom you purchased your pup to help you understand the language. To start with, it is important that you know the parts of the dog as shown on the following page.

Very probably, by the time this book is published, there will be a sixth showable color added to this Standard. It will be the *mantle* pattern found in the harlequin gene pool. This is basically a black Dane with four white stockings, perhaps a face and belly blaze, and a white chest and collar. It was once referred to as *Boston* markings, since it is the same pattern seen in the Boston Terrier.

In the section that follows, note that the breed Standard appears in Roman, while the author's interpretation is printed in italics.

A pleasing outline as shown on this harlequin is essential to the overall picture of a correctly formed Great Dane.

OFFICIAL STANDARD FOR THE GREAT DANE

GENERAL APPEARANCE—The Great Dane combines, in its regal appearance, dignity, strength and elegance with great size and a powerful, well-formed, smoothly muscled body. It is one of the giant working breeds, but is unique in that its general conformation must be so well-balanced that it never appears clumsy, and shall move with a long reach and powerful drive. It is always a unit—the Apollo of dogs. A Great Dane must be spirited, courageous, never timid; always friendly and dependable. This physical and mental combination is the characteristic which gives the Great Dane the majesty possessed by no other breed. It is particularly true of this breed that there is an impression of great masculinity in dogs, as compared to an impression of femininity in bitches. Lack of true Dane breed type, as defined in this Standard, is a serious fault.

The preceding paragraph describes the overall appearance and desired temperament of the Great Dane. It should go without saying that this is going to be a VERY LARGE dog indeed. You should keep this in mind before choosing this breed.

It is further stated that "A Great Dane must be spirited, courageous, never timid; always friendly and dependable." This is very important in a breed of this size, which once was extremely aggressive. It's even more important to keep this in mind when selecting a puppy. Reject the puppy that shies away from you or slinks off into a corner

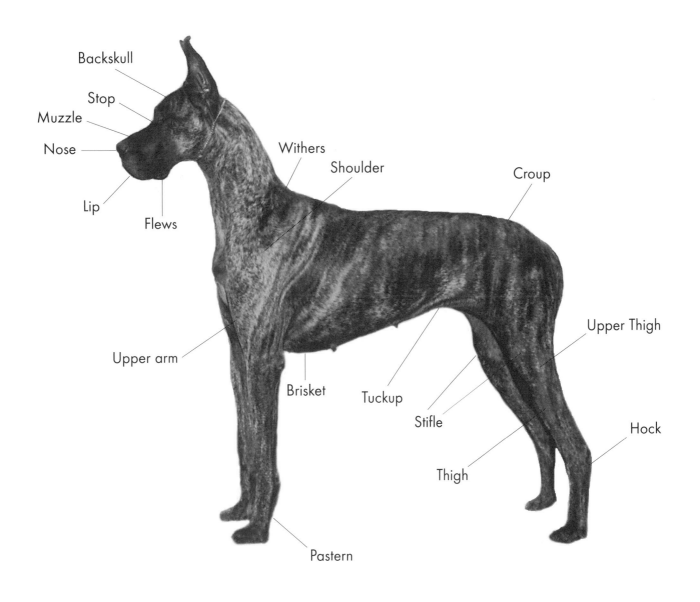

External anatomy of the Great Dane. (Callea)

and tries to hide. Also rule out the puppy that throws himself against your chest and tries to bite your chin! A Great
Dane should greet strangers in a friendly manner with a
wagging tail. An adult Great Dane should bark (or not)
when it hears the doorbell and then happily allow the visitor to enter the house once his owner has said it's okay.

When evaluating temperament, look for a dog that is
confident, friendly and outgoing. A Great Dane with a
sound temperament will stand quietly and allow itself to be
examined, while still maintaining that regal attitude. The
dog should exhibit interest in everything around him, while
being willing to take direction from his handler.

SIZE, PROPORTION, SUBSTANCE—The male
should appear more massive throughout than the
bitch, with larger frame and heavier bone. In the
ratio between length and height, the Great Dane
should be square. In bitches, a somewhat longer body
is permissible, providing she is well proportioned to
her height. Coarseness or lack of substance are
equally undesirable. The male shall not be less than
thirty inches at the shoulders, but it is preferable that
he be thirty-two inches or more, providing he is
well-proportioned to his height. The female shall not
be less than twenty-eight inches at the shoulders, but
it is preferable that she be thirty inches or more, providing she is well-proportioned to her height. Danes
under minimum height must be disqualified.

The preceding paragraph basically means that a Great
Dane should resemble neither a Mastiff nor a Greyhound.
Males should appear distinctly more masculine and be taller
than bitches. Substance means sufficiency of bone, frame
size and muscle as to give the impression of great size
without being coarse.

Although it is possible to have a lovely male specimen
that only stands thirty inches at the shoulder, it's very
unlikely that this dog will ever finish his championship.

Masculinity and femininity are evident in this study of
Ch. Sandale Wyne's Razz-Ma-Tazz, owned by George and
Georgia Williams and Sue Wyne (left) and his daughter
Smoky Bays Red Hot Pepper, owned by Tracie Fellows and
M. Cope. (Gail Painter)

Males that will become show dogs should be a minimum of
thirty-two inches tall and preferably thirty-four inches or
more. The same goes for a bitch, although it is easier for a
smaller bitch to finish her championship than a smaller
male.

HEAD—The head shall be rectangular, long, distinguished, expressive, finely chiseled, especially below the eyes. Seen from the side, the Dane's forehead must be sharply set off from the bridge of the nose (a strongly pronounced stop). The plane of the skull and the plane of the muzzle must be straight and parallel to one another. The skull plane under and to the inner point of the eye must slope without any bony protuberance in a smooth line to a full square jaw with a deep muzzle (fluttering lips are undesirable). The masculinity of the male is very pronounced in structural appearance of the head. The bitch's head is more delicately formed. Seen from the top, the skull should have parallel sides and the bridge of the nose should be as broad as possible. The cheek muscles should not be prominent. The length from the tip of the nose to the center of the stop should be equal to the length from the center of the stop to the rear of the slightly developed occiput. The head should be angular from all sides and should have flat planes with dimensions in proportion to the size of the Dane. Whiskers may be trimmed or left natural.

You should be able to positively identify a breed by its head. The head is very important in the Great Dane, as it gives this breed its distinguished appearance and regal attitude. You should be able to ascertain the sex of the dog from seeing its head. It has been said that the head should appear to be two bricks of equal length laid one on top of the other. A short muzzle or round, wide skull tends to make a Great Dane resemble a Mastiff. Conversely, a long, narrow nose bridge with no indentation (stop) when viewed from the side and a narrow back skull are reminiscent of a Greyhound.

EYES—Shall be medium size, deep-set, and dark, with a lively intelligent expression. The eyelids are

Here is an example of a correct, masculine head modeled by Ch. Homewood Sensation. There is a little too much loose skin under the neck, but the neck itself is long and pleasing. (Jill Swedlow)

almond-shaped and relatively tight, with well-developed brows. Haws and Mongolian eyes are serious faults. In harlequins, the eyes should be dark; light-colored eyes, eyes of different colors and walleyes are permitted but not desirable.

Whereas eye color has no impact on the health of the eye, a darker eye is most pleasing. Although the Standard makes no distinction, all dogs' eyes have haws. The objection is to prominent haws, which can make eyes more prone to infections and are, of course, quite unsightly. With a prominent haw, the lower lid droops and the red membranes underneath it are apparent. A Mongolian eye is exaggeratedly slanted. It should be noted here that a blue coat, being a dilute gene, and a dark brown eye will rarely appear in the same dog. The dilute attribute of this gene affects all color and pigment of the individual. A blue Dane's eye

This headstudy of Sunnyside Kiwi shows the correct planes and long, elegant head typical of the bitch. Her eyes are dark, of good size and well placed. Her ear set could be slightly higher, and the lip is just a bit too long. (Jill Swedlow)

Here is another lovely headstudy showing correct eyes as described in the Standard. (Dee Dee Murry)

color may range from very pale champagne to a medium light brown.

EARS—Shall be high-set, medium in size and of moderate thickness, folded forward close to the cheek. The top line of the folded ear should be level with the skull. If cropped, the ear length is in proportion to the size of the head and the ears are carried uniformly erect.

It is widely believed that it is necessary to crop a Great Dane's ears in order for it to be shown. This is not now, nor has it ever been, true in the United States. However, because most American-bred Great Danes' ears are cropped, breeders have not actively selected for the smaller, high-set ear. If left uncropped, many Dane ears tend to hang houndlike—low-set, very large and

pendulous. This is not an attractive look and is much out of character with the breed.

With a high-set ear, the bases are set fairly close together on top of the dog's head.

Cropping ears precludes the development of hematomas (blood blisters in the ear) and makes ears less prone to infection. Cropping also gives a much more regal appearance and is preferred by most exhibitors. However, each year we see more uncropped dogs entering the show ring. (More on the pros and cons of cropping later.)

NOSE—Shall be black, except in the blue Dane, where it is a dark blue-black. A black-spotted nose is

Correct ears on a seven-month-old puppy. (Ginette Desrosiers)

permitted on the harlequin; a pink-colored nose is not desirable. A split nose is a disqualification.

A split nose is a nose with a cleft from the top to the bottom. Most experienced Great Dane people have never seen one.

TEETH—Shall be strong, well-developed, clean and with full dentition. The incisors of the lower jaw touch very lightly the bottoms of the inner surface of the upper incisors (scissors bite). An undershot jaw is a very serious fault. Overshot or wry bites are serious faults. Even bites, misaligned or crowded incisors are minor faults.

Unless grossly malformed, an undershot *(lower incisors protruding beyond uppers) or* overshot *(upper incisors protruding beyond lowers) mouth should have no effect on the health or well-being of a Great Dane pet. Dogs do not really chew their food but tend to swallow or bolt it. A puppy with any of the mouth faults described in*

the Standard should not be considered as a show prospect. Even more important, a dog with a badly formed mouth should never be bred.

NECK, TOPLINE, BODY—The neck shall be firm, high-set, well-arched, long and muscular. From the nape, it should gradually broaden and flow smoothly into the withers. The neck underline should be clean. Withers shall slope smoothly into a short level back with a broad loin. The chest shall be broad, deep and well-muscled. The forechest should be well-developed without a pronounced sternum. The brisket extends to the elbow, with well-sprung ribs. The body underline should be tightly muscled with a well-defined tuckup. The croup should be broad and very slightly sloping. The tail should be set high and smoothly into the croup, but not quite level with the back, a continuation of the spine. The tail should be broad at the base, tapering uniformly down to the hock joint. At rest, the tail should fall straight. When excited or running, it may curve slightly, but never above the level of the back. A ring or hooked tail is a serious fault. A docked tail is a disqualification.

Basically this section calls for a long neck without excess skin hanging from the throat, as well as a length of back that is neither excessively long nor so short that smooth movement is not possible. The back should be level with a slight downward slope of the croup *(the area from the hips to the tail root). When viewed from the side, the* brisket *(chest) should be level with the elbows and should gently slope upward toward the hind legs, forming a trim waist (tuckup). If there is no waist, the dog is either not correct for this trait or is too fat. A wasp waist or extreme tuckup is also undesirable. When viewed from the front, the chest should not be extremely narrow, nor should there be large, bulging muscles on the shoulders. This fault is termed* loaded shoulders.

FOREQUARTERS—The forequarters, viewed from the side, shall be strong and muscular. The shoulder blade must be strong and sloping, forming, as near as possible, a right angle in its articulation with the upper arm. A line from the upper tip of the shoulder to the back of the elbow joint should be perpendicular. The ligaments and muscles holding the shoulder blade to the rib cage must be well-developed, firm and securely attached to prevent loose shoulders. The shoulder blade and the upper arm should be the same length. The elbow should be one-half the distance from the withers to the ground. The strong pasterns should slope slightly. The feet should be round and compact with well-arched toes, neither toeing in, toeing out, nor rolling to the inside or outside. The nails should be short, strong and as dark as possible, except that they may be lighter in harlequins. Dewclaws may or may not be removed.

When viewed from the side the shoulder blade (scapula) should form a 90-degree angle with the upper arm (humerus). There are three distinct portions of the foreleg; the shoulder blade begins at the base of the neck on the back and slopes forward to articulate (touch) with the upper arm. The upper arm then angles backward to form the elbow joint, which articulates with the lower foreleg. The foreleg drops straight to the ground. The angles formed by the scapula and the humerus (upper arm) are what form the angle of the forequarters. (This explanation is quite simplified but amply illustrates the point.) The degree of the angles here determines how far forward (reach) the dog can extend its forelegs. The straighter the angle, the greater the stress placed on the foreleg joints as these take the weight of the moving dog. A Great Dane with overly straight joints may be more prone to lameness and would exert more effort to cover the same amount of ground as a dog with a well-angulated front.

When viewed from the front, the feet should turn neither in nor out but should point straight ahead. The feet should appear catlike and rounded rather than oval in shape.

HINDQUARTERS—The hindquarters shall be strong, broad, muscular and well-angulated, with well let down hocks. Seen from the rear, the hock joints appear to be perfectly straight, turned neither toward the inside nor toward the outside. The rear feet should be round and compact, with well-arched toes, neither toeing in nor out. The nails should be short, strong and as dark as possible, except they may be lighter in harlequins. Wolf claws are a serious fault.

As in the forequarters, the hindquarter angles should also form a 90-degree angle that is composed of the pelvis and the femur (upper thigh). The lower point of the thigh (which some might refer to as the rear *knee) is the stifle joint. It is the rear legs that provide what is called the* drive *in the gait. Like the forequarters, the greater the angle, the greater the drive and the more effortlessly the dog can move. Although it is important that a dog have the correct angulation, it is also important that the dog be balanced. This means that if the dog has less angulation in the front, it is better that the rear angulation match so that the dog will move in a smooth, uniform manner.*

COAT—The coat shall be short, thick and clean with a smooth, glossy appearance.

Color, Markings and Patterns

BRINDLE—The base color shall be yellow gold and always brindled with strong black cross stripes in a chevron pattern. A black mask is preferred. Black should appear on the eye rims and eyebrows, and may appear on the ears and tail tip. The more intensive

A well-made body modeled here by Ch. Tydwind's Sail Maker, owned by Joy and Dennis DeGruccio. (Joan Ludwig)

the base color and the more distinct and even the brindling, the more preferred will be the color. Too much or too little brindling are equally undesirable. White markings at the chest and toes, black-fronted, dirty-colored brindles are not desirable.

FAWN—The color shall be yellow gold with a black mask. Black should appear on the eye rims and eyebrows, and may appear on the ears and tail tip. The deep yellow gold must always be given the preference. White markings at the chest and toes, black-fronted, dirty-colored fawns are not desirable.

BLUE—The color shall be a pure steel blue. White markings at the chest and toes are not desirable.

BLACK—The color shall be a glossy black. White markings at the chest and toes are not desirable.

The same model shows a good front...

...as well as a strong rear.

A well-made body modeled here by Ch. Tydwind's Sail Maker, owned by Joy and Dennis DeGruccio. (Joan Ludwig)

the base color and the more distinct and even the brindling, the more preferred will be the color. Too much or too little brindling are equally undesirable. White markings at the chest and toes, black-fronted, dirty-colored brindles are not desirable.

FAWN—The color shall be yellow gold with a black mask. Black should appear on the eye rims and eyebrows, and may appear on the ears and tail tip. The deep yellow gold must always be given the preference. White markings at the chest and toes, black-fronted, dirty-colored fawns are not desirable.

BLUE—The color shall be a pure steel blue. White markings at the chest and toes are not desirable.

BLACK—The color shall be a glossy black. White markings at the chest and toes are not desirable.

The same model shows a good front...

...as well as a strong rear.

©The American Kennel Club

©The American Kennel Club

©The American Kennel Club

©The American Kennel Club

HARLEQUIN—Base color shall be pure white with black torn patches irregularly and well-distributed over the entire body; a pure white neck is preferred. The black patches should never be large enough to give the appearance of a blanket, nor so small as to give a stippled or dappled effect. Eligible, but less desirable, are a few small gray patches, or a white base with single black hairs showing through, which tend to give a salt and pepper or dirty effect.

Any variance in color or markings as described above shall be faulted to the extent of the deviation. Any Great Dane which does not fall within the above color classifications must be disqualified.

For the family pet, color is basically immaterial. Just because a certain color is not competitive in the show ring is no reason that the dog wearing it cannot become a cherished family member. The only color that may carry some problems

is white. It is not uncommon for white (albino) dogs to be deaf and perhaps even blind. This can present a whole set of major training problems, and unless you are prepared to deal with this, it is better to avoid all-white Danes.

Finally, regarding color, at least one writer has cautioned that in his opinion, you should not even breed blue Danes because of their extensive skin problems. Many breeders of the blue color phase have said that although blues might be somewhat more prone to certain skin problems, they certainly are not as severely affected as to not be bred.

GAIT—The gait denotes strength and power with long, easy strides resulting in no tossing, rolling or bouncing of the topline or body. The backline shall appear level and parallel to the ground. The long reach should strike the ground below the nose while the head is carried forward. The powerful rear drive should be balanced to the reach. As speed increases, there is a natural tendency for the legs to converge toward the centerline of balance beneath the body. There should be no twisting in or out at the elbow or hock joints.

Just because a Great Dane is huge, it does not necessarily follow that it should be clumsy. A Dane that tends to fall down a great deal or lose its balance may have a health problem of some kind and should be seen by a vet without hesitation. An adult, romping Dane should appear sound and graceful. Even a young puppy should not appear overly clumsy.

Movement is the ultimate gauge of conformation. Although Great Danes are not considered to be the best movers among all dog breeds, they should exhibit a certain amount of grace and style when moving in the show ring. Admittedly, many poor movers win, but a dog that can move well will enjoy a great advantage in competition from a judge who truly understands the relationship between movement and conformation.

©The American Kennel Club

The harlequin color phase is familiar to all; less so is the mantle (right) which is recognized in Canada and soon (as this book goes to press) in the United States. (Walter J. Perkins)

TEMPERAMENT—The Great Dane must be spirited, courageous, always friendly and dependable, and never timid or aggressive.

Temperament is especially important in a breed the size of a Great Dane. A bite from this big guy can do tremendous damage, especially to a child! Although the breed, overall, deserves its nickname of Gentle Giant, there are some individual dogs that do not. This is why it is so important to buy from a reputable breeder who is willing to guarantee the temperament of his or her stock.

This trait is equally important for dogs that will be shown and bred. TEMPERAMENT IS INHERITED! Yes, temperament problems can stem from improper socialization and mistreatment. However, it's in the genes, and you should never breed or show a Dane that is shy or aggressive.

Disqualifications

Danes under minimum height.

Split nose. Docked tail.

Any color other than those described under "Color, Markings and Patterns."

Approved September 11, 1990
Effective October 30, 1990

When evaluating dogs as potential show/breeding animals, the disqualifications must be considered. Perhaps the only exception might be color patterns, such as some unshowable colors that are part of the harlequin gene pool.

In addition to the breed-specific disqualifications, remember that dogs may be disqualified from showing in AKC conformation events if they are altered, are vicious, have been cosmetically altered in some manner, and in the case of males, have only one or no descended testicle(s).

None of the disqualifications (with probably the exception of poor temperament) disqualify any Great Dane from becoming a beloved member of the family!

© Hadley James

CHAPTER 4

Finding the Right Great Dane for You

Having decided that no matter the drawbacks, the Great Dane is the breed for you, how do you go about finding that special puppy (or adult)? Whether you're looking for a pet or a show dog, a puppy or adult, it would be wise to start at a dog show, preferably a *Specialty*. A Specialty is a show for only one breed, put on by a club for that breed. Specialties often draw the best dogs in the local area, and sometimes even dogs from outside the area. (See the appendix for how to locate shows.) Take a folding chair, an umbrella and a lunch; buy a show catalog; and sit and watch. You'll probably start noticing certain dogs that appeal to you. If so, note the handler's armband number and look the dog up in the catalog. The catalog lists the registered name, sire, dam, breeder, owner and (sometimes) the handler of every dog entered. Mark those you like and after the dog has left the ring, approach the owner or handler and ask questions on the availability of puppies/dogs related to this dog. Be sure to ask if this is a good time to talk. Exhibitors are often going right back into the ring with another dog and don't have time to talk right then. Later most people will be happy to talk to you. You might find that the dogs that appeal to you are somehow related and you've found a place to start looking for your puppy.

A visit to a local dog show is wise for anyone who wants to learn more about a breed. The prospective Great Dane owner can learn a great deal just by observing the dogs and the judging.

color. If you want a dog with show potential, familiarize yourself as thoroughly as you can with the Great Dane Standard. Although it takes years of practical experience to understand the Standard, you can still develop a general idea of what to look for and what to avoid.

If the object of your search is to be strictly a pet, remember that there is nothing wrong with a pet-quality Dane puppy. The *pet* designation only means that the breeder doesn't consider that this individual will have the outstanding conformation necessary to become a champion. It is, however, perfectly suited as a beautiful pet that will enjoy a long, happy life with its new family.

Another excellent way to familiarize yourself with different dogs from different kennels is to subscribe to the *Great Dane Reporter* (see Bibliography). Often you will see litters advertised, and most breeders are happy to send videos and pedigrees on request.

Know which color you want, as few breeders work with all five colors. Ordinarily, those who breed fawn also breed brindle. Breeders of blacks often breed blues. Harlequin breeders tend to specialize, but some will also breed blacks. Each color should be bred only to certain other colors (as per the Great Dane Club of America Code of Ethics, Appendix B). Thus, if you want a harlequin, you must find Dane breeders who specialize in this

Ch. Sunnyside Daffodil was the only member of her litter to become a champion. (Jill Swedlow)

Daffi's littermate, Homewood Bronson, was sold as a pet to a loving home. This handsome Dane is an example of the fact that small imperfections make the difference between pets and show dogs from the same litter. (Jill Swedlow)

and longevity have been considered as well as physical conformation. You cannot do better than to purchase your pet puppy from such a litter.

Now that you've attended a few shows, studied the Standard, read books and magazines and have a pretty good idea of where you want to purchase your puppy, the next step is to make an appointment with the breeder to see some Danes. On your visit, make a point of interacting with the dam (or future dam) of the litter to assess her temperament. If you've made friends in the breed, it is a good idea to ask them about the reputation of your breeder of choice and his or her dogs. A reputable breeder has nothing to hide.

How can you be sure you are looking at good temperament? An adult Dane should happily greet

Most breeders have been approached by people who say they want a show-quality dog but don't want to show. I think this might be due to people just not realizing the difference. Few breeders are going to place top show prospects in homes where the dogs will never be seen again. If you don't intend to show, please don't feel you must settle for a "reject" because you're paying less for a pet-quality puppy. The pet puppy is from the same litter that was carefully planned by the breeder and that hopefully contains future champions. Health

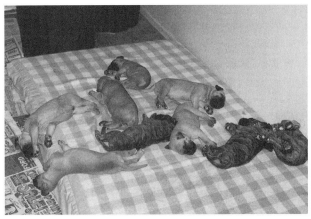

This litter was bred with health, temperament and improved conformation as the major priorities. At this age most people, even experts, could not predict which dogs would grow up to be show prospects and which would be pets. (Jill Swedlow)

strangers to his home once his owner has said it's OK. Mine typically run to the door and bark, then, once I've allowed the visitor inside, they vie with each other to see who can lean on the newcomer first and get the most attention. If the visitor sits down, it's not uncommon for him to suddenly find a Great Dane bottom planted in his lap! My Poppy is especially good at this. Actually, she prefers to drape her entire body across the caller's lap and then melt onto the lucky recipient! This is exactly the temperament you want to see in the parents of your future puppy. A Great Dane is typically friendly and outgoing, never hanging back or fearful, or worse, threatening. Although this last is certainly not the predominant temperament in the breed, temperament problems do exist. Be sure the puppy you purchase is from a background of happy, well-adjusted Danes. *Temperament is inherited.*

When you meet and talk to the breeder, be sure to ask about what, if any, guarantees she offers with the purchase of a puppy. Most guarantee health and temperament with either a replacement puppy or a full or partial refund of the purchase price. A breeder unwilling to guarantee these things might not be the best person to buy from. I always guarantee these things, but I retain the option of exactly what I want to do about replacement or full or partial refund. I've had a couple experiences with people who seemed at the time of sale to be good homes and turned out not to be. As a result, I establish these ground rules up front.

A caring breeder will not lose interest in a puppy once the check is cashed. I tell all my puppy people to call me as soon as they get home with the puppy and let me know how the puppy is doing.

Before they take the puppy, they are instructed in what to do to prepare for their new family member. They are provided with extensive instructions as to what the pup has been eating, care, vaccines and wormings and aftercare of the cropped ears. These instructions also include descriptions of common problems of health, especially growth in the Great Dane. I insist that they call me at any time of the day or night if they have a problem. I'm always available to answer questions or to help with ear taping. My contract promises that I will take the puppy back at any age or help to find the right home, should this become necessary. Concerned breeders try to keep track of every dog they've bred until the day it dies. If a breeder does this, you can feel safe in purchasing from him or her.

INTERVIEWING THE BREEDER

Much has been written about the relationship between breeders and those who purchase their puppies. However, precious little has appeared that assists the puppy buyer in knowing when he's found the right breeder. Too many newcomers to Great Danes have sad stories to tell about purchasing puppies from breeders they thought could be trusted and ending up with puppies with serious health or temperament problems. Now these things can and do occur in the best of breedings. The main complaint, however, was that the breeder who was so helpful before the sale either became unavailable or blamed the owner for the problem after the check cleared.

So, for all of the novices hoping to buy a healthy puppy with a great temperament from a breeder who will guarantee the puppy and be there as a mentor, here are some of the things you must know and questions you must ask.

First, just because a breeder owns, breeds and heavily advertises winning Danes, don't assume that these are necessarily good dogs. Don't assume that these peoples' dogs must be of the best quality, are glowing with health and have perfect temperament. On the other hand, don't assume that they aren't. The key will be in the answers to the questions you ask and the observations you make.

When you, as a prospective puppy buyer, first meet a breeder, you should expect the breeder to question you in minute detail about how you plan to house the puppy, whether you have a fenced yard, if you can afford emergency bloat surgery and if you understand the special issues in owning a giant dog. If the breeder doesn't ask these questions, look elsewhere. But in turn, you are not out of line to question the breeder.

1. The first thing I'd want to know is what, if any, health-screening tests have been performed on the parents of the litter. If you are told, "Oh, I don't need to health check because my dogs don't have any problems," *run,* don't walk, to the nearest exit. I know this sounds ludicrous, but there are still too many very well-known breeders who don't even x-ray hips on their breeding stock because they claim they have no problems! One breeder I know asserted, "I'd know by the movement if my dogs had hip dysplasia." This is simply not so. I've known three dogs personally, all known for their superior movement, that could not pass their OFA

(Orthopedic Foundation for Animals) evaluations. The breeder who doesn't x-ray doesn't know—period. To add to the confusion, some films that get sent to OFA come back dysplastic the first time and normal the second. Mistakes can occur in all phases of the endeavor. But hip x-ray is still the best defense we have, and whether or not the films are actually sent to OFA, there should at least be a note verifying the evaluation by a board-certified radiologist.

By now you probably realize that hip evaluation is a mandatory test to be done prior to breeding. If a breeder doesn't do this, take it as a red flag and look elsewhere for your puppy. The other evaluation I consider mandatory is thyroid testing. Besides certifying hips, OFA now certifies thyroid levels and has a protocol in place for doing this procedure. At the very least, a screening thyroid should be done. The thyroid is a difficult function to test, and results should be sent to the laboratories that are properly set up for this. I believe that OFA accepts results from only a couple of labs at the present time.

Testing for thyroid function in Great Danes is especially important because it is often found to be abnormal in the breed. In addition, hormones from the thyroid gland control the entire endocrine system, thus affecting everything from skin condition to reproductive to autoimmune problems.

At a minimum, a breeder should test for normal hips and thyroid function. There are other problems that also affect Great Danes. One, *von*

Willebrand's disease (VWD), is a blood disorder that greatly increases clotting time. The disease has been reported in a number of totally unrelated breeds. A simple, easy-to-screen blood test reveals the presence of VWD. Many Dane breeders also test for elbow dysplasia, cardiac soundness and juvenile cataracts.

Occasionally a Dane will be diagnosed with juvenile cataracts. Although in many breeds this is a serious health problem, often causing blindness, the question in Danes remains the same: Do they live long enough to ever be bothered by cataracts even if they have them? In any case, because cataracts do occur in Danes, the only way to control them is to screen for them.

Although cardiomyopathy is a problem in the breed, it's a difficult condition to evaluate. Obviously if a dog is suffering from it, the test will show it. However, when I had one of my bitches checked, I was told that although she was healthy at the moment, she could show cardiomyopathy when tested in six more months.

2. So assuming that the breeder has at least had hip and thyroid screenings performed, ask for documentation. Anyone can say that their dogs have been screened. This might sound harsh, but an honest breeder should have no problem with showing you written certifications. If you note any hesitation on this issue, beware.

3. Now we come to a really touchy subject. Suppose that a breeder claims to perform screenings, can produce documentation, and

can prove that this documentation does reflect the results for that particular dog. Can it be shown that the dog on the documents and the dog in the flesh are one and the same? In other words, does the dog have any kind of permanent identification? Until recently, it never occurred to me that someone might test a healthy "ringer" to substitute for a dog that had previously failed the testing. In talking to the veterinarians who have done these screening tests, I've asked them how they verify that this is the actual dog it is purported to be. They've all told me that this is not possible unless the dog is identified with either a tattoo or a microchip. Due to a personal experience with this kind of fakery, in the future I plan to microchip and tattoo every puppy I breed at the time it is cropped.

Hopefully the day will soon come when the AKC will require permanent identification *prior* to registration. This will go a long way in protecting the integrity of the registry. While most breeders are scrupulously honest, infractions do occur and it is important to be aware of this. AKC has recently instituted a rule that states that unless a dog is permanently identified by either microchip or tattoo, its OFA number for hip evaluation cannot appear on its registration certificate. This is definitely a step in the right direction. Further, advances in DNA technology will make correct identification 100 percent foolproof.

4. In the matter of temperament, the Great Dane truly deserves its nickname, *Gentle Giant*.

Breeders have wrought miracles in temperament improvements since the first German imports. Back then the breed was so aggressive that it was banned from dog shows. Unfortunately, biting incidents by Danes seem to be increasing. Top show specimens with terrible temperaments continue to be bred. Some are from highly regarded families and are used at stud by well-known breeders. Why? I've given up trying to figure it out. I've always hoped that one of these dogs would take a really *big* bite out of the people who continue to breed him/her. Sadly, that would solve nothing.

Ask if the breeder will guarantee temperament on the puppies. You must see the dam (away from her litter, please) and, if he is available, the sire. Be sure to observe them under nonstressful circumstances. Believe me, this makes a big difference in making a true evaluation. However, there's a catch to this one. Temperament is not only a product of genetics, it is also heavily influenced by environment. An aggressive dog can be made more so by a timid owner who has no idea how to cope with his pushiness. A submissive dog could be turned into a fear biter by an abusive owner. Conversely the aggressive dog can become a reliable family companion and guard in the right hands, and the shy dog can be brought to its best by a competent owner.

Because control is relinquished once the dog leaves the breeder, *I do not* guarantee temperament in writing. For example, if I thought a problem had been caused or aggravated by the dog's treatment in its new home, there is no way I'd place another dog in that environment. Instead I would take back the dog, refund half or perhaps all (depending on the circumstances) of the purchase price, and consider the matter concluded. In one circumstance when we had a temperament problem in a dog that I knew had been properly raised and nurtured, I replaced the dog with a puppy from another (unrelated) litter. I make it clear in my contract that I have the final word in these cases. As a new buyer, you will need to go on your instinct here. If the breeder strikes you as being truly concerned with good temperament, then you're probably safe in going with her stock. Just don't fault her for failing to unconditionally guarantee this trait.

A responsible breeder knows the potential temperament of her puppies. Rely on her to help you pick the best temperament for your situation. A family with small children will do best with a puppy who is submissive enough to take direction willingly, but who is outgoing enough to romp and play happily with the kids. A dominant personality might best suit a single person or a family of adults only. In any case, a family must have the ability to properly train the dog, not the other way around.

5. OK, you've got the big stuff out of the way. The other questions are often dependent on exactly what quality of puppy you want. If you plan to show, you want to be reasonably sure that the puppy you get is truly of show quality. Ask the breeder about her recent successes in the ring. Hopefully you are familiar with

Once these puppies leave their birthplace, the breeder no longer has any real control over how well they will be socialized and trained. (Jill Swedlow)

Danes related to the litter and their breed quality. Ask how many of the puppies are already reserved. This is important if you're serious about a good show prospect. If most puppies are spoken for, perhaps you should consider waiting for another litter, where you could perhaps get first- or second-choice puppy. Be aware that in the case of an outstanding litter, there might not be a real "pick." One person might be looking for one set of traits, and another might choose something else, yet each puppy might have show potential.

Another advantage of waiting for another litter is more time to become acquainted with the breeder and the breeder with you. No breeder wants to sell a bona fide show prospect to someone who wants a "show" puppy but

has no intention of showing. Many people think that a pet-quality puppy is inferior. Not true. But don't be surprised if you have to prove your sincerity to the breeder, regardless of the quality you're looking for.

6. Obviously you want to see that the breeder's facilities are clean, well kept and free of odor. Although puppies tend to mess up as quickly as we clean up, there's no excuse for a house that reeks of urine and feces. Puppies should be clean, active and healthy looking. They should also readily approach visitors with interest and curiosity. If they hang back or slink away, this is not a good litter, or it hasn't been properly socialized. In any case, you would be wise to hang back and slink away yourself.

7. Ask if the breeder has a written contract. Read it thoroughly before you sign. Your puppy should come to you with the *blue slip*, which is actually the AKC individual registration application. Additionally the breeder should provide you with a four- or five-generation pedigree, a list of what the puppy has been eating, a feeding schedule, plus several days' supply of food. You should also receive a health record including all vaccines and wormings the puppy has had to date, as well as what is due next and when.

8. The breeder should extend as a minimum a forty-eight hour health guarantee and take the puppy back with a full refund if it is found to be ill by a veterinarian. Additionally, a breeder should be willing to take the dog back at any age if you can no longer keep it. These innocent

The conscientious breeder will try matching the right puppy to the right home. A more submissive temperament will be best with children. Children must also be taught how to properly interact with a puppy and should never be left unattended with the dog. (Colleen Leahy)

babies didn't ask to be born. The breeder is entirely responsible for their existence and well-being. A breeder who isn't willing to shoulder this responsibility shouldn't breed.

9. The breeder should actively encourage you to ask questions, call at any hour with any size problem and take an ongoing interest in the puppy once it's living in your home. Most breeders will be happy to do so.

And to my fellow breeders who are wondering, *Well, what about us? What about the times we've sold pups to people who seemed great who turned out terrible?* Read on—your turn comes next.

THE BREEDER'S TURN TO QUESTION YOU

You, too, must be ready for a barrage of questions, and some might be very personal. Most breeders want to know if you have a fenced-in yard. If you have children, the breeder will probably insist that they accompany you on your first visit. This is often a very reliable indicator of a home's suitability for a puppy. If the kids are wild and undisciplined, I won't sell them a puppy. Naughty children equal naughty puppy, and naughty puppies can do a *lot* of damage in a short time. If a puppy grows up undisciplined, it won't be pleasant to have around. If it's not pleasant to have around, it will either be exiled to the back yard or dumped at the first opportunity. Temperament may be inherited, but a lot can be done to hurt or hinder it through an inappropriate environment.

You may be asked about your yearly income. Bloat surgery alone can cost over $2,000. The breeder wants to know that this puppy will get the very best care, come what may.

Even someone involved in Danes for years as a breeder/exhibitor should not be surprised to be asked for references. I've had bad experiences from not checking references. Consider this sad story.

One puppy, "Ben," was purchased by a veteran breeder on the recommendation of a mutual friend. After asking the buyer to come see the puppy, or at least wait for snapshots, I told her on arrival that if she didn't like him for any reason to give him a few days' rest and return him. She agreed, and Ben was shipped by air. He arrived safely and the buyer said she was thrilled with him.

Each time we spoke, the buyer assured me that she was thrilled with Ben and all was well. Then, gradually, she mentioned problems. He was too heavy-boned, he hadn't grown, was cowhocked and, worst of all, he was not the same puppy her friend saw! Then, suddenly she phoned threatening to euthanize him if she didn't get a full refund because he had osteodystrophy.

As Ben had been co-bred, I requested time to advise my partner of the situation. In the end we had to send the money to an attorney before the puppy or his papers was released to us. He was sent back collect and I brought a friend to the airport since I wanted a witness to his condition.

When he emerged from his now-too-small crate (remember—he "hadn't grown"!), his coat looked like a fleet of moths had been at it and he was crawling with fleas. He was cowhocked, flat-footed and down on his pasterns, but he certainly wasn't at death's door.

We went to my vet the next day. After checking for internal parasites, the vet discovered that Ben had about everything imaginable—some indigenous only to the state where he had lived. He had been fed a high protein diet, calcium and other supplements contraindicated for growing Great Dane pups. All this could have easily brought on hypertrophic osteodystrophy. While he was away, Ben spent most of his time crated so had no exercise to speak of.

I put Ben on a low-protein diet, vitamin C, no calcium and he was free to run and play. His fleas were under control and he was treated for the internal parasites. Soon he was back up on his pasterns, his feet and coat both improved. Ten days after his return, I showed him at a Specialty match where he placed second in a class of nine!

What really happened to Ben I'll probably never know. But from what I could ascertain the buyer was unfamiliar with Ben's growth pattern. He had much greater bone than she was used to, plus she kept him crated much of the time, overfed and oversupplemented, probably throwing him into a mild case of HOD (see chapter 6, "Keeping Your Great Dane Happy and Healthy"). Had she told me what was happening and communicated her concerns, we could have fixed the problem. I'd told her from the beginning that I'd buy him back under any circumstances.

The moral of the story—an established breeder should be as ready to answer a seller's questions as a first-time pet buyer must.

ALTERNATIVES TO A PUPPY

Whatever your needs for a dog are, starting with a puppy is not your only option. There are many good reasons for considering an adolescent or a young adult.

If you want a show dog, you will have a much better idea of what you're getting by purchasing an

Ben, the day I picked him up at the air-port. (Jill Swedlow)

Ben at approximately seven months. (Jill Swedlow)

older animal. The problem here is that few breeders will sell a show-quality dog that is old enough for its potential to be beyond speculation. If they do, the price will probably be higher than that of a puppy. Bargains rarely happen, and most people get what they pay for.

Rescue Dogs

If you don't plan to show or breed, a rescue Dane might be your ideal answer. Most breed clubs maintain a rescue committee that helps place dogs that, for whatever reason, can no longer remain in their present homes. By considering an older dog, you might well save that dog's life. You will also

not have to go through some of the problems of puppyhood. On the other hand, you might adopt a dog with problems that made it a rescue candidate.

As in finding a reputable breeder, you also need to be careful of the rescue organization you contact. It's pretty safe to say that breed club rescues are reputable. A good rescue operation will screen a dog as much as possible. It will first learn why the dog is being given up. Is it destructive? Does it have a temperament problem? Does it get along with other dogs and other animals? Is it okay with kids, men, women? Is it ill? Are the owners getting divorced or moving where the dog won't be allowed? Some of the reasons are valid; others are simply ridiculous. Whatever the reason, the object is to rehome the dog.

A reputable rescue organization, whether club-affiliated or not, will make certain that the dogs it places are properly screened for health and temperament, will provide the potential adopter with as much information about the dog as possible, and will attempt to match the right dog with the right person. They will screen a potential adopter for all essential details of the home environment, and whether or not he or she can afford to properly care for a Great Dane.

CHOOSING YOUR NEW GREAT DANE

Regardless of why you want a puppy, health, temperament and personality are all important matters that deserve your attention.

When you come to view the litter for the first time, the breeder may or may not lock the dam away. Some bitches are extremely protective with their litters, and others will allow one and all to play with them. Don't fault the bitch either way. She has a right to protect her babies.

The age of a litter makes a significant difference in the puppies' reactions to strangers. Puppies under twenty-one days old will not show much response to people. After twenty-one days, they suddenly develop an interest in their surroundings and begin to show curiosity and investigate anything that interests them. This is always one of my favorite ages. At the end of day twenty, the puppies are sort of playing with each other, acting like they *might* see me and doing a lot of sitting and staring. The

next morning they greet me with avid interest and wagging tails. Toys and strange objects are happily investigated. Climbing out of the whelping box becomes job one! As they grow, they become a lot more active in pursuing such interests.

When a visitor approaches the litter, the puppies should show interest and a willingness to check out a new friend. They should not cower away or indicate fearfulness. There should be no discharge from the eyes, noses or ears of any of the puppies, and all should look and smell clean. They should be active if they aren't sleeping, which they do most of the time. Their coats should be shiny and soft.

If you are observant, you can get a feel for the personality of the individual puppies. The one that runs to you, climbs up your chest and bites you on the chin is a very confident *alpha* personality. This is the puppy who will need a firm hand and discipline as he grows up. He is probably *not* the best choice for a home with small children. This puppy is going to try to be the boss and will view the kids as littermates. In his perception, this gives him the right to dominate the children. Puppies dominate their littermates by growling and biting. This is not what children should have to endure.

The puppy who approaches readily, tail up and wagging, and who cuddles up and licks your face or hand or invites you to play is going to make a great child's dog, pet and obedience dog. This is the dog who will be submissive enough to obey but confident enough to happily accompany you on any outing or family activity.

The puppy who hangs back a little, then approaches quietly with tail at half-mast and head somewhat lowered would be a good choice for a person who wants a dog that will be somewhat quiet and willing to learn. Perhaps a good choice for an elderly person who no longer has the physical strength to deal with a very rambunctious Dane. With some patience and intensive socialization, this puppy will become a well-trained, happy companion.

The sad puppy who cringes in the corner and cannot be persuaded to approach you should be avoided. This dog can easily become a fear biter. Such a dog has no confidence and will be frightened by just about everything in its environment. If you can imagine what it would be like to go through life terrified of everything, you will probably conclude that it would be a kindness to euthanize this individual. People unfamiliar with canine temperament often mistake this personality for evidence of abuse. This is seldom the case.

Rely on the breeder to help you choose the right puppy. An experienced breeder is very familiar with her lines and has a good idea of how each pup's personality will develop. The breeder wants to help choose the right puppy because she wants you to have the one that will best fit into your lifestyle and remain a lifelong companion. By giving her this freedom as you look over the litter, you also avail yourself of her experience and will never regret it.

If you are purchasing a dog that is to be a pet or performance dog, you can expect the breeder to encourage you to spay or neuter the dog, or perhaps it will already have been done.

Additionally, AKC now has a limited registrationcategory. The breeder checks a box on the

Puppies should happily approach you and show interest in you. Here's Narcissus at about four weeks old. She was the personality kid from day one! (Jill Swedlow)

registration application that renders dogs with limited registration ineligible to produce registerable offspring. If the dog later develops into a show/breeding prospect, and you and the breeder want to show or breed it, the breeder may change the limited registration to full registration.

Understand, however, that ugly ducklings rarely grow into swans in the dog world. If your dog is not a show prospect or lacks solid breeding potential, you will be doing yourself, the breed and your dog a big favor by neutering it.

When approached by a stranger, a puppy with a correct temperament should show interest and curiosity. There may be reserve but never a suggestion of shyness.

SELECTING A SHOW/BREEDING PROSPECT

If you want a puppy who shows promise of having all the physical attributes necessary for show competition, you must go beyond the previously mentioned requirements. The dog's personality should be outgoing and confident, or at least the dog should approach you readily and happily. A puppy that is too submissive or shy should neither be shown nor bred.

In my opinion, the show-prospect puppy is best selected between ages seven to nine weeks. My own puppies seem to display most of the traits at seven weeks that they will show at maturity. Of course there is always some risk with selecting a show prospect as a puppy. Even the most promising puppy can fail to meet its potential as an

adult. One of the most common problems occurs in males. The puppy might have it all together, winning right up through the puppy classes. He could even take points as a puppy. His biggest problem is going to be small size, but this will not show up as a glaring fault when the pups are under six months of age. Even though the Standard requires a male to stand at least thirty inches at the shoulder, to be truly competitive a dog should measure over thirty-three inches. A thirty-inch male in the Senior Puppy (nine to twelve months) class doesn't stand out as he will once he ages into the adult classes. This does not mean that selection should be made on size

The wise puppy buyer will rely on the breeder to help in the selection of just the right puppy to meet the buyer's needs. With an attractive group like this, that would be very welcome help indeed. (Mike Johnson)

There should be no discharge from the eyes or nose, and puppies should appear alert and happy. This lovely litter belongs to Melody Grund. (Melody Grund)

only. It's just an example of how conformation can change as a puppy matures.

Although you want your show-prospect puppy as faultless as possible, no dog is perfect, and even the best will have some blemishes. It is wise to rely on the breeder, as most know what to expect of their puppies as they mature. If you have your eye on a couple of pups, the breeder might be able to explain why you should choose one over the other.

There are some faults that might be apparent in puppyhood but will correct as the puppy grows. There are others that you should avoid in a puppy intended for show or breeding.

Possible Faults of Youth

- **Cowhocks:** Puppies can go through some pretty weird stages as they grow, and cowhocks are sometimes one of them. If a puppy of my own

breeding had cowhocks, I would suspect that it would mature into a cowhocked adult. In other lines, puppies might outgrow this.

- **A roached topline:** Rather than appearing level, the topline (or top of the back) shows a convex curve usually from midpoint to tailset. If not severe, this is often a fault of youth.

- **Higher in the rear than at the withers:** Almost all puppies go through the stage where they grow taller behind than in front. Most will catch up in front as they grow.

- **Narrow front, east/west feet:** This can, and often does, correct. As the chest matures, drops and widens, it pushes the elbows outward, causing the toes to point forward as they should.

Here are some faults *not* to excuse in a show/breeding prospect:

- **Undescended testicles:** They *can* descend later, but this isn't a given.

- **An even or undershot bite:** Malocclusion almost always stays the same or becomes worse.

- **Small bones without any evidence of large joints at the pasterns:** A puppy with small bones and a slight build will probably grow into a "weedy" adult, although not always.

- Forefeet that are severely east/west and severe cowhocks.

- Shyness or an overly aggressive temperament.

- Any of the disqualifying faults listed in the Standard.

Which Sex?

For a show dog, sex can make a difference, although it is not certain that one is preferable to another. There have been top-winning Great Danes of both sexes for many years. The males (dogs) exhibit an awesome grandeur, while the females (bitches) have an unmistakable air of elegance.

If you have no desire to become a breeder, a dog would probably be your best choice. Dogs don't come into season, go through false pregnancies and blow their coats right afterward. They are generally larger and more impressive than bitches. This is a real plus for a Dane that has earned his championship and is competing at the Group level. Many judges, especially those not directly experienced with Great Danes, will frequently gravitate to a dog for their Best of Breed choice.

Generally dogs suffer a drawback in that higher overall quality is most often found in bitches. Bitches don't tend to go through as many "ugly" stages as their brothers and are often sounder movers than males. Notwithstanding, if you want to become a breeder, you must of course begin with a bitch, not a dog.

Regardless of which sex you choose, the traits you look for are similar, with the exception of masculinity in the dog and femininity in the bitch. If you know which sex you want, remove all the pups of the opposite sex and the obvious pets to another location. This will be less confusing than trying to observe the entire litter together. If you are considering several similar puppies, identify each puppy with a different-color collar.

First, just watch the puppies move around and play. Most litters have at least one standout that always catches your eye. Interestingly, this is not always the best one. Attitude counts for a lot. This is why (in my opinion) some dogs become champions who shouldn't. That showy attitude can hide a multitude of physical faults. You look at the dog and at first glance think, *Oh, that's gorgeous!* Then if you continue to *really* look at the dog, the faults become apparent. So this is something to consider only if you want to show. If you can find a puppy that has *both* correct conformation and natural presence, grab him and run!

Obviously you will be looking for a puppy that most closely adheres to the Great Dane Standard. It should have balanced angulation front and rear; good topline; a long, nicely arched, well-set-on neck; and a head showing ample breed type. The puppy should have good bone and proportionate length of leg. Although puppies often move like, well, puppies, there should be some indication of good reach and drive when gait is viewed from the side. When viewed coming or going, the action shouldn't look like that of an egg beater. Many puppies just constantly play and act up and don't really settle into good movement until they're a year or so old. So it takes patience to make a full evaluation.

CONTRACTS

Once you've decided on the love of your life for, hopefully, the next ten years, you must discuss a contract with the breeder. Even if the breeder is your best friend, look at a contract as a simple way to record the points of your mutual agreement. That way, two years later when you're about to breed the bitch, share handler expenses, or whatever, you'll both have a written record of the original agreement.

It is said that a contract is only as good as the people who sign it, and I've found that to be true. However, it helps to at least know what guarantees you can expect. The AKC *requires* the following information to be present on a contract/sales agreement:

- Birth date
- Sire
- Sire's AKC number
- Dam
- Dam's AKC number
- AKC number/litter number of the puppy/dog being sold, microchip/tattoo
- Sex
- Color/markings
- Breeder(s)

The following is a copy of the contract I use here at Sunnyside Farm. Contracts differ somewhat depending on whether it covers a show or pet puppy and whether the puppy is to be co-owned.

Purchase Agreement for a Show-Quality Great Dane Puppy

This is a legal contract entered into by Jill Swedlow hereinafter referred to as Breeder and "Purchaser,"

the purchasers (hereinafter to be referred to as Owners) of the below described Great Dane.

Birth date:
Sire:
Sire's AKC#:
Sire's permanent ID, if any:
Dam:
Dam's AKC#
Dam's permanent ID, if any:
Reg. name to be:
AKC reg./litter no.:
Sex:
Color/markings:
Breeder(s):

The purchase price of the above described Great Dane is $0,000.00, to be paid in full when the puppy is taken to his new home.

Conditions and Guarantees of Sale

1. If at any time in the future the Buyer decides to rehome the dog, she/he must offer the dog to the Breeder at one half the purchase price. If the breeder does not want the dog, she has the right to final approval of any future owner. If the dog is placed with another owner, that person or persons are equally bound by and must agree to and sign this contract and must be so advised and so agree before any transfer of ownership may take place.

1A. Buyer agrees to have the hips OFA (Orthopedic Foundation for Animals) certified free of hip dysplasia once the dog is two years of age. Buyer further agrees to test this dog for VWD,

thyroid (OFA), eyes (CERF) and cardiomyopathy prior to any breeding that may take place,
and to send copies of these tests (microchip of
dog to be included on papers) to Breeder.

2.　Your SHOW QUALITY Great Dane is guar-
anteed in the following manner up to the age
of three years.

2A.　(PLEASE NOTE THAT THE FOLLOWING
GUARANTEE IS EFFECTIVE ONLY IF
THE OWNER HAS COMPLIED WITH
THE FEEDING INSTRUCTIONS
ATTACHED HERETO.) Any SHOW
QUALITY DOG which has been diagnosed
by two qualified veterinarians (mutually agreed
upon by Breeder and Owner, both to be paid
by Owner) as having hip dysplasia or wobblers
syndrome will be replaced by a dog of equal
or better quality from the next litter bred by
Breeder, Owner to pay for ear cropping and
any shipping expenses.

2B.　If this Great Dane fails to develop into a show
dog capable of finishing its championship
within a reasonable amount of time (this to be
determined by evaluation of three unbiased
Great Dane breeders and/or AKC approved
Great Dane judges in the event that Buyer and
Breeder cannot agree), the Breeder will replace
this dog with another of her breeding from the
next available litter.

3.　Breeder retains the sole right to refuse to
replace any defective Dane with another Dane
and may, instead, refund one half the purchase
price should she feel that the Dane was not

given the type of home environment and care
which she feels to be necessary.

4.　The parents of your Great Dane have been
chosen with good temperament being a top
requirement. Because temperament can be
greatly influenced by environment, and there is
no way to control this environment once the
dog has left Sunnyside Farm, Breeder retains
the right to decide whether to replace the dog
or refund money because of inherited temperament problems, (i.e., viciousness or shyness) at her discretion, based on her evaluation
of the situation in which the dog displayed
unacceptable temperament.

5.　RESPONSIBILITIES OF OWNER

A.　I (Owner) guarantee that this Great Dane is
to be a house dog who will live with and
be treated as a member of my/our family. I
have a fenced yard and proper environment
in which to safely raise a puppy and house
an adult Great Dane.

B.　I (Owner) agree to follow the feeding plan
attached hereto during the rapid growth
period from puppyhood to age 1½ years, or
at least keep the protein percentage at 24%
or lower and not supplement with vitamins
or calcium with the exception of vitamin C.

C.　If this Great Dane has been purchased as a
show dog, I (Owner) understand that it is
up to me to do my best to properly train,
condition and show this dog to its AKC
(or other) championship. To this end I will
socialize the dog and attend puppy matches

to accustom the dog to all the sights and sounds of travel and shows.

D. I understand that it is important to properly socialize and expose the puppy to strangers and unfamiliar sights and sounds. I understand that it would be a good idea to enroll in a puppy kindergarten class and a show handling class or obedience class once the puppy has had at least two of its permanent vaccinations for parvovirus and DHLP.

E. If this Great Dane has been purchased as a pet I understand that it is the Breeder's policy to issue limited AKC registration papers which prevent any future offspring from being registered with the AKC unless specifically reinstated by the Breeder. I further agree to spay or neuter this Pet Quality puppy before it reaches a year of age.

F. The Breeder has explained to me the expense and time required to show a dog to its championship (when possible) and I agree to do this to the best of my ability if I have purchased a show quality Dane. The Breeder has also explained the cost of possible emergency bloat surgery and I can and will see that this is performed if it is in the best interest of the Dane.

We have read and understood and fully agree to the above.

Date:

Owner:

Address:

City, State, Zip:

Phone:

Jill Swedlow, (Breeder)
Breeder's address, phone and the date

Not all contracts need to go into as much detail as this example, but you need at least *some* information in writing.

Along with the contract, you should receive the registration application, commonly called the *blue slip*. This is sent to AKC along with a small fee in order to register the puppy. The breeder will show you where to sign.

Some breeders will withhold the blue slip until the puppy has been paid for in full. AKC says that the blue slip must accompany the animal, but this is rarely enforced.

You should also receive some information about what and how much to feed the puppy, general care, housebreaking and an invitation from the breeder to contact her with any questions or concerns. Here is what I send out with each of my puppies.

GENERAL INFORMATION ABOUT YOUR NEW GREAT DANE PUPPY

Feeding Your Puppy

Great Danes are classified as a giant breed. They reach their ultimate height usually by the age of two years but are very close to it at a year. Because of this rapid growth rate, they are prone to many skeletal growth problems. Recent studies have found that if you can slow the rate of growth, especially through the age where it is fastest, you can help prevent problems such as hip dysplasia, wobblers syndrome, and hypertrophic osteodystrophy (HOD).

To slow the growth on my dogs, I feed a dog food of 24 percent protein or less. Specifically, your puppy has been eating Innova mixed with Eagle Brand canned. Only about 15 percent of the meal is canned. DO NOT FEED SUPPLEMENTS SUCH AS CALCIUM, COTTAGE CHEESE, HIGH-PROTEIN MEAT or any additive that will throw off the balance of the food you're offering. Next to lower protein, a calcium/phosphorus/vitamin D balance is essential. Throw the balance off, and your puppy is on its way to bone problems.

Vitamin C is one supplement that you should definitely give. It is one of the few supplements that can do no harm, and it is thought to be beneficial to growing dogs. Give 500 milligrams in the morning and evening meals for a total of 1,000 mg per day. If you notice diarrhea, you might need to lower the amount. Your Dane should eat its food in two smaller meals per day rather than one large one. Water should always be available. The puppy has been eating three meals a day of the following:

Two cups of Innova mixed with approximately ¼ cup of canned Eagle Brand a.m. and p.m. Add hot water to kibble. You can add 500 mg vitamin C twice a day and probiotics if desired.

Vaccination Issues

The major veterinary schools have recently issued a new protocol for vaccination of puppies. This is due to the fact that more evidence is building to indicate that giving multiple vaccines and modified live vaccines may be responsible for producing autoimmune problems in the pups or as they mature and can also actually cause the disease against which they're supposed to protect. They recommend that after the initial vaccination series, the dog only be boostered once every three years instead of yearly. Since no study has ever been done to prove how long immunity lasts in the dog, the one-year interval was an arbitrary one.

I have taken this one step further and instead of just vaccinating, I have an immunity titer run on my dogs. Reliable immunity tests exist for parvovirus, distemper and rabies. I believe that Michigan State is one of the few schools who will do this test on the blood sample. If titers are high, then I don't vaccinate.

There are two drawbacks to doing a titer. They aren't cheap. The most expensive was the rabies titer for which I just paid $80.00. Also, you can get a false negative. In that case you would just have to vaccinate to be sure. In my opinion, it's cheaper to avoid health problems with my dogs than to have to face them later on.

Modified live vaccine (MLV) is also contraindicated unless facing a major parvo outbreak or something similar. The MLV is more likely to cause the disease it's supposed to protect against.

It is further recommended that vaccines be separated. This might be difficult as most vets carry only multiple vaccine "cocktails" consisting of up to seven different vaccines. I feel that to assault the undeveloped immunity system of a young puppy with this is dangerous and I don't do it. I give my own vaccines (with the exception of rabies) and it's difficult to find the separate ones.

Dr. Jean Dodds has performed extensive research into the connection between vaccines and autoimmune diseases. She recommends the following vaccination protocol:

AGE OF PUPS	VACCINE TYPE
6 weeks (no earlier than 5 1/2)	Distemper + measles (without hepatitus)
6–8 weeks and 10 weeks for puppies not receiving measles earlier for puppies not receiving measles	Distemper + or - parainfluenza (without hepatitis)
7–8 weeks & 10–11 weeks	killed canine parvovirus* same schedule & product
12 weeks	distemper+hepatitus +parainfluenza+ or - leptospirosis (without parvovirus)
14 weeks & 18–20 weeks	Distemper+hepatitis +parainfluenza + or -lepto+killed parvo*
16–24 weeks	killed rabies vaccine

During parvovirus epidemics or for highly susceptible breeds such as Rottweilers, newer modified live vaccines may be needed at more frequent intervals.

Even more recently, the need to vaccinate for leptospirosis has been questioned because the risks of the vaccine have begun to outweigh the benefits.

Leptospirosis is an infection caused by a bacteria found in the droppings of animals including rats, mice and cattle. The bacteria is contracted orally, most often from drinking contaminated water. It can be passed from one animal to another.

Alan Brightman, professor of clinical sciences Kansas State University, says that leptospirosis is a devastating disease that destroys internal organs, often causing kidney failure or liver disease. It is not found often anymore, though.

Kansas State's canine vaccination protocol dictates that puppies receive the distemper, hepatitis, parainfluenza and parvovirus vaccinations. These vaccines often are administered together in a "cocktail." Brightman said these are given to puppies at least six weeks of age and are repeated every three to four weeks until 16 weeks of age to make sure they take effect. Kansas State veterinarians do not recommend giving the leptospirosis, coronavirus or lyme disease vaccinations.

According to Bill Fortney, assistant professor of clinical sciences, it is not uncommon for dogs to have a reaction to vaccines, causing other difficulties or death. One of the problems with the leptospirosis vaccine is that it causes more reactions than the others.

Fortney cited the following reasons for not administering the leptospirosis vaccine to puppies:

- Puppies sometimes have reactions to vaccines and there are more reactions to the leptospirosis vaccine than most others.

- Leptospirosis is not often seen anymore.

- The vaccine does not protect the puppy well.

- The vaccine costs around $7.

A recent pilot study at Purdue University has made it clear that more in-depth research into the relation between autoimmune disease and vaccination is definitely warranted.

My suggestion to *you* is to discuss these issues with your veterinarian. If your vet hasn't heard of the above, or refuses to consider alternatives, find one who will.

Parasites

If your puppy has already been treated for worms, it will be shown on the dates listed below. Since fleas do not live in my locale, there is no need for me to have treated for tape worms. If you live in an area where fleas are a problem, you will probably have to watch for this problem in the future. Tape worms look like grains of rice in the stool or around the anus.

It would be wise to take a stool sample into the vet to check for any other types of worms that might be present and to be sure that the initial wormings were effective. Always have your veterinarian worm your puppy unless you have experience with this.

Your puppy was found to be positive for roundworms and was treated with Strongid on 0/00/00.

General Care

Great Danes are not suited to being backyard watchdogs who get little or no attention and rarely get in the house. (Of course, had I thought you would do that I wouldn't have sold you one of my puppies!) They are happiest and thrive when they are house dogs who are considered members of a family. Canines are, after all, pack (family) animals. Although they are naturally pretty well behaved, they still need discipline and respect for their "pack leader" as well as *all* humans. To this end I highly recommend that

you and your puppy attend obedience classes, and yes, they do have them for little puppies.

I also recommend that you purchase a crate for your puppy (keeping in mind the adult size). Your pup is already used to sleeping in a crate with its littermates, although I haven't locked them in it. This becomes like their own little private house where they can be away from the bustle of the family for some rest. It also protects the house from them while you cannot be watching them. But the best thing it does is assist with housetraining. A Dane is naturally clean and does not want to mess its bed. Most puppies from three months on can make it through the night without messing the crate. After this is accomplished, they easily get the idea that outside is the place to go. DO NOT, however, use the crate continually. Overnight or a few hours during the day is enough.

Provide a large outside fenced yard where your dog can romp and play. Exercise is important for growing puppies. If you have other dogs (larger than the puppy) and children, make sure that they don't knock the puppy down or hurt it. Instruct your children on how to treat the puppy, and make sure they know that a growing puppy needs many hours of sleep to grow properly. Don't let children tease the puppy.

Be sure that from the start you continue to lead break your puppy and take it places in the car with you. Go to shopping malls and public places so the puppy will become accustomed to different sights and sounds. Encourage strangers to pet and play with the puppy. Don't allow the puppy access to other dogs until he has had at least his first adult vaccination. This is also true for attending puppy matches or shows.

Ear Care

When a Great Dane has his ears cropped, that is not the end of the procedure. For ears to stand properly, they must undergo many tapings, sometimes until the dog is over a year old, but most ears are up by five to six months, sometimes sooner. If you're inexperienced at aftercare, either I will help you or find someone in your area who can.

Life-Threatening Emergencies: A Word About Bloat and HOD (Hypertrophic Osteodystrophy)

HOD is a condition affecting young, rapidly growing dogs usually between 3½ and 8 months of age. The symptoms are very high fever, swelling and inflammation of the joints (usually the pastern) and tremendous pain. Even a lethargic puppy with a slightly elevated fever should be checked by a vet. If caught early enough, this disease will probably subside quickly.

Unfortunately, many vets fail to recognize the disease and the puppy is neither diagnosed nor treated correctly. Immediate diagnosis is made by x-ray. The treatment consists of injectable vitamin C and steroids to combat the joint inflammation, Banamine to combat the pain (the injectable form is preferred) and antibiotics to combat any secondary infections (pneumonia is the most common) that

may take hold when an animal is badly stressed is an effective treatment regimen.

Bloat usually occurs in dogs over one year of age but is not unheard of in younger dogs. The symptoms include attempts to vomit but producing only foam. The stomach and/or rib cage appears distended and continues to enlarge. The dog is in obvious distress and is usually panting and restless. *TIME IS OF THE ESSENCE.* The stomach is filling with gasses and beginning to rotate. This means that gas cannot leave the stomach and enlargement continues. As the stomach rotates, the blood supplies are cut off and the animal begins to go into shock. The vet will usually try to pass a stomach tube to ascertain if the stomach has already turned and to relieve the gas pressure if it hasn't. (Occasionally a tube can be passed into a rotated stomach.) An x-ray will confirm rotation. The dog must be stabilized before surgery (the only permanent cure) can be performed. Even then, it is not uncommon for a dog to die of heart complications after a successful surgery.

The above are extreme emergency situations, especially those regarding bloat. Don't waste any time getting veterinary help. Your veterinarian should be familiar with the health issues affecting Great Danes, and your choice of veterinarian should be made from the beginning with this in mind. In this way, in the event of any life-threatening emergency, you know your dog will be in competent hands.

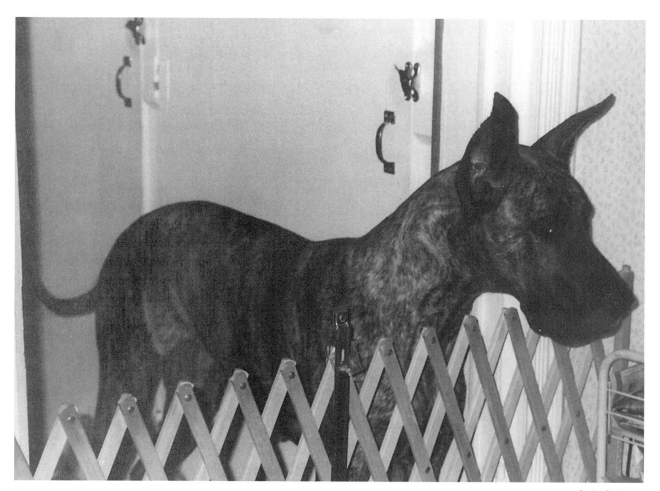

CHAPTER 5

Living with a Great Dane

Sharing one's life with a Great Dane is an experience filled with fun, love, frustration and, at the end of the dog's life, heartbreak. I'm often asked by non-Dane owners how I can stand to lose them so soon. (The average for the breed is seven years, although many Danes manage to beat the average.) I answer that the pleasure they give while I have them makes them well worth the pain of the loss. I simply cannot imagine living with any other breed, and most Dane owners agree.

But on to the fun stuff! You're about to bring home your new Great Dane puppy, and you need to make some preparations ahead of time. If the breeder hasn't already suggested this, you *definitely* need a crate. Unless the technique is overused, crating is *not* cruel. To a dog, his crate is his den—his very own place where he can sleep, get away from household commotion, and be at peace during meals and at any other times as needed. A crate to *you* is a safeguard for both your dog and your house and a wonderful tool to aid in housebreaking your puppy.

GETTING THE RIGHT CRATE

Purchase a crate large enough to house your Dane when he's full grown. This means the crate you buy should be *at least* twenty-eight inches wide, forty-eight inches long and thirty-six inches high. If you plan to have one crate double as a car crate, be sure it will fit in your vehicle and still be large enough for your dog. Regardless of the size crate you select, you must section it off while the puppy is small so that he has only enough room to stand and turn around. (Some crates have dividers that make this simple.)

This puppy sees her crate as her private little home. Rather than being cruel, crate training offers many advantages for both the puppy and the owner. (Fran Lass)

Since Danes do not normally soil their beds, the puppy will whine to let you know he has to go out and relieve himself. If the crate is too big, he'll simply move to the area away from his bed and relieve himself there.

There are two basic crate types—solid and wire. The solid crate is best suited for shipping dogs. It has solid sides that protect the dog from injury during transport. Shipping crates are made in both fiberglass and metal. The latter are usually very expensive, but they are durable and most usually can be folded for storage. Fiberglass crates are strong but less durable than metal models. A solid crate breaks down by only half its size. You should consider a solid crate only if you intend to ship your dog by air a great deal. Because they are enclosed, solid crates don't allow air to circulate as well as wire models.

Wire crates allow surrounding air to circulate and so cool the crated dog. If it becomes necessary to provide shade or more warmth, you can either make or purchase a crate cover. The wire crate also allows you a full view of the dog. This is especially good if you're traveling in the car and you want to be able to visually check your dog from time to time.

PROPER USE OF CRATES

Crates are convenient for the human members of the family. For this reason, it can be tempting to overuse them. Please, for the sake of your dog, *don't!* He can spend the night in the crate and a brief daytime interval in it when you must leave the house for a couple hours or when you cannot be right there to watch him. It's much better, though, to provide him with a safe, outdoor area where he can play in fresh air and relieve himself when necessary if you must leave him for any length of time during the day. Of course, you'll also provide him with a comfortable indoor area— either a doghouse with a soft bed or access into a room of the house or garage through a dog door. Great Danes *must never* be left outdoors in extreme weather, hot or cold.

A crate is a wonderful tool for housebreaking. Teach your puppy that this is his bed where he spends the night. Have him close by your bed so you'll hear him when he needs to go out. Most puppies from age nine weeks can make it through the night. But give him the benefit of the doubt if he acts like he wants out during the night. When he cries or whines, let him out, take him outdoors to where you want him to relieve himself, and then *stay with him* until he's done his duty. As soon as he has, *praise him generously!* He needs to know that this is why he came outdoors and that you are very happy with him. Soon he'll learn what is wanted, relieve himself and be ready to go back to bed.

It's much easier to prevent accidents indoors right from the start, and a crate greatly facilitates this. Remember that a puppy will have to relieve itself upon waking, after play and after eating. It's up to *you* to be watchful and anticipate when your puppy needs to go out. If you are consistent in your training, you'll have a housebroken puppy within a week. This doesn't mean you can leave him loose and unattended in the house for hours on end, but if you're around for him to tell you, he'll let you know when he wants out. If, by four or five months your puppy still needs to relieve himself in the middle of the night, withhold water two or three hours prior to bedtime.

EARLY TRAINING AND SOCIALIZATION

Set house rules for the puppy right from the beginning. If he's to stay off furniture, don't hold him in your lap while you're sitting on the sofa watching TV. If he's to stay out of certain rooms,

he stays out from the beginning. If you don't want him begging for food while you are eating, enforce this from day one. If you think that once won't hurt, you're wrong! It's much easier to prevent the unwanted behavior than to correct it once it has become a habit.

Enroll your Dane puppy in a puppy kindergarten class once he's had at least two permanent DHLP and parvovirus vaccinations. He'll probably be around four months old by that time and will benefit from the socialization with other dogs and people. Take him in the car to shopping malls and walk him around. Encourage strangers to approach and pet him. If you plan to show him in conformation, enroll him in conformation handling classes. Take him to a few puppy matches. Give him as broad an experience as you can. Dogs who spend their whole lives in a house and back yard

If you allow your Great Dane puppy on the sofa, be prepared to do it for the dog's life. (Brad Vickrey)

To a young puppy, curling up on a sofa is no match to snuggling into loving arms. This six-week-old Daynakin puppy clearly proves the point.

and give the person a doggie treat to offer the pup. At the first indication that the puppy is going to approach the stranger, *praise him.* If his initial shyness is due to inexperience and not a faulty temperament, he'll soon learn that friendly strangers are positive. It would be a good idea to have a friend who is unknown to the puppy to act as the friendly stranger and keep repeating the experience until the puppy is happily approaching the stranger expecting to be petted.

After your puppy has completed puppy kindergarten, you might want to enroll him in an obedience class. If you do, and you're also intending to show in conformation, I recommend that you do not teach the automatic sit. Although many obedience instructors insist that the dog knows the difference, it has been my experience that this can confuse the dog. If you want to compete in both conformation and Obedience, I suggest you complete one course of training and then the other. It's also easier on you and your Dane if you concentrate on obtaining a title in only one area first. Competition can be very stressful for dogs, even for the naturals. Trying to achieve success in both conformation and Obedience at the same time is asking a lot of your dog.

Great Danes are, for the most part, naturally well mannered. Perhaps this is one reason so many Dane owners tend to be very lax in the discipline department. In many cases their dogs get away

can be terrified if they have to leave their property. This is unfair to both you and your dog.

If your puppy shows unreasonable fear of something or someone, *don't* make the mistake of "comforting" him. If you pet and hug him in an effort to reassure him, you're really teaching him to react in a fearful manner to this situation. For instance, say you're walking along the sidewalk and a stranger approaches from the opposite direction. Your puppy begins to hang back and tries to get away from this person. The correct response on your part is to give a mild correction and tell the puppy "No." Enlist the assistance of the stranger

Maxine Schlundt's Julie seems to think that the dishwasher makes a great place to sleep!

can learn to the extent you require. (Also see chapter 10, "Obedience Trials, Performance Activities and Other Fun Things," by Lyn Richards.)

Most Danes learn very easily. Occasionally Great Danes are accused of being "dumb," perhaps because they tend to perform many Obedience exercises at a more leisurely pace than other breeds. Take my word for it, Great Danes are *not* dumb. My Daffodil was so smart that I had to put bungie cords on the refrigerator and baby locks on the trash cupboard and the others that contained food. Daffi could open *anything,* including doors and gates, as could her daughter Kiwi.

Being a rather lazy trainer about teaching formal Obedience, much of what my dogs learn occurs during everyday living. For instance, if I

with a whole variety of peccadilloes. But if a dog this size is undisciplined and unruly, he's a time bomb awaiting detonation. We hear of more biting incidents by Danes at the present time than was once true. Surely, this must be taken as a distressing trend. Although poor temperament can certainly be inherited, I wonder how many biting incidents could have been prevented if these dogs accepted all humans as superiors.

EARLY OBEDIENCE TRAINING

Although I do not consider myself an expert on obedience training, I'll offer a few training guidelines here for your new puppy. There are many excellent books on the subject from which you

Exhibiting your puppy at matches is a wonderful way to prepare for the show ring and socialize the puppy at the same time. (Jill Swedlow)

don't want them to rush out a door, I'll give them the signal for *stay* (hand open, palm toward their face) as I go through the door. I praise them if they've shown any inclination to stay behind. Of course the first time I do this is when they're babies and they have no idea what I want. I let them know by gently bumping their nose with the open palm while saying "Stay" or "Wait." It doesn't take long before I can go through the door without anything more than the hand signal. (I must admit, though, that if it's the door to the garage, and they think they're going in the car, all is lost! Then they get some pretty *firm* nose bumps!)

Down, sit and stay can all be taught during the course of daily routines. Down works well while you're watching TV. You might want to initially use food as a lure to get the puppy into the different positions. Then gradually require him to remain in the sit or the down longer and longer until you release him. Don't ask for a full minute down the first time. If you ask your puppy to obey the house rules as they come up, his training will seem painless to you both.

I always try to start my puppies on some elementary lead training prior to their going to their new homes. This helps eliminate some of the stress that they encounter upon changing families. I usually start by fitting the entire litter with buckle collars to which I'll attach a foot-long lead. The puppies grab each others' leads and collars, and the feeling of pressure around their necks becomes part of a game. For the next step I clip a six-foot leather lead onto the collar and simply follow the puppy around wherever he leads. I'll carry a food treat and get down on the ground and call the puppy to me. I keep a mild tension on the lead, but not enough to frighten. When he comes to me, he gets the treat and lots of praise. Soon I can walk with the puppy, call him to me, and as he moves to follow, I put a little more tension on the lead. It doesn't take long before the puppy realizes that a small tug leads to a treat if he comes in my direction. From this we graduate to taking short walks away from the house. Again, I usually let him lead while I follow. There are so many interesting new sights and smells to investigate that the pup usually forgets about being on a lead. Gradually, the puppy will learn good walking manners on the lead.

If you intend to show your puppy, this is the time to begin training for the conformation ring. Ideally you want your dog to *love* the show ring.

Training for the conformation ring should be fun for your puppy. This puppy is getting a food reward for standing squarely and paying attention to the handler. (Jill Swedlow)

The show collar needs to be kept high on the neck just behind the ears. This helps minimize any loose skin and keeps the head high. (Jill Swedlow)

The author's Kiwi lying on her soft bed made of three king-size pillows contained in a cover. (Jill Swedlow)

The best way to accomplish this is to train the puppy so he thinks that dog shows and conformation training are the best things in the world—after *you,* of course! I start teaching baby puppies to bait (stand and look at a treat, preferably with ears up) at about the same time as they are able to stand. I let them sniff a small treat and, of course, they want it! The second, the *very second,* the puppy is standing still with all four feet on the ground (it doesn't matter where the feet are), give him the treat. Keep this up and before long the puppy will associate the fact that he's standing still and looking at the treat with actually *getting* the treat. Once the puppy has the idea, you can start placing his feet where you want them. Front feet

should be even and facing straight ahead with the elbow directly underneath the withers. The hind feet should be placed parallel also, with the hocks perpendicular to the ground.

You must also accustom the puppy to having the collar placed high up under his neck without fighting it. He must allow his mouth to be opened by a stranger and his teeth examined. Male puppies must not sit or cower when their testicles are manually examined by a judge. By frequently examining all these areas and working him with the collar high on the neck, the puppy will not resent this when he goes to his first show.

Daily living with a Great Dane takes a little more forethought than living with a smaller breed. Danes get *very BIG!* This means that they can reach *very HIGH!* This means that such things as your dinner are not safe if left unattended in an accessible location. I don't care how much training your Dane has had, I have yet to hear of one that was reliable around available food. It's better still if the prize is the owner's food! In this house, everything edible goes into or on top of the refrigerator, or in the drawers or cupboards. I once had a Dane steal an entire ham that was thawing in the sink and eat it down to the bone before he was discovered. One evening Kiwi nabbed a huge and *very hot* stuffed potato off the countertop (tinfoil and all) when I just turned around for a second! I was standing *right there!* Daffodil used to open the refrigerator, food cupboards and the trash and would help herself. The fridge sported a bungie cord and the cupboards were all fitted with baby locks. Years ago Ch. Tallbrook's Bit'O Honey ate an entire five-pound bag of sugar! It's a wonder it didn't kill her. Years later her great-great-great-great-great granddaughter, Poppy, did the same to a 20-pound bag of sugar. That adventure didn't kill her either, but she didn't get it all!

The size of the adult Great Dane also places his tail at a dangerous height if you're a piece of bric-a-brac. The damage is caused when the tail is wagging hard and sweeps everything off the coffee table. Watch out for toddlers around the wagging tail of a high-spirited Dane, as that tail is hard and can be like a whip. It isn't unusual for a child to get swiped across the face with the dog's tail. And

Great Danes can fit into surprisingly small spaces. Here (from left) Can. Ch. Windsor Clasibawn Daynakin, Daynakin's Briana, and Am. Can. Ch. Daynakin's Bringold Gretchen, Am., Can. CD, squeeze in for a ride with Benjamin, their Bulldog buddy.

children are not the only ones at risk. A wagging Dane tail is also placed just right to make a profound impression on some sensitive, vulnerable adult male body parts. Get it?

SPECIAL DOG, SPECIAL BED

Because of their large size and weight, Great Danes need soft bedding to avoid developing calluses on their thighs and elbows. It's best to use nonabrasive cloth on your Dane's bed rather than canvas. A soft blanket or synthetic sheepskin is the best choice. You can also buy a bed made from orthopedic three-inch-thick foam. The cover, which unzips for washing, is made of the same synthetic sheepskin on one side and cloth on the other. Of course, you might decide to allow your Dane access to your furniture, in which case, forget the bed!

Some owners allow their Danes to sleep in their beds with them. This is fine for only one or two Danes. With any more than this, it becomes too much. The reasons are many, but I won't elaborate. I ask only that you trust me and benefit from personal experience—mine!

If you have a Dane with aggressive tendencies or one that does not accept you as pack leader, *do*

not allow this dog on furniture of any kind. In his frame of reference, this makes him your equal and you do not want to encourage this. He is *not* your equal, *you* are *his* leader.

If you use a crate, be sure that the bedding is very soft and comfortable. A base of four-inch foam would be best, with a sheepskin cover. Beds of this type are great around the house. Be sure it's big enough for the puppy as he grows to adulthood—at least twenty-eight inches by thirty-six inches and bigger if possible.

Living comfortably with one or more Great Danes in your home is basically common sense combined with enough knowledge to properly train and control your dog. A dog that knows its place and what is expected of it is a happy dog. This will, in turn, make you a happy Dane owner.

© Hymmen/Henderson

CHAPTER 6

Keeping Your Great Dane Happy and Healthy

All breeds (mixed breeds, too) can and do have indigenous health problems, and Great Danes are no exception. Because many of these problems can be inherited, it's imperative that breeders screen their breeding stock prior to making breeding decisions. Many of the problems affecting the skeletons of Great Danes occur during the very fast growth stages of puppyhood. It's been shown by several scientific studies that these problems can be prevented or controlled by paying close attention to both the amount and protein content of the food, and the body condition of the puppy as it grows. The type of exercise the puppy receives during this time is also very important.

Although I continually stress that Great Danes are not outdoor dogs, they *do* need exercise—and plenty of it. It's "enforced" exercise that is not a good idea, especially for a puppy. My Danes romp and play on an acre and a half of lawn and forest, and they *use it!* Exercise is very necessary in building strong bones, muscles and ligaments. Allow your Dane, both puppy and adult, all the exercise he wants. He knows when it's time to stop.

A Great Dane's health starts with the breeder. Hopefully you have purchased your puppy from a breeder who routinely health checks breeding stock prior to mating. This means much more than simply getting veterinary health certificates. Both parents should be checked for hip dysplasia, normal thyroid function, normal cardiac function, absence of von Willebrand's disease and normal eyes. The breeder should also select for long life span within the pedigree. With this background in the parents, the likelihood that the offspring will live long, healthy lives is greatly increased.

Health in Great Danes is also heavily influenced by how the puppy is raised. Puppies of large and giant breeds kept fat and supplemented with calcium, phosphorous and vitamin D during the early rapid growth stages are far more likely to develop hip dysplasia, OCD and other growth-related and inherited illnesses. If your puppy is kept lean and eats a high-quality food of 24 percent protein or less during its growing period, you're doing the best you can to help him achieve good health. (See chapter 7, "Caring for Your Great Dane.")

Young puppies need plenty of room to exercise and play. They will usually know how much is enough and stop at the right time.

HEALTH PROBLEMS THAT CAN AFFECT GREAT DANES

Gastric Torsion, Volvulus or Bloat

This disease is, in my opinion, the worst problem that can befall any Great Dane. One minute you have a normal, healthy, happy dog and twenty minutes later it's dying. Aside from this is the helplessness you feel since the only real way to help is to get the dog to a vet ASAP!

The causes of bloat are still unknown. Purdue University is currently conducting research into the cause of bloat, as have other organizations. Purdue has recently released information concluding that up to 25 percent of all Great Danes will bloat, making the breed most likely to succumb to this terrible disease. It has been suggested that feeding foods containing soy, allowing the dog to gulp its food too fast, allowing the dog free access to water, allowing the dog to exercise one hour before or after eating or feeding only once a day contributes to the onset of bloat. So far none of these theories have been proven. The latest findings suggest that nervous dogs or those under stress are also more likely to bloat.

As puppies grow, their need for recreational space grows with them. Here two adolescents enjoy a good game of tag with a favorite toy as the object of the chase.

My dogs have free access to water, exercise at will (although they all tend to sleep well after meals), I do not soak their food prior to feeding and they *all* eat fast. I don't feed soy and I do feed twice a day. The one sure (well, *almost* sure) way to prevent bloat is to have a preventative gastropexy performed on the dog. I do this with every bitch I spay. Happily, I have not had a dog bloat in many years.

What happens when a dog bloats? First the stomach begins to produce large amounts of gas and swells up. For some as yet unknown reason, the gas cannot be passed by the dog. As the stomach continues to enlarge, it begins to turn on its axis until it has made a complete, 180-degree turn.

(Picture a towel with a melon wrapped in the center. Then flip the towel so it's twisted, end to end.) This is termed *volvulus* or *torsion*. Once this occurs, the blood vessels and nerves are occluded and the stomach tissue served by these blood vessels begins to die. This in turn produces toxins that are spread throughout the body, and the dog goes into shock. Cardiac involvement is common.

Most dogs are well past puppyhood when they bloat, but it *can* happen to animals as young as four months. This, however, is very rare. The symptoms include abnormal stomach (abdominal) distention. The dog will attempt to vomit but can only bring up foam. The dog will be restless, will perhaps pace or even dig and be unable to find a comfortable position. The gums may appear pale. If you even *suspect* bloat, *get to the vet as fast as possible.*

Treatment consists first of establishing if it really is bloat. Most vets will first attempt to pass a tube into the dog's stomach. If the tube cannot be passed, torsion is likely, but it's possible for the dog to be in torsion and the tube to still be able to pass. An x-ray will confirm whether or not the dog is in gastric torsion. If the dog is in torsion, the vet will stabilize its vital signs prior to performing surgery. Often successful surgery is performed and the dog dies of cardiac involvement a few hours later.

The surgery is (or certainly should be) a gastropexy. If the vet only tacks the stomach to the inside of the abdomen, this tack will become ineffective within approximately six months. There are two types of gastropexy with which I'm familiar.

The first method is called an *intercostal* (between the ribs) *gastropexy*. The procedure partially removes a strap of muscle from the stomach wall. This belt of muscle is then passed through the diaphragm, around a rib, and back to the stomach. As the area heals, it forms adhesions that securely attach the stomach to the abdominal wall.

The second method consists of sewing the stomach wall into the *linea alba* (the center line of the abdomen). As with the other method, adhesions form during healing that secure the stomach to the abdominal wall. The first method is perhaps a bit more secure, but it is also far more invasive. My vet uses the second method as a preventative gastropexy performed during the spay.

If the dog has had a bloat episode, it is also common for the vet to cut the muscles of the *pyloric sphincter*. This valve is found between the esophagus and the stomach. During a bloat episode, this valve does not open to allow gas or food to be regurgitated out of the stomach as it normally should. It is thought to be involved in the actual onset of bloat. Cutting this valve will prevent it from clamping down.

Although it is possible for the dog to bloat again, it cannot torsion. It is the torsion that is most life threatening. However, this is a rare occurrence.

Is the tendency to bloat inherited? Probably. It would certainly seem so when a breed has a 25 percent chance of having it. Until more is known of this disease, we can only listen to the experts and do all we can to prevent it. And if a dog *does*

bloat, speed in obtaining help for him will greatly improve his chances for survival.

As mentioned, I do a preventative gastropexy on my bitches when I spay them. They are usually about four or five years old at this time and have had one or two litters. If I had a male, I would also do this. It's a lot easier on the dog to have this surgery performed when in good health instead of under emergency circumstances.

Cancer

Cancer is one of the major causes of death in all dogs. Unfortunately this also applies to Great Danes, with *osteosarcoma* (bone cancer) being the most common. Besides osteosarcoma, Danes can also have *lymphosarcoma* (cancer of the lymphatic system), *fibrosarcoma* (cancer of the connective tissues and a very slow-growing cancer that does not metastasize) and various other cancers. If the cancer is caught soon enough, chemotherapy and/or radiation can often extend time and quality of life a year or more, especially in the case of lymphosarcoma. Amputation of an affected limb can also be an option, but I wouldn't do it unless the dog is sound enough to maintain itself on three legs. I know of young amputees that did wonderfully. Each case is individual and must be evaluated accordingly.

Cancer treatment can be very expensive, stressful, and might not provide the dog with an extended, good quality of life. I had always thought that I would not put money into this. Because of cancer in my family history, I just didn't consider chemotherapy or radiation as options for my dogs.

Then my six-year-old Poppy was diagnosed with lymphosarcoma and I was devastated. After talking to my vet and some friends whose Danes went through chemotherapy, I decided to go this route with Poppy.

At this writing, Poppy has gone through thirteen chemo sessions. After a couple of initial eight-hour bouts with vomiting and general malaise, she's doing *great!* She's acting like a puppy again—playing with her toys, knocking her daughter Skylark to the ground and standing on her and "talking" her way through life! Lymphosarcoma responds beautifully to chemo in most cases.

Prior to Poppy's diagnosis, Jonquilla was diagnosed with fibrosarcoma in her left forefoot and pastern at eight years. That was two years ago, and except for a slight limp and a clubfoot caused by the cancer, she is also doing great with no special treatment. The only option given for her was amputation. She was beginning to show rear-end weakness at the time, and I decided against amputation. I'm so glad I did.

Two of my other Danes had osteosarcoma. The first, Amber, was diagnosed at ten years and lived about six more months. She was euthanized because I refuse to allow these wonderful animals to suffer needlessly. My other was eleven-year-old Pepita. Her cancer was in a foreleg. One of the side effects of osteosarcoma is that it greatly weakens the bone. Because of this, the dog might get up one day and the bone could spontaneously break. The last thing I wanted was to have something like this happen to my darling Peeps. But she was basically feeling fine and only limped slightly, so I couldn't bring myself to euthanize her at that

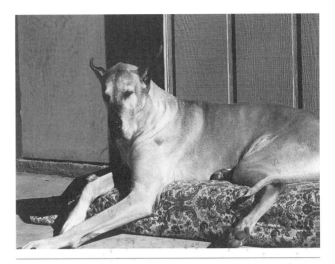

Although Pepita died of bone cancer, medication kept her very comfortable right up to the end. When she showed that the pain was too great, she was humanely put down.

time. My veterinarian gave me a very strong injectable pain medication that I could give as needed. It kept her comfortable until she could be euthanized; she was put down about four months after diagnosis.

Hip Dysplasia (HD)

Hip dysplasia is an inherited laxity in the hip joint. This laxity keeps the joint from fitting correctly, which in turn, can cause painful arthritic changes in the hip. There are various degrees of HD, from mild, causing little or no pain, to such extreme malformation that the hip joint must be replaced or the dog euthanized. Although it is possible for a dog to develop hip dysplasia even with several generations of normal hips behind it, it is not very likely.

Be aware that HD *cannot* be determined simply by observing a dog's movement. Sadly, there are still too many very well-known breeders who do not x-ray hips. Their excuse? "Oh, we don't x-ray because we don't *have* hip dysplasia." That's highly questionable at best. If you are looking at a puppy bred by someone who won't certify the health of his or her breeding stock's hips, do yourself a good favor and look elsewhere.

Hypertrophic Osteodystrophy (HOD)

Most often affecting male puppies between four to eight months of age, this disease causes acute and painful inflammation in the joints of the legs— usually the forelegs. The puppy will be lethargic and may run a fever up to 103° or higher. The degree of pain can be from mild with a reluctance to eat, to extreme with the puppy refusing to stand and screaming. The joints are usually painful to the touch.

Unfortunately many veterinarians are not familiar with HOD and often misdiagnose it. This is one reason it's a good idea to discuss some of these breed-specific problems with your vet before you need to deal with them. Diagnosis is by x-ray, symptomatic history and observation.

Treatment consists of medication to reduce pain, fever and inflammation. Most cases resolve themselves quickly. It has often been thought that HOD is caused by lack of vitamin C. Treatment at one time included use of IV cortisone and vitamin C, and perhaps some vets still use this approach.

This is one reason I give 1,000 mg of vitamin C daily to all my Danes. It can't hurt.

A friend had an affected bitch that was in severe, screaming pain, and since there was little to lose, she was given an injectable form of the analgesic Banamine (a horse medication). This gave her immediate relief.

Many breeders also recommend immediately reducing the protein content of the food to between 17 and 18 percent. In mild cases, this is often enough to correct the problem.

If you even *suspect* HOD, do the following:

1. Immediately give 2,000 mg of vitamin C orally.

2. Have your vet take x-rays of the legs. Insist if necessary. This is the only way to diagnose HOD.

3. Give IV Banamine. (Reduce dosage by the dosage given for horses, usually by 1,000 lbs.) If Banamine is not available, give Rimadyl. Give IV vitamin C if possible. Give IV cortisone.

4. The dog should be put on a wide-spectrum antibiotic to prevent secondary infection. It is these infections that cause death by HOD. Pneumonia is the most common cause of death because the dog just lies around. If you're puppy *does* just lie around, make sure he is moved from side to side periodically during the day if he's not moving on his own.

5. Reduce protein in diet to 21 percent or lower.

6. Continue vitamin C orally at the rate of 2,000 mg morning and night.

If HOD is caught at the first signs of lethargy and fever and treated as outlined here, recovery time should only be two or three days. However your puppy might not be out of the woods. Relapse, up to twenty-one days post HOD, is still possible. Keep the puppy quiet (indoor play only) and don't stress him in any way. This means no shows, no car rides, except for vet visits, until after the twenty-one-day period. After that, all being well, your puppy may resume normal activity.

Since HOD only seems to occur during the most rapid growth phase, it seems reasonable to assume that it is somehow linked to the growth rate. This is another good reason *to keep dietary protein low and body condition lean.* The best cure is always prevention:

• Keep your puppy on a low-protein diet for at least the first year (24 percent or lower).

• Give oral vitamin C daily—500–1000 mg a.m. and p.m.

• Never supplement the diet with anything that will throw off the balance of the food. Especially *do not* add calcium, vitamin D or phosphorous in any food product or tablet supplements. This means no added yogurt, eggs, cottage cheese or dairy products more than 15 percent of the volume of dry food.

Here's another view of HOD that has enabled many people to help their puppies through what the author calls "pseudo-HOD." This article first appeared in *Great Dane Reporter* magazine.

Keep in mind that this article was written by a breeder, not by a vet. If you even *suspect* HOD you should take your dog to a veterinarian. If the vet is not familiar with HOD, I hope that perhaps the following article may be of help.

HYPERTROPHIC OSTEODYSTROPHY (HOD), OR A BLOOD INFECTION (SEPTICEMIA)

BY HAZEL GREGORY (VON RIESENHOF)

My first experience with HOD, hypertophic osteodystrophy, was back in 1962 with a Great Dane litter. The best thing I can say about that long, sad and frustrating ordeal is that the learning experience for myself, as well as for my veterinarian, has been undeniably valuable down through the years. The hopelessness of that situation led me to believe that as a serious dog breeder, the need for a better understanding of the nutritional needs and the chemistry of a dog's makeup as well as genetics was of utmost importance. Thus a long and diligent study of animal and human nutritional needs is, to this day, a constant quest—a study of both medical and Mother Nature's facts and theories. I do believe it was this serious study of large, fast-growing dogs' nutritional needs as compared to the commercial dog foods available that has perhaps saved my Great Danes from a repeat episode of HOD as described in veterinary medical publications. Unfortunately that long, twenty-year dry spell was soon to end.

It is my hope that this true story will help dog owners and veterinarians recognize that the symptoms of HOD and what I call "pseudo-HOD," a blood infection, or septicemia, are quite nearly the same. My proof of this claim is a story that needs to be told.

My story starts back in September of 1984, the weekend of the Dallas/Fort Worth Kennel Clubs' dog shows and the Great Dane Specialty. My husband and I lived about a two-hour drive due west of Dallas. I had puppies to sell and I had buyers that wanted us to meet on that dog show weekend. Fortunately I had a friend in Dallas that had room at his home for my puppies and I. The Dallas Great Dane Club's Specialty party was to be at his home and I was looking forward to a fun weekend.

My friend had told me that his prize female puppy was sick with HOD. His vet said it was a classic case—but the prescribed treatment didn't seem to help much. I hadn't seen a case of HOD since the 1960s. We discussed the pain, high fever, diet and the helplessness of coping with HOD. I couldn't believe HOD was back again. That weekend my friend's puppy was rushed back to the vet and although they did all they could, the puppy died. My friend's disappointment and sadness was obvious, but like most dog people he knew one had to learn to hang in there and move on. That weekend I had sold several of my puppies to good show homes.

Four of the puppies had gone home with their new owners: one to Dallas, one to Houston, one to Alaska, and one to Wisconsin. Three puppies came back home with me. One of these, a male, was to be lead and house trained for his new owner.

The following Wednesday, while working with the male puppy, I noticed he didn't act up to par. I reasoned that he hadn't quite recovered from the stress of the weekend trip and strange surroundings. On Thursday the puppy was not any better but was still eating, had no temperature, but was playing less. By Friday morning the puppy was very sick, completely down with a raging fever. I rushed him to the vet where I had to leave him as I was to be gone for the weekend on a judging assignment. The vet had just opened her new clinic. She was young, eager to succeed and had a brilliant, inquisitive mind. I felt confident that the puppy would be fine and that I would get a call on Monday to come and get him. I did get that call on Monday. The vet said that it took a high dose of antibiotic by IV to bring the fever down but he would be fine now. The pup's fever was gone, he was eating, had bright clear eyes, looked and acted fine except that he couldn't walk. His rear just collapsed when he tried. The vet said, he'd be OK. In a few days he'd be stronger and able to walk. She said he'd had more than enough antibiotics to get whatever caused the problem and to take him home to rest. I did just that. The pup ate well and his eyes were clean. He would struggle to stand but fell over when he tried to walk. His hind legs just would not work. By Wednesday the puppy's fever was back again, full force! I took the puppy back to the vet and left him there.

The next day the vet talked to her professors at Texas A&M Veterinary School; she then called me to come to the clinic because we needed to talk. Dr. Pierce said A&M suspected HOD. This was her first case of this disease.

The x-rays she took were inconclusive at that point. (Note: X-rays usually don't show much at this early stage.) My reaction was instant. From what I had learned, HOD is not contagious. HOD is a nutritional chemical imbalance. I explained to the vet about my friend's HOD puppy and told her that my puppies had been at his kennel. My previous experience with HOD and this experience were very different. Could there be a connection or is this just coincidental? We talked about the calcium-phosphorus blood serum ratio. It was normal. I asked her if this could be a spinal infection.

Her antibiotic treatment had brought the fever down even if only temporarily. I suggested trying Chloromycetin. I had learned years ago that Chloromycetin was the only antibiotic that crossed Mother Nature's natural barrier that protects the brain, the spinal cord, mammary glands and bone marrow. The vet said, "…with the rear end being affected it could be a myelitis; at this point the lab tests and the x-rays are inconclusive. If it is myelitis, Chloromycetin is the drug to use. We'll have to make periodic blood tests to watch for a possible blood eclasia, which is unlikely but a necessary precaution when using this drug." (Since then I have been informed that a blood eclasia does not occur in dogs, only humans.)

If this treatment wasn't successful and it was HOD, more x-rays would prove such as it progressed. Note again, early stages of HOD do not always show joint swelling. Fever and joint *soreness* come first.

I left the puppy at the vet's and he was started on Chloromycetin, the dosage to be 25 mg per pound of body weight three times a day. The puppy stayed in the clinic through the weekend. The vet called on Monday and asked that I come in to see what I thought. It was amazing! The puppy was running around the clinic acting and looking like he had never been sick. The vet said that the Chloromycetin was responsible and I was to keep him on it for ten days to two weeks, after which he would be fine. He was, but for this puppy it was only the beginning of more HOD troubles to come.

Within the week I received a phone call from the puppy buyer who lived in Houston. Her puppy, Beau, was from a different litter and was also with me during that Dallas weekend; he was approximately two months older than the other puppy. I sold Beau as a top show puppy; his pedigree was excellent. It was a great home for this puppy. I kept his litter sister, my Daria Jane, ten years young, fat and healthy to this day. This new puppy owner said her puppy started acting sick shortly after they got home from Dallas. They had treated him with antibiotics. He improved for awhile but then got sick again. He lay around a good deal and he cried if pressure was applied to his joints. At this point he could hardly walk, and his new owner was very concerned. Her vet in Houston suspected the beginning of HOD but his x-rays were not yet conclusive. He would be x-rayed again in seven days. I told her about my sick pup and suggested she start her puppy on Chloromycetin, which she did. Beau showed signs of feeling better while on the Chloro. He was only on the Chloro two or three days when his second x-rays were taken. The x-rays were sent to a radiology lab to confirm the diagnosis, again a classic case of HOD. The vet said to stop using the Chloro as it can't help since HOD is a nutritional (mineral) imbalance. The new owner was very upset as she liked this puppy. Her husband, an orthopedic specialist, told her, "as bad as the puppy's legs are he will never be right." The vet's prognosis was also very discouraging.

I was frantic! By this time I was convinced that we were dealing with an infection that produced the same symptoms as HOD. I wanted the puppy treated with Chloromycetin. I offered to refund the purchase price if she would meet me halfway between Houston and Dallas and return the puppy (an eight-hour round trip for both of us). She agreed. When we met to make the exchange I was handed a copy of the lab report that had arrived that morning. We were stunned! It gave the diagnosis of HOD but it also said, "New findings suggest hematogenous (blood) infection as a cause. Do not treat as prescribed for HOD, use antibiotic instead. WOW—I knew I was on the right track!

I brought Beau back home, took him to Dr. Pierce and began the Chloromycetin treatment. It required three series of ten days on and ten days off before we were sure that the infection was defeated. This was the recommended treatment when a chronic situation is suspected. Beau had a serious case. He had been treated with other antibiotics before HOD was suspected, which I learned later usually suppresses the infection but will not cure it. Chloromycetin is the drug that works. All Beau's joints were much more swollen than the first puppy's and they took a long time before returning to normal.

Periodically during Beau's recovery the vet and I discussed the case. He was as surprised as I was regarding the lab report and will confirm the facts of this case as well as other similar cases he has since treated. A copy of this lab report was also sent to my vet. He was equally amazed and also supports this form of treatment.

This Great Dane, Beau, grew to his full potential, finished his AKC championship, produced fine puppies and never showed any negative aftereffects of his so-called HOD.

(Note: A month later a litter brother to my friend's bitch that had died came down with so-called HOD. This dog was also cured with Chloromycetin. Two other puppies, littermates to my puppy, the one in Alaska and the one in Wisconsin, had the same HOD symptoms several months later. When I received their owners' frantic telephone calls I sent out copies of the lab report. Both dogs were cured after treatment with Chloromycetin.)

Remember all these dogs were exposed to my friend's bitch that died of HOD.

Periodically through the years I have received many telephone calls from people all over the country who heard that Hazel Gregory knows how to cure HOD. All the calls have been word of mouth reference through Great Dane people. Usually their dogs are in terrible condition by the time they call me and their vet is willing to try "whatever it takes." These vets and owners have all been astounded by the positive results attained when Chloromycetin is administered.

Several vets have called me because they were skeptical but agreed to try the Chloromycetin treatment after we talked; I usually sent a copy of the lab report to them. Later on they (all but one) acknowledged successful results. This vet refused to treat as I suggested. He could not accept what I told him and said he didn't like to use Chloromycetin. This is a comment I often hear when talking to veterinarians. The puppy's owner said the vet did prescribe half the required dosage for five days only. That helped a little but wasn't enough. After the five days the puppy went back down and eventually had to be put to sleep.

More recently I have heard from an Irish Setter breeder. She had two different dogs diagnosed as having HOD. She was told by a friend to call me. Her vet willingly started the treatment as suggested, again with successful results. One of the puppies had a more severe case and had to receive two series of treatments. This Irish Setter breeder showed me her dog at a recent dog show. She said his legs had large knobs and swollen joints before treatment. When I saw him his legs were fine; he was a beautiful dog. This lady and her husband are well-known and respected breeders and professional handlers. They, as well as many others, have encouraged me to write this article. It seems that the dreaded symptoms of so-called HOD are continuing to occur randomly in not only Great Danes but in different giant, large and medium-size breeds. More often than not those afflicted dogs' prognosis leads to a painful, hopeless, heartbreaking end.

The reason I call this terrible disease pseudo-HOD is because, as I see it, the symptoms are the same as true HOD but the cause and treatment are totally different. The lab report to which I have previously referred seems to prove me correct regarding antibiotic treatment with reference to a blood infection. (Also see Ref. 3.)

Notice the antibiotics list does not emphasize that Chloramphenicol (generic name for Chloromycetin) is the drug of choice. But remember the Mother Nature barrier; Chloramphenicol is the only one listed that gets to the core of the infection—the bone marrow where blood is made. As I see it, the preliminary use and periodical changing of different antibiotics create a seesaw effect and possible chronic condition. Then as the infection hangs on, the joints become inflamed and calcium deposits start to build up on the outer extremities of the long bone just above the joints. When this happens, the pup is well into the disease, perhaps one or two weeks. X-rays are then taken and HOD is diagnosed. HOD, medically speaking, is listed under the heading of "Disease of Undetermined Etiology" (see Ref. 7) which basically says the cause or cure of HOD is unknown. Veterinarians are advised that treatment should be directed toward controlling fever and reducing pain using analgesics and/or corticosteroids. Prognosis is grim. Antibiotics are used only to control possible secondary infections such as tonsillitis.

With my vet's help I have obtained several pertinent veterinary medical documents on HOD research and findings. These date back to the early '70s, '80s, and into the '90s. Actually very little scientific help is available that shows consistent facts and findings that work or help. They all basically have the same conclusion. Medical science does not have any scientific proof as to the cause or treatment of HOD (see Ref. 4). All these documents are listed in the References below. Over the years, whenever I received a phone call asking about HOD, I have always suggested the same treatment and diet. It always works—I only ask for a follow-up progress report. So far I've had 99 percent success. The treatment I recommend is:

1. Always work with your veterinarian. Do not give vitamin C supplements while the dog is on antibiotics.

2. Start immediately on Chloramphenicol, 25 mg per pound of body weight three times a day for ten days to two weeks. Example: A forty-pound puppy gets 1 gram three times day—do not underdose.

3. For fever and inflammation, use only as needed Ascriptin and/or Phenylbutazone.

- Try not to use any cortisone shots or pills.
- Give plenty of rest in crate or x-pen with soft bedding and water always available.
- Do not force exercise—only free choice.

Diet

1. Mix and feed twice a day—a.m. and p.m.— always at the same time. Continue with a regular good-quality dog food—protein should range from 20 to 25 percent, fat should range from 8 to 10 percent. Add a small amount of an enhancer such as chicken.

2. Important: To each feeding add two to three tablespoons of the following tonic formula.

Tonic Formula

To mix tonic formula use equal amounts each of pure apple cider vinegar and honey.
  Example:
  1 pint apple cider vinegar
  1 pint honey
  Note: Slightly warm (not hot) honey mixes more easily with warm vinegar—store at room temperature.

- Do not free feed dry dog food.

- Do not force feed.

- Do not feed high-powered, high-fat, high-protein, low-roughage (stress type) food.

Stay with this kind of diet plus the tonic, which is an old-time recipe used for years as an arthritis remedy (see Ref. 8).

Remember the old saying, "An apple a day keeps the doctor away." IT WORKS! This overall general tonic is the best formula I've found in raising fast-growing, large-boned dogs. The apple cider vinegar helps keep the calcium intake in a soluble state so it can be more easily absorbed into the system. It also helps dissolve and flush out acid crystals that build up in the muscles and joints.

A must-read for dog breeders is Dr. D. G. Jarvis's book *Vermont Folk Medicine*. This book was my start in learning how to appreciate the many benefits of natural foods and healing. Up until then my studies were more concentrated on vitamin and mineral requirements and supplements. I can't imagine raising Great Danes without the help of apple cider vinegar and honey tonic. All our dogs—youngsters, oldsters and in betweens—and even my husband and myself have a daily shot with a glass of ice water. It tastes like apple cider—GOOD!!

References

1. Watson A.D.J., Blair, Farrow B. R. H., et al. *Hypertrophic Osteodystrophy in the Dog.* Aust. Vet 4 49 (9): 433–439, 1973.

2. Crondalen. *Metaphyseal Osteopathy (Hypertophic Osteodystrophy) in Growing Dogs: A Clinical Study.* Small Animal Practice 17(11): 721435, 1976.

3. Watson A. D. J. *Hypertrophic Osteodystrophy: Vitamin C Deficiency, Overnutrition, or Infection.* Aust. Vet Pract 8(2): 107–108, 1978.

4. Woodard 4. *Canine Hypertrophic Osteodystrophy, A Study of the Spontaneous Disease in Littermates.* Vet Pathol 19(4): 337–354, 1982.

5. Alexander J. W., Roberts R. E. *Symposium on Orthopedic Diseases.* Vet Clinic North Am (Small Animal Practice) 13 (1): Feb 1983.

6. Lewis P.D., McCarthy R. J., and Pechman R. D. *Diagnosis of Common Development Orthopedic Conditions in Canine Pediatric Patients,* The Compendium. Small Animal Vol. 14, #3, 287–297, March 1992.

7. *Textbook of Veterinarian Internal Medicine Vol. 2,* 3rd ed. Sec. XV, "Joint & Skeletal Disorders," Chapter 121, "Skeletal Diseases," pg 2391, by Stephen. Ettinger DVM.

8. D.C. Jarvis, MD. *Vermont Folk Medicine.* Fawcett Crest, NY.

Cervical Vertebral Instability (CVI), or Spondylolithesis, or Wobblers Syndrome

Wobblers syndrome is caused by an instability or malformation of the cervical (neck) vertebrae. This puts pressure on the spinal cord, which causes a lack of coordination (ataxia) in the rear legs. In severe cases the forelegs are also affected and in some cases the dog cannot walk at all. There is usually no pain associated with this disease. What actually causes the malformation is unknown, although an inherited tendency is a major suspect. Although the tendency can be inherited, it can also be brought on by injury.

The usual age of onset is around seven or eight months in Great Danes, but it can occur much earlier or later. I had one puppy whose movement I never liked from the moment she could walk. By six weeks she was an obvious wobbler. She'd totter along until one of her littermates crashed into her and over she'd go. But she'd pop right back up and continue playing. She was such a little fighter that I just didn't have the heart to euthanize her. I placed her in a great home with a friend who was well aware that she might never see her first birthday, but who was willing to give her the chance. Well, our sweet Sadie made it to age ten! She lived a

Although diagnosed with wobblers syndrome, it certainly didn't slow Sunflower down! She's playing with one of her favorite toys, a stretchy old bike tire.

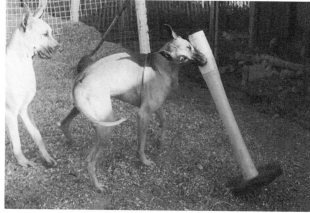

Even with wobblers syndrome, Flower lived a happy life. She could pick up heavy objects and carry them wherever she pleased.

long and happy life, and by the time she was two years old she had compensated so well for her malady that it was barely possible to tell she was a wobbler.

I had another that was a completely normal male until one day when he was playing with the other dogs. I heard him yelp and when I looked over, there he lay on his side, unable to rise. He was paralyzed! A friend helped me get him into the car and off we went to the vet. By the time we arrived fifteen minutes later, he rose and walked on his own. However he was a severe wobbler at that time. So severe that I didn't feel I could handle him along with all my other dogs, so he was euthanized.

The prognosis for wobblers is varied. There is a surgery that fuses the affected vertebrae to each other, thus stabilizing this part of the spine. Unfortunately this then puts more stress on the adjoining vertebrae, and it is common that they, too, will also become malpositioned. Most vets will not recommend the surgery, and I fully agree.

I have had personal experience with three wobblers. Sadie lived a happy, pain-free life for ten years. My first, a bitch I purchased, was diagnosed at seven months. The vet did a myelogram and sent her home on steroids and anti-inflammatories, and in a neck brace. She was so terrified of the brace that I couldn't stand watching her fearful response. Yes, I know she would have become used to it, but I wanted her to be able to live as a normal dog. I removed the brace and we never looked back.

She was affected at first in the hindquarters and later (at about age three years) in front. She lived until age five, when she was euthanized. She had become incontinent and would fall over when she squatted to urinate. She had also developed pancreatitis and it was just time for her to go. Life was no longer a pleasure to her. Although she bounced around like a flubber ball, she was able to lift heavy objects in her mouth, ran and played and had a wonderful, happy, albeit short, life. The third wobbler was mildly affected and lived until age nine. None were treated any differently than a normally healthy Great Dane.

Wobblers syndrome has many degrees of severity. There seems no way to accurately predict just how one will do in the future. No one was more surprised than I when Sadie continued to improve and lived a long, normal life. I'd give this advice to anyone having to face this problem:

- Don't have the mylogram performed unless there's some real doubt that wobblers syndrome is the problem. If a slipped disk or some other malady is the cause of the symptoms, surgery is often warranted. But if it is wobblers, and you're not going to put the dog through surgery, why do the testing? Mylograms can have unwanted side effects and can be fatal if dye gets into the brain.

- Do keep your dog on the lean side.

- Don't despair over a grave prognosis. An honest veterinarian will tell you that no one can know for sure what's going to happen.

- Do allow the dog to live as normal a life as possible.

Osteochondrosis Dessicans (OCD)

Affecting the shoulder joint, OCD can also be termed a developmental disease. It is an irregularity in the cartilage of the shoulder joint, which sometimes develops into a cartilage flap. This flap can sometimes become detached and float around in the joint capsule. It is then termed a *joint mouse*. When not obstructing movement, there is no pain, but when it interferes with the workings of the joint, the dog will show a marked limp. The cartilage flap can also cause pain. OCD is often bilateral but because there is pain in both shoulders, the dog will limp on the more painful side. OCD usually affects dogs of about seven to eight months of age.

Surgical treatment is fast, effective and *expensive*. It is also grounds for disqualification at AKC conformation shows. So if you have an affected show-potential puppy and are considering this surgery, also consider that a judge might disqualify your dog upon seeing the scar. Recent studies have shown that if there's no joint mouse involved, enforced rest and treatment with Adaquan and Cosequin and an anti-inflammatory might be equally as effective as surgery.

Breeders must evaluate each case before breeding an affected animal. It is thought that the tendency for OCD is inherited and that actual occurrence is triggered by injury. There's also evidence to suggest that pushing the growth of giant breeds during puppyhood contributes to the development of OCD. The one dog I owned that had OCD was bred once, to his cousin. Of the three pups resulting, none developed OCD.

Cardiac Problems

Although Great Danes can and do develop other heart problems, the most common cardiac problem affecting the breed is cardiomyopathy. Most frequent in males, the developing condition usually goes undetected until severe symptoms occur. Sudden weight loss, lack of energy, exercise intolerance and abdominal distension are common. Clinical signs are atrial fibrillation, and grossly enlarged, flabby ventricles are often noted. The heart is no longer able to pump blood efficiently. Prognosis is never good. Few dogs live much longer than three months postdiagnosis, although some have lived up to a year.

The Orthopedic Foundation for Animals (OFA) now certifies dogs that are free of *congenital* heart defects. This test is done by ausculation. A veterinary cardiac specialist uses a stethoscope to listen to the heart of a dog over the age of twelve months. Most congenital diseases, such as valvular and subvalvular aortic stenosis and patent ductus arteriosus, are accompanied by a heart murmur. If a murmur is present, the owner is then advised that the dog should undergo more extensive testing to discover the cause and, thus, the heart disease. It is important to realize that a dog who has received OFA cardiac certification is not necessarily free of cardiomyopathy. A dog who tests clear of cardiomyopathy in January may well test positive in June. This factor makes it difficult to screen for this problem, as several litters may already have been born when the sire is diagnosed with cardiomyopathy. In any case, it is still very important for breeders to screen for this devastating disease.

Von Willebrand's Disease (VWD)

This inherited bleeding disorder is found in a number of breeds and has been positively diagnosed in Great Danes. The definitive test for this is a simple blood test. Dogs affected by VWD should not be bred.

Cataracts

Although apparently not common in the breed, juvenile cataracts have been diagnosed in Great Danes. Unless you suspect that the dog cannot see well, you probably won't be aware that it has a cataract until it's examined by a board-certified veterinary ophthalmologist. The eyes must be dilated and then the lens (the clear, oval part behind the iris) examined by a special opthalmoscope. Cataracts occur in all sizes and shapes and affect either one or both eyes. Sometimes a vet can determine if an individual case is an inherited cataract; sometimes this is not possible, though, as cataracts can have many causes. Although some types of cataracts can affect vision at a young age, some vets say that most Danes probably won't live long enough to be adversely affected.

The Great Dane's relatively short life expectancy does not mean that breeders shouldn't test for cataracts. The Canine Eye Registry Foundation (CERF) will register dogs that have passed their eye exams. This certification is valid for only one year, since cataracts may appear at any time during the dog's lifetime.

Panosteoitis

If your Dane *has* to have *one* disease and you are allowed to choose it, this would be the one to select. *Panosteoitis, pan, pano,* or *traveling lameness* is an inflammation of the long bones of the legs that can affect the growing puppy at from four to eight months of age. Normally it will begin with a mild limp in one limb and then will migrate to another limb, affecting each limb in turn. During its active phases, the disease can be diagnosed via x-ray. The beauty of this one is that it is self-limiting, usually disappearing by the dog's first birthday or perhaps a little later.

Usually, there is little pain associated with pan, but if needed, your vet can prescribe an anti-inflammatory to ease your puppy through the worst times. The cause of pan is unknown and there is no medical cure other than the passage of time. Count your blessings if this is the only problem your puppy encounters.

FINDING A VET FOR YOUR DANE

Sadly, there are relatively few vets who are totally familiar with problems affecting giant breeds. Some have no idea what they're dealing with even when presented with a classical case of HOD or even bloat.

If the breeder of your puppy cannot help you locate a good vet, I would suggest that you start searching by calling up and interviewing vets in your area. Ask about their experiences with emergency situations such as bloat and HOD. What experience have they had with giant breeds? If a vet refuses an interview, move on. Ask owners of other large breeds where they take their dogs. Locate and get directions to the nearest emergency clinic *before* you ever need one.

When you *do* find a vet you are happy with, take his advice and ask *him* your medical questions. It's fine for owners of Great Danes to share information, and in many cases, they have more solid knowledge than many veterinarians. If, however, your dog has diarrhea, it only makes sense to take the dog and a stool sample to your vet rather than risk following the advice of other laypersons.

VACCINATIONS

Hopefully, your new puppy will have had *at least* his six-week measles/distemper shot and one parvo shot by the time you bring him home. He might have also had a couple of his adult vaccines. If at all possible, ask your veterinarian not to give your Dane puppy the seven-in-one combination shots. The celebrated Jean Dodds, DVM, has done extensive research on this practice and feels that using combinations contributes to autoimmune problems in dogs. She recommends that killed virus vaccines be used and that the parvo be separated from the DHLP. Your veterinarian should also vaccinate your puppy against any endemic diseases for your area. Rabies vaccine, of course, should be given at four months and boostered according to your veterinarian's directions.

Because of the possibility that some autoimmune problems could be associated with vaccination, you might want to have an *antibody titer* done on your dog. This is a blood test that will ascertain what antibodies your dog has in his blood. If he has a working immunity to a disease, this will show up on the test. If his antibody count is high enough to establish immunity, there is no reason to revaccinate at that time. Although antibody tests can be expensive, they can make it unnecessary to risk your dog's health by giving annual boosters.

Many accredited veterinary teaching institutions have now revised their vaccine recommendations as shown in the box on page 75.

A Brief Description of Serious Diseases

Canine Distemper

Distemper is a highly contagious, viral disease that once killed thousands of dogs. Although today's vaccines are extremely effective, dogs still die from this disease. Distemper can affect the respiratory, nervous and gastrointestinal systems. It can occur at any age but is most devastating to very young and very old dogs. Symptoms include a thick, yellowish discharge from the nose, matter in the eyes, high fever and refusal to eat. Pneumonia can develop and encephalitis can result from the high fever, which sometimes leads to brain damage.

Canine Leptospirosis

Leptospirosis is a bacterial infection that may lead to permanent kidney damage. It is spread through the urine of infected wildlife, such as mice or rats. The bacteria attacks the kidneys, causing kidney failure. Symptoms include fever, loss of appetite, possible diarrhea and jaundice. Antibiotics can be used to treat the disease, but the outcome is usually not good due to the serious damage to both kidneys and liver that is caused by the disease. Leptospirosis is highly contagious; other dogs, animals and people are all susceptible.

Infectious Hepatitis

Infectious hepatitis is a highly contagious virus that primarily attacks the liver but can also cause severe kidney damage. It is not related to the form of hepatitis that affects people. The virus is spread through contaminated saliva, mucus, urine or feces. Initial symptoms include depression, vomiting, abdominal pain, high fever and jaundice. Mild cases may be treated with intravenous fluids, antibiotics and even blood transfusions; however, the mortality rate is very high.

Parvovirus

Parvovirus, or *parvo* as it is commonly known, attacks the inner lining of the intestines, causing bloody diarrhea that has a distinctly unpleasant odor. It is a rampant puppy killer and is extremely contagious. It can even be transmitted on one's shoes. In puppies under ten weeks old, the virus also attacks the heart, causing death, often with no other symptoms. The virus moves rapidly, and dehydration can lead to shock and death in a matter of hours.

If puppies are started immediately on IV fluids and antibiotics (to prevent any secondary bacterial

NEW VACCINATION PROTOCOL BEING RECOMMENDED BY COLORADO STATE UNIVERSITY

In January 1998 the CSU Veterinary Teaching Hospital began offering its clients one additional vaccination program. We are making this change after years of concern about the lack of scientific evidence to support the current practice of annual vaccination and the increasing documentation that overvaccinating has been associated with harmful side effects. Of particular note in this regard has been the association of autoimmune hemolytic anemia with vaccination in dogs and vaccine-associated sarcomas in cats... both of which are often fatal. A booster, or the annual revaccination recommendation on the vaccine label, is just that ...a RECOMMENDATION, and is not a legal requirement except for rabies. The only commonly used vaccine that requires duration of immunity studies to be carried out before licensure in the U.S. is rabies. Even with rabies vaccines, the label may be misleading in that a three-year duration of immunity product may also be labeled and sold as a one-year duration of immunity product.

Based on the concern that annual vaccination of small animals for many infectious agents is probably no longer scientifically justified, and our desire to avoid vaccine-associated adverse events, in January of 1998 we began recommending a new immunization protocol to our small animal clients.

This program recommends the standard three-shot series for puppies (parvovirus, adenovirus 2, parainfluenza, distemper) to include rabies after sixteen weeks of age in dogs. Following the initial puppy immunization series, dogs will be boostered one year later and then every three years thereafter for all the above diseases. Similar programs to this one have been recently adopted by the University of Wisconsin, Texas A&M and the American Association of Feline Practitioners.

Other available small animal vaccines may need more frequent administration (bordetella, Lyme, etc.) and may be recommended for client animals on an "at risk" basis. Recent studies clearly indicate that not all vaccines perform equally and some vaccine products may not be suitable for such a program.

---

infection) and are aggressively treated symptomatically, they have a fair chance of recovery. Dogs that have been infected with parvo are immune for life.

Coronavirus

Corona is another virus that is rarely fatal to adult dogs but can frequently cause death in puppies. Symptoms include vomiting, loss of appetite and a yellowish, watery stool that might contain mucus or blood. The stools carry the shed virus, which is highly virulent.

Parainfluenza (Kennel Cough)

Parainfluenza, a disease of the respiratory system, can be caused by any number of different viral or bacterial agents. Highly contagious, it is easily spread in a kennel situation where many dogs are confined within a restricted space, thus the common name of *kennel cough*. Symptoms include a cough, of course, caused by inflammation of the trachea, bronchi and/or lungs. Antibiotics may be prescribed to prevent pneumonia, and a cough suppressant may quiet the cough. Most cases are mild, and many dogs recover spontaneously having received no treatment whatsoever.

Lyme Disease

Lyme disease is bacterial in origin caused by a spirochete *(Borrelia burgdorferi)* and is spread through direct contact with ticks. The most common host is the deer tick, which is very small and often escapes notice. Arthritis-like symptoms may occur, and one of the first symptoms in the dog is lameness. If untreated, the lameness subsides but returns and grows progressively worse. In humans the disease usually begins with a rash and mild, flu-like symptoms. The dog, likewise, may have had a rash that went undetected because of the coat. If treated early with antibiotics, most patients will recover without complications, but the disease is often either undiagnosed or misdiagnosed. Always check yourself and your dog for ticks after an outing in grass or woods. In case of illness, keep any ticks found imbedded in the skin in alcohol for further examination.

Rabies

A highly infectious virus, rabies is usually carried by wild animals, especially bats, raccoons and skunks. Any warm-blooded animal, including humans, can be infected. The virus is transmitted through the saliva, through a bite or break in the skin. It then travels throughout the body. Behavior changes are the first sign of the disease. Animals usually seen only at night will come out during the day; fearful or shy animals will become bold and aggressive or friendly and affectionate. As the virus spreads, the animal will have trouble swallowing and will drool or salivate excessively. Paralysis and convulsions follow. Once rabies symptoms appear, there is no cure and the disease is always fatal.

Parasites

All dogs, puppies and adults are susceptible to parasites, both internal and external. Most bitches carry the encysted form of roundworms (ascarids) in their bodies, although the worms aren't in an active phase. When puppies are born, they will almost always have the worm larvae in their bodies, as they contract them prenatally via the bloodstream through the placenta.

The breeder should have a stool sample checked when the litter is four weeks old to ascertain what kind of parasite, if any, the pups have contracted. The whole litter should then be treated with the appropriate drug to eliminate the parasite.

Besides roundworms (probably the most common), puppies most frequently will have tapeworms (spread by fleas), hookworms and whipworms. Giardia and coccidia are microscopic intestinal parasites rather than worms and are not uncommon. Both can cause diarrhea, vomiting and general unthriftiness. While coccidiosis is easily eradicated with an oral antibiotic, giardia can be frustrating and take a long time to clear up. Information on giardia is difficult to find. The problem seems to be that the treatment of choice doesn't always get rid of it completely and repeat outbreaks are common. Dogs appear to eventually build up their own immunity to the condition.

Great Danes don't have any more trouble with fleas and ticks than other dogs. Occasionally one dog may seem to be especially bothered by fleas. Usually such a dog will have a flea-bite allergy. The new flea treatments, both oral and topical, used in conjunction with flea larva nematodes (they attack the flea larva) that you can spray in a back yard, and indoor exterminating efforts have all but eliminated fleas for those who are consistent in this war.

SPAYING AND NEUTERING

It is a kindness to your dog and to the breed in general to sterilize a dog that will not or should not be used for breeding. A bitch that is spayed prior to her first season will probably never develop breast cancer. Alter your male early, and prostate cancer is also unlikely.

Bitches in season can be messy. They can also be very sneaky, and it is quite common to find out that the six-foot-high chain-link fence that you had so much confidence in is not unbreachable. Now your beautiful Great Dane bitch has mated with a "you-don't-dare-think-what" and you want to spay her immediately! Surprise! You'll be risking her life if you do. A bitch should not be spayed during heat or sixty days after going out of heat. This is because the hormones that bring her into estrus and then keep her in a false pregnancy postestrus also keep her blood from clotting as quickly as it normally does. This can allow capillary bleeding that continues

seeping at the incision site. I almost lost a bitch this way before I knew better.

Your male dog should be castrated while he's young. Neither dogs nor bitches *need* to have a litter or be bred. Your dog will be much happier and healthier if he's altered when the unspayed neighborhood bitches come into season. You won't have to worry about prostate problems due to sexual frustration or the constant whining, pacing and panting to be allowed out to visit the girl next door.

Here are some valid reasons *not* to breed your Dane:

1. **The kids can see the miracle of birth.** Children can learn about birth from books and videos. Enough can happen during the birth process that children should *not* see—or hear! This does not justify bringing a litter of perhaps ten puppies into the world needing loving homes. Take a trip to the local animal shelter and see the sad results of the many litters born for just this misguided reason.

2. **She/he should have one litter before she/he is spayed/altered.** WRONG! There is absolutely *no* medical, physical or emotional reason that a dog or bitch needs to reproduce itself except to continue the species. With a pet-quality dog (or even some show dogs) this myth especially does not apply.

3. **You want to recoup your investment.** This makes serious, experienced Dane breeders laugh. I doubt there are many breeds more expensive to breed than Great Danes.

4. **It's expensive**—even without counting the expense of showing your bitch and just starting

with the medical health screenings. All Danes that are even being considered for breeding should, at the very least, have their hips x-rayed to rule out hip dysplasia. More and more breeders are now screening for cataracts, von Willebrand's disease (VWD), normal thyroid, cardiac profile and elbow dysplasia. These tests will probably cost somewhere around $500. A routine check for any uterine or vaginal infections will help ensure a live litter. Add $100. The stud fee to a good-quality stud who is right for your bitch and has passed all his health screenings will run about $500. If a cesarean section becomes necessary, add at least $350 and probably more. Assuming there's no need for a section (there rarely is in Danes), you now have a nice healthy litter of, oh, say eight puppies. By the time the puppies are six or seven weeks old, you'll probably go through at least fifty pounds of dog food a week. Add in the first vaccines (about $20 per puppy from your vet, less if you give your own), and that's about another $160.

Soon you must arrange to have the ears cropped. For this you can easily add $150 per puppy. And, if you've bred a bitch and have no market for her puppies, you might end up supporting several of these for four or five months or longer. Gets expensive, doesn't it? To make matters worse, with no ready market for what you have bred, you cannot hope to get the $1,200 that is about average for a show-zpotential puppy from top show stock at the present time. You'll be lucky to get a small portion of that figure for your puppies. Are you

prepared to keep, feed and properly care for several six- or seven-month-old puppies until you can find the right homes for them? Do you realize what your dog food bill will be for this period? You *certainly* wouldn't want to resort to taking your puppies to the pound. The chances that they'll survive there are almost nil. Do you want this on your conscience? Still think you're going to recoup your investment? Better stick with an altered pet.

5. **She's/he's just so nice, all my friends want one of her/his babies and I want another one just like her/him.** I refer you to myth number three. Those friends who just have to have one of the pups have a strange way of backpedaling when the time comes to actually purchase the puppy. They're hoping that you'll give them the puppy. And there's no guarantee that you'll have a puppy even remotely like your dog or bitch. So is it worth all the expense and toil to go this route? It's much cheaper and easier on all concerned to just go to a reputable breeder and buy another dog.

6. **Perhaps the best reason not to breed your bitch is that you could lose her.** This happened to some good friends who had purchased a lovely bitch from me. She was bred and then died of bloat four days after her litter of seven was born. Ed and Wendy fought to save that litter for several long, sleepless weeks. Several times they feared that they'd lose some of the puppies. As they mourned their beloved Heidi, they fought all the harder to save her babies. They *did* save them, but if they had the

choice to make over, knowing they'd lose Heidi, they would never have bred her.

EMERGENCIES AND FIRST AID

Recognizing a problem is the first step in managing an injury. With a Great Dane, it's most important because this is a very stoic breed. A Miniature Poodle with a thorn in its paw is likely to scream and hop around on three legs like it's been shot. A Dane is more likely to limp slightly and perhaps quietly lie down and lick the injury. You must be observant. Before you treat a seriously injured dog, even though it's your own, you should muzzle the dog. Keeping a suitable muzzle around is an excellent idea. Lacking one, you can use any soft cloth, a belt or whatever is handy for the purpose.

Life-Threatening Emergencies

Bleeding

This is one of the most obvious signs of an injury and can also be one of the deadliest. Wounds that slowly seep blood are probably not life-threatening. Wounds from which blood is actively pumping or spurting are very dangerous, and the bleeding must be stopped immediately. Direct pressure on the wound is the best method. If you're alone, make a pressure bandage by wadding up some cloth, gauze or other absorbent material and then binding it to the wound with a cloth or tape while transporting to the vet. If there is a foreign object lodged in the wound, it's best to leave it to your vet's attention. A major blood vessel could be involved, and removal could cause more bleeding.

Bloat

Although bloat is covered in depth earlier in this chapter, it can't hurt to relist the symptoms. If your dog is "off," just not himself, watch him closely. The abdomen usually, but not always, appears distended. There will be attempts to vomit but the dog will only bring up foam. The dog might be restless or try to dig. Do not muzzle a dog in bloat. If you even suspect bloat, get to the vet immediately. Bloat is a life-threatening emergency.

Poisoning

There are far too many poisonous substances to mention them all here. However, some of the more common ones are certain house and garden plants, antifreeze (dogs are attracted to its sweet taste), certain household cleaners (especially those containing pine tar), insecticides and herbicides. Symptoms of poisoning are retching, vomiting, diarrhea, salivation, labored breathing, dilated pupils, weakness, collapse or convulsions. Sometimes several symptoms may appear together. Contact your vet immediately. If you cannot contact him or get to an emergency clinic, contact the National Animal Poison Control Center hot line at 800-548-2423.

Choking or Obstructed Airway

If your Dane is pawing at its mouth, gagging, trying to cough and acting like it's terrified, it may either have an obstructed airway (major emergency) or be choking. The first thing you must do is to look into the dog's mouth to see the obstruction and if you can remove it. If it's stuck tightly in the throat, performing the equivalent of the

Heimlich maneuver on the dog may save its life. To do this, have your dog standing and grasp both sides of the rib cage and squeeze your hands together sharply. The idea is to get the lungs to force enough air up the throat to dislodge the object. If this doesn't work, try the abdominal thrust by laying the dog on its side and, using your palms together, press in quick, sharp motions just behind the rib cage.

If the dog is choking on the object but can still breathe, get it to the vet as quickly as possible.

Bee Stings

A bee sting becomes a life-threatening emergency if your dog is allergic to bee venom. If the dog is stung and begins raspy breathing sounds, get to the vet immediately. Keep some liquid Benadryl™ on hand for just such emergencies. Just before you leave for the vet, give the dog the adult dosage recommended on the bottle. Also remove the stinger immediately, as it will continue to pump venom into the dog. Do this by scraping the stinger out with a fingernail rather than trying to grasp it. This way you won't inject any additional venom.

If the dog does not seem to be in any respiratory distress, remove the stinger and give a dose of Benadryl. If you have any kind of cortisone cream, you can apply this to the sting site.

Snakebite

This is, of course, a major emergency and the dog should be immediately transported to the vet. If you cannot see the typical puncture holes of a viper bite, you'll see the swelling and the dog will be in pain or worse. The speediest possible response is imperative.

Cardiac Arrest

If your dog loses consciousness and you suspect cardiac arrest, place your thumb under one front leg and your four fingers in the other armpit to determine whether or not the heart is still beating. This places the chest between your fingers. If the chest is too large for you to do this, use both hands instead. Reach up to feel for a heartbeat. If you cannot feel a heartbeat, put your ear on the dog's chest to listen for one, then check for a pulse either in the side of the neck or inside the hind leg where the leg meets the body. A normal pulse rate is eighty to 140 beats per minute.

Cardiopulmonary resuscitation (CPR) can be performed on a dog by first examining the dog's mouth to make sure the mouth and airway are clear. Then close the mouth, and holding it shut, blow three short breaths into the nose while watching to see if the chest rises. Then, with the dog on his side, press down with two hands on the chest to stimulate the heart and force air in and out of the lungs. Chest compression should be rapid, and you should stop about every thirty seconds to see whether the heartbeat has resumed. Get the dog to an emergency clinic, giving the described CPR all the way, unless the dog begins breathing on his own.

Non-Life-Threatening Injuries

There is nothing so sad as an injured dog. But you should be able to distinguish between true emergencies and injuries that are simply in need of urgent care. Having worked as a veterinary technician for several years, I'm always amazed at how many pet owners have no idea of what constitutes a true emergency.

Animal Bites

Few injuries sustained in dog fights are life-threatening. Most confrontations are "full of sound and fury; Signifying nothing." However, a few puncture wounds are likely. Most are only skin deep and nothing to worry about. Any wound, of course, does bear watching for infection.

Wild animal attacks are not unusual, even in city or suburban areas. Coyotes are bold and in many areas have lost their fear of man. They are even seen in highly populated city areas from time to time. Dogs are very inquisitive, and Great Danes are natural hunters who will most likely attack the wild animal first. Wild animals such as skunks, opossums or raccoons have little chance of escaping from a Great Dane but can inflict nasty bites and scratches. They can also carry rabies. Do not neglect your dog's immunizations against this dreaded disease, especially if your dog can have an encounter with wild animals.

If a skunk sprays your dog, it can be very painful to his eyes, the area that seems to be just where the skunk takes aim. Wash your dog's eyes with warm water, and apply a few drops of vegetable or olive oil to them. If you have any ophthalmic ointment on hand, that will also suffice to ease the pain to the eyes. The usual treatment for the overpowering skunk odor is a bath in tomato or lemon juice, which can be followed by a soap and water bath. The one time I had to try this remedy, it was basically worthless. Commercial products now available guarantee to get rid of the skunk odor on dogs.

Once, at about two in the morning, one of my dogs was thumping around in the hall just outside my bedroom. As I got out of bed to investigate, I was suddenly hit by the unmistakable odor of *skunk!* At the same time, the other four Danes came thundering up the stairs, each smelling worse than the other! I immediately chased them all downstairs into the kennel and locked them out of the house. I only had V8™ vegetable juice in little cans and some tomato sauce. I opened every can I had, grabbed the first victim, and into the shower we went. (I have a walk-in "dog shower" in the kennel that has proved to be a godsend for such emergencies.) One by one, I scrubbed each dog with the tomato sauce and V8, shampooed them, and then locked each one in the indoor/outdoor kennels. The odor was everywhere.

Once all the dogs were bathed, dried and locked into their kennels, I pulled the sliding door shut in an effort to keep the house from smelling any worse.

By the next morning I was fairly inured to the stench, and it *had* dissipated somewhat. The girls were quite indignant at their overnight confinement and were jumping up and down anxious to be out. I opened the gate to the backyard and let them all out of their runs. They went galloping off up the back hill to an area behind the house of lawn and fenced-in old-growth forest, which they love to investigate. I went into the kitchen to prepare their breakfast. Suddenly the skunk odor became much stronger, and when I turned, all five girls were standing behind me, each with a dead baby skunk in her mouth!

It took about a week for the odor to clear from the house, but for about the next three or four weeks, the dogs still had some lingering fragrance whenever they got wet.

Away from Home

When planning an outing in the country with your dog, take a few precautionary measures and a small first-aid kit—if not for you, for your dog. Include a muzzle; knife; eye ointment; pliers; some antiseptic, such as peroxide, meat tenderizer or ointment (for insect stings); and should you anticipate meeting a porcupine, a small bottle of vinegar. If you are going into an area where you know there are poisonous snakes, take along a snakebite kit.

If your Great Dane accompanies you on a trip into an area where he might encounter a porcupine, it is helpful to know what to do if your dog's curiosity gets the best of him. With the porcupine, there's no contest. If your Dane ends up with quills in his body, get to a veterinarian right away, because the quills will invade the tissues more and more as the dog moves around. If you are far away from a vet, you will have to remove the quills yourself as soon as possible. This should be done gradually and will be very painful to your dog, which might necessitate the use of the muzzle. If one is unavailable, you can use a strip of soft fabric to tie around the muzzle—first on top, and then bring under the muzzle, tie again, bring the tails of the cloth up around the head behind the ears, and tie yet again.

Tie it snug but not so tight as to cut off his air. It's best to carry a manufactured cloth muzzle with you.

Beginning in the chest area, cut off the tips of the quills at an angle to release pressure, making them easier to remove (vinegar can also be used to soften the quills). Use an instrument such as pliers (if none are available, your fingers will have to do) to slowly twist out each quill. Do not jerk them out. As they are removed, clean the wound with an antibacterial agent such as peroxide.

Bone Fractures

Although serious, bone fractures are seldom life-threatening unless a punctured lung or cut artery is involved. Immobilize the limb or whatever part of the body is injured as well as you can and transport to the dog to the vet. A rolled-up newspaper taped around a limb makes a quick and easy makeshift splint. Don't try setting the bone yourself, especially if it protrudes through the skin.

Heat Stroke

Every summer, at almost every dog show I attend, I hear this announcement over the public address system: "May I have your attention? There is a dog in a blue van, license plate DUMBJERK, who needs his owner's attention. It's very hot out here today, folks, please check your dogs!"

Now I ask you, just how much intelligence does it take for people to remember that even cars with windows open can heat up dangerously in the summer!? Wouldn't you think that people who show and love dogs, who purport to have their best interest at heart, would be super aware of this problem? There's always one idiot in the crowd.

Great Danes do not take heat well. Especially the blacks, blues or dark brindles. Symptoms of heat stroke include rapid panting, difficulty breathing, vomiting and collapse. Check the gums for color; they might be blanched. If you can find a container big enough, place the dog in the container and fill it with cool, but not cold water. Or cover the dog with towels and keep cool water running over the dog. In lieu of all these procedures, wet the dog as best you can, and place cold packs (with ice) in the armpit, groin and under the throat. Offer water in small amounts. Get the dog into a cool environment as soon as possible.

Burns

Immerse the burned area in cold water immediately. Transport the dog to the veterinarian.

Fever

Fever can be a symptom of many diseases. In a Great Dane between the ages of five and nine months, it could be a symptom of HOD. In any case, a dog with a fever needs veterinary attention. Your vet is going to want to know the dog's temperature. You can take your dog's temperature using an ordinary rectal thermometer. Normal temperature for a dog is between 101 and 102 degrees Fahrenheit. Shake the thermometer down below 98 degrees and apply a small amount of Vaseline™ to the end. If you have an assistant, have him hold the dog's head. Lift the tail and insert the thermometer into the anus approximately two inches. Hold on to it while the temperature is being taken. After about two or three minutes, you'll have an accurate reading. Wipe the thermometer off and read the temperature. Always clean the thermometer with alcohol after use.

Vomiting

Vomiting is often a normal occurrence in a dog and should not cause alarm if it only happens once. But continued vomiting coupled with other symptoms, such as fever or diarrhea, is cause for medical attention. Note the presence of any foreign objects in the vomitus, such as plant material, glass or small stones.

Diarrhea

Like vomiting, occasional loose stools are probably not a reason for alarm. However, continued diarrhea needs attention. It can be a symptom of anything from intestinal parasites to parvovirus.

While diarrhea by itself is not an emergency, it can cause dehydration. For this reason, it's a good idea to not allow your dog to go more than a couple days with this problem before seeking veterinary advice. Dehydration itself *can* become an emergency, especially for young puppies. You can check to see whether a dog is seriously dehydrated by pulling up the skin on its back. If the skin feels plump and quickly returns to its original position, the dog is probably not seriously dehydrated. However, if the skin feels pliable and remains pulled up, that is an indication that the animal is becoming dehydrated. Dry or tacky gums may also indicate dehydration. The dog probably is too sick to be expected to drink enough water to correct the condition. Take him to a veterinarian who, if she confirms dehydration, will inject fluids that are slowly absorbed into the body.

CHAPTER 7

Caring for Your Great Dane

"GROWING" A GREAT DANE

At first glance this heading might seem stupid… but is it? Don't they just grow up like any other dog? Well, no. Great Danes are a giant breed. The amount of growing they must do before reaching adult size in comparison to say, a Golden Retriever, is enormous. In only a year, almost full skeletal size is reached. Compare that to the very slow growth of a human, who essentially reaches the same size and weight at adulthood. With bones forming and reforming so quickly, it isn't surprising that much can go wrong in a short time.

We once thought it was necessary for giant breeds to consume huge quantities of protein, calcium, phosphorous and vitamin D to reach their full adult potential. Several extensive research projects have strongly indicated that excess nutrition and, worse, excess supplementation can be the causative agents in the many growth problems seen in the giant breeds. Now informed breeders strive to keep growth steady but *slow*. Great Dane menus are properly balanced when protein is kept to around 21 to 25 percent, especially during the rapid growth stages of puppyhood.

At five weeks. (Jill Swedlow)

At five months. (Jill Swedlow)

And as an adult. (Jill Swedlow)

I start puppies on solid food at whatever age they look like they need it. Some of my bitches have enough milk to raise pups up to a year on nothing else if they'd put up with it! Only a couple have seemed to need help. One litter I bred appeared a bit lean, with hip bones and ribs easily seen and felt at about three weeks. I feed puppies the same diet I feed their mother but grind it into a powder in a blender. In this case it's Innova at 24 percent protein, 12 percent fat. The first meal consists of human baby cereal, usually rice and powdered bitch's milk

Great Danes achieve the dynamic growth to their adult size in about eighteen months. There is little wonder that they are so prone to growth-related problems.

replacer. To this I add a couple of crushed Lactinex™ *(Lactobacillus acidopholus)* tablets, which help digestion and help to prevent diarrhea so common during the weaning process. Lactinex can be purchased in any drug store pharmacy. After a few meals of this, I begin adding baby-food beef. Gradually I add the Innova kibble, ground to a powder, a little at a time to each meal. I also begin adding Eagle Brand™ canned meats—beef, chicken, lamb or liver—to the diet. As the pups get better at eating on their own, the amount of added milk replacer is gradually decreased until, by four weeks, it is removed completely. At the same time the volume of canned meat is increased. Once the puppies are about five weeks old, they will be gradually introduced to whole, soaked kibble. When I first begin solid food, I offer it in the morning and evening, allowing mother to fill in between feedings. Again, depending on condition, I play it by ear for when I add a noon meal. I've never had a litter that would eat four meals a day. Three have always sufficed. By the time puppies are about seven or eight weeks old, they will usually leave some of the noon meal. Once this occurs I just discontinue it. I've never had a problem doing this. They're allowed to nurse (if their mother will cooperate) up until they are six weeks old.

Because most dog foods are completely balanced for all stages of growth, the delicate balances will be upset by the ill-advised addition of calcium and other unnecessary components. If the kibble you feed does not have added vitamin C, you might want to use 500 mg in the morning and evening meals. Although dogs can manufacture their own vitamin C, it can't hurt to give them a little extra. I give the full group of antioxidant vitamins (C, E & A), Co-Q-10, probiotics (to help digestion) and Source™ (micronutrients from a kelp source).

I like to keep my dogs on as natural a diet and as free from chemicals and pollutants as possible. Because of this, I've done some research on exactly what goes into different dog foods. For your dog's sake, learn to read and interpret dog-food labels. One of the most helpful books on this subject is the *Official Publication of the Association of American Feed Control Officials.* You can obtain a copy from the treasurer at AAFCO, Capitol Square, Atlanta, GA 30334. Contact them for the current price.

You will learn that poultry meal and poultry byproducts are most definitely *not* the same. Any ingredient that is designated as a *byproduct* is probably composed of beaks, feathers and feet—basically unusable protein sources for dogs. Poultry *meal* means that the whole chicken has been used. Also, protein levels can be misleading depending on the source of the protein. A dog-food label can list 28 percent protein, but if it's derived from leather dust, the dog will never be able to use it. The first ingredient listed on the label must contain the highest percentage of the food. Therefore, if you see poultry meal as the first ingredient, the chances are that it's a higher quality food. If grains make up the bulk of the first ingredients, beware. This is not to say that just because grain is the first ingredient listed that the food is not good. Many manufacturers offer different types of foods for different stages of life. If the protein content of a food must be lowered, this is often accomplished by increasing the percentage of grain.

Learn about the use of preservatives in dog food. Avoid foods that contain any kind of chemical preservatives. Ethoxyquin is common in some foods and has been proven to cause cancer in mice. It was originally used as a preservative for *rubber.* Also, avoid any food that contains tomato pomace. This is the leftover parts of tomatoes after everything good is taken from them for human use. Now, this in itself isn't particularly bad, but this part of the tomato, especially the skin, contains the highest concentration of insecticides of almost any byproduct you can name. The risks are obvious.

As I learned more about ingredients that can be contained in pet food, I discovered that even if preservatives aren't listed on the dog-food package, they can still be in the formulation. This is because if certain ingredients contained in the meal were in the base product, they don't legally have to appear on the label. I've also learned that certain "meat meals" could easily contain protein sources and chemicals you would not knowingly feed your dog.

I'm not trying to come across as an expert on canine nutrition here, but these are things that I've learned and they have worked for me for some time. Before I stopped feeding the higher protein foods, I never had a litter without some major growth problems. Panosteitis, osteochondrosis dessicans and wobblers syndrome all raised their ugly heads at times. Since feeding a 24 percent protein (or less) formulation, only one pup showed a mild case of panosteitis. It might just be coincidence, but the change in diet must be considered. Some or all of these conditions can surely be inherited. However, if there is an inherited predisposition to these problems, it certainly can't hurt to slow puppies' growth and perhaps bypass the problem.

It's also worth mentioning that recent studies have shown that it isn't even so much the level of protein that can cause growth problems, but also the body condition of the growing puppy. Until he's at least ten months old, a Great Dane puppy should be maintained on the lean side. The ribs should be easily felt but be only faintly visible.

At one year, the puppy's major growth period is over, although it will continue to fill out and the skeleton might still grow a bit. Now you can be a little more liberal when adding other foods to your young Dane's meals. Balance is no longer so critical as it was while the rapid growth phase was in force. Feed twice a day throughout the dog's life as a preventative against bloat. I've always added table scraps or leftovers to add variety to the diet. Occasional additions of cottage cheese in small amounts and often yogurt are always appreciated. (Interestingly, the bloat study being conducted by Purdue University reveals that Danes fed a *variety* of different foods are less likely to bloat.)

The diet my dogs are fed contains added probiotics. As a fortunate result, my dogs *no longer are troubled with gas!* For a breed as prone to bloat as the Dane, this can only be a plus. The other real plus in my mind regarding their food is that this manufacturer uses only human-grade ingredients in the formula. More recently I've begun to believe that fresh, whole foods are of real benefit in dog feeding. To this end they also get fresh ground beef; raw, whole eggs (with the shell); yogurt; cottage cheese; and—to satisfy the urge to chew—whole, raw carrots; apples; and raw beef bones. These extras are not furnished daily and not at the same time. In this way the dogs are always looking forward to something special. Eggs are fed both raw and cooked, and are thoroughly washed in soapy water and rinsed prior to feeding if fed raw. Each dog is limited to no more than one or two raw eggs per week, as they can restrict the dog's access to certain nutrients if fed in greater quantity.

Occasionally Great Danes will help themselves to whatever tempting morsel they can reach, and they can reach many. It should always be a routine matter for Dane owners to put anything edible in a secure, Dane-proof spot. Otherwise your large canine friend will find any edible left unsecured!

There is much to know about dog feeding and nutrition, and the subject fills volumes written by preeminent world authorities. There are some especially interesting books on natural feeding. If you want to learn more about modern dog feeding, refer to the listing of books in the bibliography at the end of this book.

FEEDING A GREAT DANE PUPPY

Let's now consider the practical side of feeding your puppy. When you take delivery from the breeder, you should either be given a few days' supply of the food your puppy has been eating or have the same food at home. If you plan on staying with the same diet, simply continue the current routine. If you intend to switch the puppy to another product, do this gradually over about a week. The breeder will tell you how much food your puppy eats and how often.

Most puppies between the ages of seven and eight weeks will eat between two to three cups of food twice a day. As your puppy grows, you will know when to increase the amounts by your pup's body condition. Although most new Dane owners are obsessed by their dogs' weight and height, it really doesn't matter at this point. What does matter is whether or not you can see (barely) and feel (easily) the puppy's ribs. This is the ideal body condition for a growing Dane.

As your Dane matures, he'll require less food because he's no longer growing at such a prodigious rate. For example, Skylark, the tallest bitch I've ever owned, ate twelve cups of food a day at about seven months of age! She stayed lean on it, too, and also spent a great deal of time running up and down the back hill. Skylark was a very busy puppy. At three years old, 135 pounds and standing approximately thirty-four inches at the shoulder, she eats a scant three cups twice a day. She's still pretty active but not as much as when she was younger.

In contrast was Narcissus, who at ten years, weighing about 110 pounds and standing approximately thirty-one inches at the shoulder, stayed fat on one-and-a-half cups of kibble twice a day. My Poppy is a good example of average food intake. She gets two cups of kibble twice daily. At six years old, she stands thirty-two inches at the withers and weighs 120 pounds. Males will probably eat more; six to eight cups of food a day is usual.

The amount of food you feed will depend on its quality. This is why it is so important to feed a very high-quality food. There is no need to overload a dog's stomach with huge quantities of food or to pick up the large volume of inevitable results. It is truly false economy to buy a lesser quality food. You will make up the difference in cost by the large quantity you must feed. You might find yourself feeding twice as much of a poor-quality food. Also, less-expensive foods contain lower quality ingredients, vitamins and minerals. Few contain probiotics, which should be considered essential for Great Danes. In dog feeding as in many other things, you get what you pay for.

Because it helps to prevent the dog from gulping air as it eats, elevating the feed dishes is an excellent idea. (It is thought that gulping air may contribute to bloat episodes.) There are many ways to do this. You can place the dish on a chair, or you can buy an elevated, adjustable food-dish stand or dish holders that clip to a chain-link fence, an exercise pen or a crate, depending how and where you intend to feed your dog.

Do not free feed your Dane, and feed him in the same place at each meal. It's important to know exactly how much he's eating regardless of the amount of weight he carries.

As with all dogs, clean, fresh water should be available at all times.

Keeping fresh, clean water available at all times is imperative. As with food pans, it is wise to elevate the water bucket off the ground to prevent the dog from taking an unnatural position and to discourage excess intake of air, which could lead to bloat.

EXERCISE

Great Dane puppies are fragile beings. That big-boned, fifty-pound baby can be more easily harmed at this age than many other breeds. It's great to play ball with your puppy. Tug of war is also a favorite, but let the *puppy* do all the tugging. If you roughly yank and snap the tugged object around, you could harm the puppy's neck or back.

Enforced exercise for puppies is a bad mistake. Of course you can go for short walks on lead, and this is encouraged. Especially if you go to a public area where strangers can pet and meet the puppy.

Snacks are always welcome when Great Danes gather. Here (from left) the author's Kiwi, Cricket, Amber and Daffi beg for handouts.

do not do well in extreme heat or extreme cold. If you *must* jog with your adult Dane, work up to the distance slowly. Do not jog with your dog on days much over 70 degrees or under 40 degrees. Danes, especially blacks, blues and dark brindles, are especially susceptible to heat stroke.

TO CROP OR NOT TO CROP

Cropping is often an emotional issue. If you have the choice, it should be an informed one. Most Danes in the show ring are cropped; however, this is *not* a competition requirement, and the Standard describes both cropped and uncropped ears. Many first-time Dane owners have no idea what they're facing with the aftercare of a cropped puppy. You need some information to make an intelligent decision—one you hopefully will be glad you made.

Uncropped Ears

First, it's interesting that in the natural world, there is not *one animal* species with drop ears! The erect ear is nature's way of keeping an open ear canal so that air can reach inside. This helps prevent infection. Drop ears are more susceptible to infection than erect ones. They are also more likely to develop a hematoma if the head is shaken hard. The ear tips can snap like a towel and cause the blood vessels in the tips of the ears to break. They

But jogging with a Dane puppy or hauling it alongside a bike is asking for trouble. A Dane puppy gets his healthiest exercise from playing on his own (or with another dog) in a fenced yard. He can run and play until he's tired, and then he can go sleep for however long he wants. *He* sets the limits. If you have a larger puppy or adult dog, make sure that it isn't playing too rough with the pup. I've seen puppies badly injured because larger adults were playing in the same area and knocked a puppy flying.

Many people ask about jogging with their adult Danes, but they should remember that Great Danes are not endurance dogs. They were meant to quickly run down and then hold their prey until their masters arrived to make the kill. They

When playing tug of war with a young puppy, allow the puppy to do all the pulling. Jerking a youngster around may damage the neck or spine and could lead to wobblers syndrome. (Jill Swedlow)

bleed into the ear tissue and cause painful swelling. Sometimes this swelling breaks open when the dog shakes its head and blood flies everywhere. Hematomas are difficult to heal and often keep reopening. The ears must be taped down over the top of the head and a bandage applied to keep them there. Because this irritates the dog, he scratches at it, often reopening the wound.

Although cropping is not necessary for a show dog, uncropped Danes have a different look compared to cropped animals. The alert attitude of an uncropped dog pales in comparison to the same attitude on a cropped dog. All else being equal, a judge might tend to lean toward the cropped animal when making his placements.

Cropped Ears

There is more to owning a Dane with beautiful, cropped, properly standing ears than simply purchasing a cropped puppy or having him cropped after you have purchased him. The actual surgery is only half the story. The aftercare usually lasts until the puppy is five or six months old but can continue for up to a year or even longer. If you live close enough to the breeder, he or she will often continue to tape and train the ears for you or will teach you how to do it properly. If you don't live close enough to the breeder and she cannot recommend anyone local, you're on your own. The following instructions should successfully see you through this task.

Objections to ear cropping often come from the impression of a poor crop done by a veterinarian with no idea of how to properly crop ears. Not every vet is good at it. Cropping is more often learned through the vet's personal experience as the breeder of a cropped breed, or by being properly taught by a vet with years of experience with show crops. And *he* might have been taught by a breeder!

Great pain and disfigurement can result if the ear is not properly cut, stitched, and either racked or taped to some kind of support. And, if the aftercare giver has no knowledge of how to properly tape and train cropped ears, a great deal of unnecessary damage and pain can result. Any time you see a beautifully cropped Dane, the chances are that the breeder has arranged for the cropping of the litter and has used a talented vet for the actual surgery.

It's not a good idea to allow a larger dog to play with a youngster unsupervised. Here Lark is starting to get a little too rough with her son Mac. (Jill Swedlow)

Ear taping consists of wrapping the ears with tape in such a way that they stand erect. The tape is usually left on for a week or ten days, removed for a couple of days, and then reapplied. This is done consistently until the ears are standing. It's time-consuming but, in my opinion, worth it.

If you decide to have your Dane cropped, it is imperative to use an experienced veterinarian who comes highly recommended by breeders who show. I'd rather see a Dane uncropped any day over one that has been mutilated by an incompetent surgeon. There is nothing uglier than a bad crop. It can also be an unnecessarily painful experience for the puppy if the vet doesn't know what he's doing. The issue of pain is the most common reason used by those opposed to cropping. If done by a competent veterinarian, there is little pain involved. Certainly no more than the pain of a hematoma.

Your dog's breeder will probably be able to refer you to the right vet. If not, ask the vet how many crops he does, whether they are show dogs, what kind of aftercare he recommends and whether you can talk to a few of his clients. Also arrange to view dogs he has cropped. If he's not willing to answer these questions, look elsewhere. You want a vet who will agree to crop the ear all the way to the end in a long show crop. This will take longer to stand, but it's well worth the final result.

Veterinarians will differ on the best age at which to crop a puppy. Some prefer that the puppy be between eight and twelve weeks of age, with a body weight of at least twenty pounds. Others will want puppies cropped as young as six weeks.

Another consideration is the type of anesthetic used. My own feeling is that if the veterinarian won't be using an inhalant anesthetic, I would rather not have the puppy cropped. With certain anesthetics, there's just too little control if something goes wrong. When on inhalants, a puppy is also hooked directly to oxygen and a respirator in case it should stop breathing. The vet can put it on pure oxygen and breathe for it in an emergency.

Preferences for methods of stabilizing the ears immediately after cropping will vary among practitioners. Few will change their methods on request,

Skylark plays with daughter Blossom. Blossom is now old enough to be at little risk when playing with her mother. (Jill Swedlow)

but here are some of the options. My personal experience has always been with racks. They are formed out of stiff wire (often wire coat hangers) and shaped so the ears can be taped erect to them directly on top of the head. If properly taped, these racks cause little discomfort to the puppy for the two weeks they are left on. My only real objection to racks is that they can get caught on projecting objects. I've seen a pup get them stuck in the ground and severely twist its neck when playing. One of my own did this, and she developed into a wobbler. It might have just been coincidence, but I've always felt that this episode had something to do with it.

Some vets will tape the ears flat over the top of the head and then apply a bandage. I don't care for

this method, as I think it tends to cause the ears to cup over the top of the head when they're taken down. I've seen this done but never had a pup treated with this method.

The other method I've seen uses Styrofoam cups stacked one on top of the other and then reinforced with tape. They are set on top of the head, and the ears are taped directly to their sides. I think that this looks like the best method of all. People I've discussed it with recommend it highly. The cups are loose enough to give when pushed around in play, and because they are very light in weight, the pups seem to hardly know they're there. My last litter had this done, and I will use it again in the future.

Aftercare of the Ear

Once your puppy has been cropped, the racks or cups are off, and the ear is healed, it's time for the aftercare to begin. Without proper aftercare, the ears are unlikely to stand properly. First, be sure that the ears are completely healed. If there are one or two areas with scabs still intact, be sure not to tape over them or place a tiny bit of cotton sprinkled with antibiotic powder at the site so the tape won't stick.

There are probably as many aftercare methods as there are breeders. The two basic differences in most methods are that one type completely encloses the ear and the ear canal, and the other leaves it open to the air. I don't care for the

It is not imperative that a Great Dane have cropped ears. As an example, Holland's ears are of the correct size and set for this attractive natural look. (Colleen Leahy)

enclosed method—it's not only extremely irritating to the puppy, but it often causes infection or oozing under the more enclosed areas of tape. I much prefer and recommend any method that allows good air circulation. My own method and directions follow.

Here's What You'll Need

- A length of one-half-inch fabric *boning* material (available in yardage shops). Cut these long enough to reach from the top of the bump of the ear to just past the ear tip (see Figure 7.2 on page 97).

- Johnson & Johnson's Zonas™ adhesive tape. A one-inch and a one-and-a-half-inch roll. You'll probably get this from your vet or from a hospital supply store, although some drug stores carry it. I recently noticed something called Sports Tape™ by Johnson & Johnson in the drug store. It seems to be the same as Zonas.

- Benzoin compound. Available from your drug store.

- Cotton swabs.

- Bandage scissors.

- Antibiotic powder or BFI powder.

- Alcohol.

- Cotton balls.

- Three-fourth-inch diameter plastic hair curlers (or lightweight half-inch PVC pipe) cut about one-and-a-half inches long. (A knife heated on the stove cuts the plastic easily.)

- Surgical glue or ear cement. Use this only if you are having trouble getting the tape to stay in place after a day or two. If you do use this, use it very sparingly. Only a dot or two on the inside and outside of the ear should suffice. When you remove it, be sure to use adhesive remover.

- Adhesive remover.

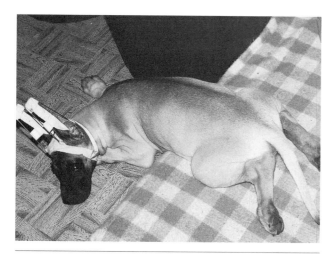

Many veterinarians use the rack, shown here, to hold the ears erect immediately after cropping. (Jill Swedlow)

This puppy's ears are in training tapes minus the brace across the top of the head. Once ears can stand this well, there is no need for a brace. (Jill Swedlow)

The author's Gala in Styrofoam cup molds. (Jill Swedlow)

Now Follow These Steps

1. After you've cut the rollers, use your scissors to cut away any rough edges from the cut ends.

Take the wide tape and cover this roller completely, tucking the excess at the ends inside the roller. Then take the one-inch tape and wrap it around the roller *sticky side out.* Set aside.

2. Cut two pieces from the one-inch tape that extend about one-fourth inch past the stay (boning) material you've already cut. Lay one piece of tape down sticky side up. Center the stay on the tape. Lay the next piece of tape on top of the stay with *its* sticky side up, making a "sandwich" of tape, stay, tape. Repeat with the second piece of tape.

Now put the stay onto the roller with the other side of the stay against the roller. Place the stay against the roller so that the bottom of the stay is even with the bottom of the roller, as shown in Figure 7.1. As the ear grows, the stay can be placed higher on the roller each time so that it is a little longer than the ear.

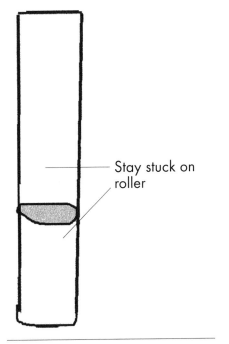

Stay stuck on roller

Figure 7.1

3. Cut two pieces each of one-and-a-half-inches-wide tape long enough to wrap twice around the base of the ear, approximately ten inches long. (If you cannot find one-and-a-half-inch tape, use two pieces of one-inch tape connected along the long sides.) Cut two pieces each of one-inch tape, approximately nine inches, six inches and three inches long.

4. Prepare the ears. Clean the ears well with alcohol and dry thoroughly. Next, using cotton swabs, paint the ears with the Benzoin compound. Paint the inside of the ear from the bump to the tip (see Figure 7.2). Paint the outside of the ear to the tip, and pay particular attention to the outside of the base. Allow the area to dry until tacky—about two or three minutes.

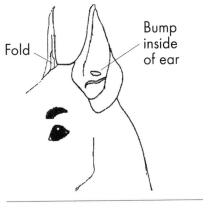

Fold

Bump inside of ear

Figure 7.2

5. Shake a small amount of the antibiotic powder in the little fold at the base of the ear on top of the head. This will help prevent the infections that usually start here.

6. Set one of the roller/stay appliances in the inside of the ear just resting on the bump. Smooth and apply pressure until adhered firmly (see Figure 7.3).

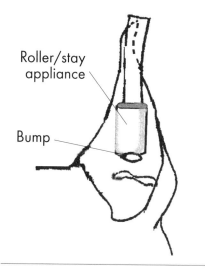

Roller/stay appliance

Bump

Figure 7.3

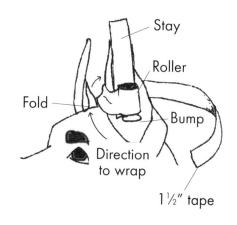

Stay

Roller

Fold

Bump

Direction to wrap

1½" tape

Figure 7.4

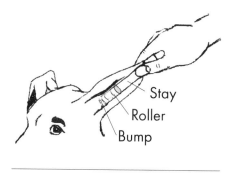

Stay

Roller

Bump

Figure 7.5

7. Wrap the nine-inch-long piece of one-and-a–half-inch tape around the base of the ear and curler, as shown in Figure 7.4. It is important to keep tension on the ear at this point. You want the base pulled out from the head so you can tape it properly in order for it to stand (see Figure 7.5). Wrap in the direction of the small ear fold at the base of the ear. Wrap it snugly but not too tight and angle the tape down into the base of the ear where it meets the head (see Figure 7.6).

8. Take the nine-inch piece of one-inch-wide tape and wrap it around the ear and roller, starting about one-fourth inch above the top of the roller. The six-inch piece goes around the ear in its middle, and the three-inch piece wraps the very tip.

9. Repeat the procedure on the other ear. (Note that the ear will be pulled more tightly into the roller than shown in the illustration.) For the first couple of tapings after the cropping incisions have healed, the sutures are removed and the rack is off, it's a good idea to brace the ears across the top of the head.

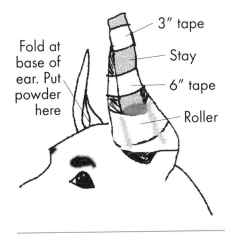

Figure 7.6

10. **Brace the taped ears** (see Figure 7.7). Cut a piece of "stay" material wide enough to span the space between the ears without rubbing the ears themselves, usually about three to four inches. Cut a piece of one-inch tape long enough to reach from one ear to the other, circle the ear, return to the first ear, circle it, and wrap about halfway back to the other ear. Ears should be held erect and allowed to turn into a naturally held position, usually slightly out from the side of the head. You'll need an assistant here to hold the ears while you tape. Start taping at the front of one ear, span to the other, circle it around the back of this ear to the front span, and then insert the stay and sandwich it between the two pieces of tape. Continue the tape around the second ear and back across the front. Be very careful not to

twist or turn the ears out of their natural resting position. Cut a short piece (about two inches) of one-inch tape and wrap around the span between the ears a couple of times so the stay will remain in place. You're done! Leave the ears taped about a week, then take the tape off and allow the ears to rest for a day. Repeat until the ears are standing.

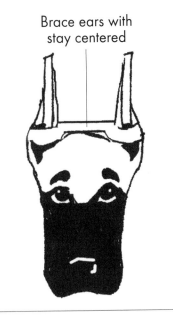

Figure 7.7

If the ears constantly flop forward or hang out to the side, you have not taped the bases close enough to the head. You can try putting another wrap of tape around the base and see if that works. If it doesn't, you'll have to retape the whole ear.

CHAPTER 8

Grooming Your Great Dane

Because one of the Great Dane's most appealing traits is its ease of grooming, this chapter is one of the shortest in the book! There is, of course, a minimum grooming requirement for health and general well-being. A certain amount of grooming beyond normal maintenance is also necessary for the show ring.

It is very important to start these procedures while the puppy is still very young, especially in the care of nails and teeth. This will save you considerable grief (and possibly expense, since you won't need the services of your vet or a groomer) when your dog is an adult. Some breeders start acclimating puppies to nail care and other grooming operations when the puppies are able to stand.

NAILS

For pet Danes, nails should be kept short enough so they do not click on the floor when the dog is walking. For show dogs, the nail should be very short—about one-half to three-eighths inch is about right. To keep nails this short means beginning with tiny puppies still in the whelping box. I clip nails for the first time when the puppies are about two days old. This continues weekly for life. If this regimen is followed, there will never be a worry about clipping the nails back drastically, because they will never get too long.

Keep nails short by using either a specially made dog nail clipper, nail grinder, or a Dremel™ grinding tool. Be careful not to cut into the *quick* (the vein present in each nail), as this could cause the dog considerable bleeding and pain. For this reason a grinder is my tool of choice, as it will cauterize the nail if the quick is cut. If you use a nail clipper, take only small amounts at a time until you see the quick. Have some form of coagulant on hand for those occasions when you *do* get into the quick. Sooner or later you will—especially if your Dane has dark nails.

DENTAL CARE

Whether or not your Dane will ever have his bite and teeth examined by a judge in the show ring, he will probably have to submit to such an examination by the vet. As with nails, you must start this conditioning while the puppy is very young. Get your puppy used to having your hands in his mouth by gently rubbing his gums and playing with his tongue. Don't allow him to mouth *you*, however! After they get used to it, most dogs enjoy having their gums rubbed. You can purchase doggie toothpaste and toothbrushes in a pet store or from a mail-order catalog. These are very helpful in preventing the buildup of plaque. You can also invest in a wide variety of chewing items, which dogs love and help keep teeth clean. Also, raw beef femur bones are wonderful chew toys for youngsters and adults. Just make sure your puppy keeps these outdoors until the worst of the grease and fat are eaten.

It's easy to scale your Dane's teeth should it become necessary. If you make scaling a regular part of his grooming, he'll probably never need this done by the vet, so he'll avoid general anesthesia. Buy a scaler at the pet store or through some of the pet-supply catalogs and learn how to use it.

All you need to do at first is just lift the lips away from the teeth and scrape away the tartar from the outer surfaces of the teeth, working away from the gums. Getting to the tartar inside is more difficult, and you might need a helper for this. However, if you've been consistent with your scaling and giving the dog the synthetic chewing items and natural bones, there should be almost no tartar buildup inside the mouth.

COAT CARE

This is one of the best aspects of Great Danes—no long hair to become tangled and matted, and no trimming! Most Danes will shed twice yearly. During this time, the hair will continue to fall for several weeks. You can speed this along by using a rubber curry comb or a rubber mitt. This pulls out all the loose hairs, and the dogs love it.

For the Great Dane exhibitor, it never seems to fail that your dog's coat will look like it's been attacked by a fleet of moths just prior to an important show weekend. However, if you can easily pull the hair out in a clump with your fingers, there's a way to get the entire coat out quickly. Be sure you choose a warm day, because the dog will be wearing his "oil" bath for several hours.

Mix Alpha Keri™ bath oil and some bubble bath containing coconut oil. It's a good idea to do a small patch test on the skin under the belly first to make sure your dog isn't allergic to the ingredients. Attach a hose to a faucet where you can control the temperature, and adjust it to warm—Danes *hate* cold water.

Now combine one part Alpha Keri with two parts *very warm* water. Wet the dog thoroughly with the warm water from the hose and then "squeegee" most of the water out of the coat with your hand. You can also buy a sweat scraper made for horses for this task. Then completely saturate the coat with the Alpha Keri mix. Do not dry or squeegee. Leave the dog outdoors with this mixture on his coat for about five or six hours.

Mix the bubble bath with equal parts water. Sponge generously over the coat and work into a lather. Rinse thoroughly with water from the hose as warm as the dog can stand it. Towel dry (or blow dry if desired). Once the coat

This handsome brindle models the good grooming that has gone into him for his appearances in the show ring. His ears and whiskers are closely clipped, and every inch of him is immaculately clean. Because a dog is smooth coated does not mean that grooming is optional. For pet or show dogs, good grooming is never optional. (Gayle Painter)

is completely dry, brush out the loose hair with a rubber curry comb. You won't *believe* how much hair comes out. The dog is now "greaseless" and can be allowed in the house.

Repeat this every day for about three days. Most of the old coat should be gone and the new will be coming in. It really works!

REGULAR BATHING

If possible, bathe the dog outdoors with warm water using the hose you've attached indoors. An adjustable spray nozzle that turns the hose on and off is helpful. Wet the coat down thoroughly, then lather with the shampoo of your choice. Rinse very well, making sure you leave no soap residue on the coat. You can either dry the dog with a towel and hand-held dryer, or you can just let 'em rip through the back lawn! (Why *do* dogs get so silly when they're wet?) If the weather is bad, of course, you'll have to bathe indoors. A bathtub can be a real hassle in dealing with a giant breed, but you might have no other options.

If you aren't showing, it's unlikely you'll need to bathe your Dane more than once every few months. Danes are very clean. Too-frequent bathing can strip the coat of needed oils, thereby contributing to dry skin and a dull coat.

EARS

Cropped or uncropped, ears need a certain amount of attention. A small amount of hydrogen peroxide on cotton balls and swabs is perfect for this task, but you can also use an ear-cleansing solution made for dogs from your vet or local pet store. Dampen (do not saturate) a couple of cotton balls with peroxide or ear cleaner and gently swab the entire inside of the ear, reaching into the canal as far as your finger will reach. Then use the swabs dampened with solution to get into the smaller areas on the outer ear that are difficult to reach with the cotton. *Do not* poke the swab into the ear canal itself! If you go too deep or the dog suddenly moves his head, you could do a lot of damage. Leave this task to your vet should it be needed.

GROOMING FOR SHOW

Other than a bath prior to the show, the bulk of show grooming a Dane concerns the ears and face whiskers. If at all possible, have the breeder, a handler or some other experienced person show you how to do this the first time. Also, please don't wait

Ch. Paquestone's Mistydane Quasar, owned by Jack Henderson and Georgia Hymmen and bred by Raymond Paquette, is a multiple Specialty winner.

until the puppy is six months old or more and about to attend his first show to get him used to the sound and feel of having clippers against his face. A six-month-old puppy is much harder to restrain than an eight-week-old!

First a word about whiskers is very necessary. The long hairs, or whiskers, that extend out from the dog's muzzle, above the nose, under the jaw, above the eyes and at the moles on the side of the face are actually sense organs called *vibrissae*. These sensors help the dog to "see" in the dark and prevent injury to his eyes or other tender areas. It is

Ch. Michaeldane JB Advent, CD, TDI, CGC, bred by M. Chiles, J. Kleim and T. Muller and owned by J.P. Yousha.

also thought that these sensors help canines to locate their prey when hunting. Because they *are* useful to the dog, some people don't want to cut them off, even for show. There is no AKC rule or Great Dane Club of America policy that requires you to do this. The main reason for clipping the whiskers is to clean up the face and give the dog a more "groomed" look.

Although I personally love the look of the whiskers, I also love the look of the head without them. I compromise by clipping whiskers just prior to a show and allowing them to grow out between times.

If you do decide to clip, here's how it's done. Use an electric small animal clipper fitted with a #40 blade. I use the Oster A5. You must be very careful when you start clipping the whiskers, as you don't want to gouge into the surrounding body hair. Just skim the surface of the body hair as you clean each whisker off. On the lips, it helps to stretch them downward while clipping. When working on the under jaw, hold the lips up so you can see what you're doing. When clipping the feelers above the eye, gently place your other hand over the eye so it's shut. The dog is not as likely to jump or shy away when it can't see the clippers so close to its eyes.

The insides *(only)* of cropped ears usually must be clipped. I clip against the hair from the tip of the ear down toward the base. Carefully clip all the long hairs inside the base of the ear. If the hair is a little longish along the ear edges, clip this too while holding the ear stretched upward with your other hand. Be *very careful* that you don't cut into the edge of the ear, as copious bleeding can result. This is where that mishap is most likely to happen.

Some exhibitors and handlers use clippers to trim any long hair on the skin of the flank between the body and the stifle. I always seem to do a poor job of this, so I leave it alone. Using barber's shears or thinning shears, you might want to carefully clip any longer hairs that adorn the back of the thigh. I usually don't do this unless the hair is really long, but it adds a perfect finish to the overall look.

A quick nail trim, ear cleaning and bath, and your Great Dane is ready to do you proud—in the show ring or for public admiration.

CHAPTER 9

Showing Your Great Dane

Entering the world of dog shows is like stepping into a whole new dimension. (There was once a time when I considered dog shows stupid, and I am now a seasoned exhibitor. After I began showing, there was a time I thought I'd never want to judge, and now I've changed that tune!) So... if you think that dog shows sound interesting and that you might like to participate, read on. You'll be able to base your decision on some inside knowledge.

The *intent* of the first dog shows was to select the best specimens of a breed. Those dogs were often widely bred from and would perpetuate (hopefully) the best qualities of their respective breeds. To an extent, this is still true, but more often than not, most people participate because they love dogs, it's fun and they have the chance to make a win. Strictly speaking, a knowledgeable, objective breeder does not need the opinion of a judge to evaluate her breeding stock.

HOW DO AKC DOG SHOWS WORK?

Basically there are three kinds of conformation shows—Specialty shows, Group shows and all-breed events. Specialty shows are put on for one breed by a club devoted to promoting that breed. There are many Great Dane Specialty clubs operating in all parts of the United States, and those sanctioned by AKC to do so hold shows for Danes only. A Specialty may be held as an independent event or in conjunction with a Working Group or all-breed show. As the name suggests, all-breed shows are open to every AKC-recognized breed.

A dog show is basically an elimination contest in a closely structured format. Winning dogs go on to the next level until they are defeated, with the last undefeated dog at day's end being named Best in Show.

The first level involves competition among individuals of the same breed, so let's consider this here. There are six regular classes in the format. These are further divided by sex, age and, often, color. All dogs (males) that are not champions are judged first, followed by all the nonchampion bitches (females). For further details about eligibility, see *Rules Applying to Registration and Dog Shows*, published by AKC; free single copies are available on request.

The classes follow:

- **Puppy:** Dogs at least six months old and under a year. At most larger shows and at Great Dane Specialties, this class is further divided for puppies under and over nine months.

- **Twelve to eighteen months:** Dogs in this age range.

- **Novice:** Dogs that have never won a blue ribbon in any higher class, have no more than three firsts in the Novice class, and have never gone Winners or Reserve.

- **Bred by exhibitor:** Dogs bred and owned by the handler or a member of his or her immediate family.

- **American bred:** Dogs born in the United States as a result of a mating that took place in the United States.

- **Open:** All dogs of any age or country of origin, including champions. Great Danes of any color may be shown in Open. However, most shows divide this class into Black, Blue, Brindle, Fawn, Harlequin and, coming soon, Mantle.[1]

Following the judging of all regular classes in each sex, the first-prize winners of the same sex return to the ring to compete against each other for Winners. Whichever dog is selected Winners Dog (or Bitch) receives the allowable number of championship points based on the number of dogs actually present and competing. Next, the exhibitor placed second to the Winners returns to the ring to compete with the remaining first-prize winners for Reserve Winners. The Reserve Winners does not receive any points unless Winners is disallowed for some infraction.

Once all regular class judging has been completed, all champions of record and dogs that, according to their owners' records, have completed their championship requirements enter the ring to compete for Best of Breed. Also competing for Best of Breed will be the Winners Dog and the Winners Bitch. Many years ago this class was named *Specials Only*, meaning it was for champions competing for special prizes. The name has stuck, and you will often hear this class referred to as the *Specials* class and champions identified as *Specials* to this day.

---

[1] *The mantle pattern is found in the harlequin gene pool. Basically, it's a "mantle" or "cloak" covering most of the body, except for a blaze on the face, a white chest and collar and four white "stockings" on the legs.*

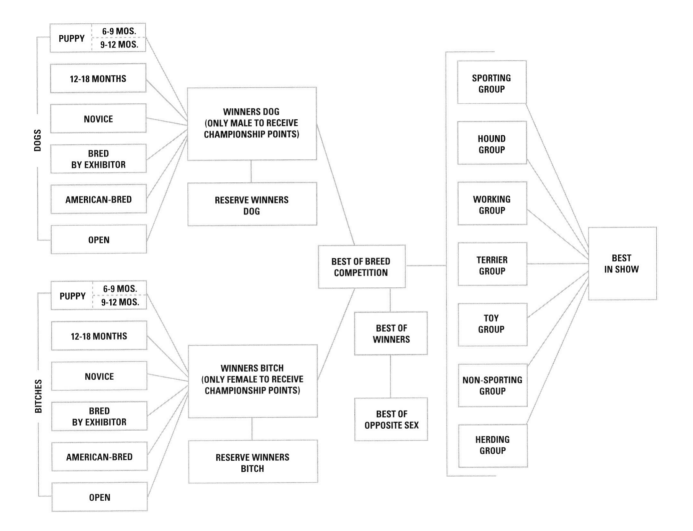

From this class the judge selects one dog as Best of Breed (BB), a Best of Winners (BW) and a Best of Opposite Sex (BOS). Only the Winners Dog and Winners Bitch compete for Best of Winners. If the bitch goes Best of Winners (beating the dog) and there were more points in the dog classes, the bitch gets the extra points. The Winners Dog, however, does not relinquish the points he won. This means that she could obtain a major win that she would not have earned otherwise. Obviously, if either Winners Dog or Winners Bitch wins BB, it automatically is BW.

The dog or bitch that wins Best of Breed is, in the judges opinion, the best example of its breed on that day. Finally, the judge also chooses a Best of Opposite Sex. This animal must be the opposite sex to the BB winner. The BB Great Dane may now compete in the Working Group. The dog that wins the Group goes into Best in Show (BIS) competition against the winners of the other six groups. Obviously the winner here is Best in Show.

HOW DOES A DOG BECOME A CHAMPION?

To become an AKC champion, a dog must win a total of fifteen points under three different judges. Included in these points must be at least two *majors* won under different judges.

How many points a win is worth depends on how many dogs were defeated on that day. Point schedules vary for different regions, reflecting the average numbers usually present. The AKC changes point schedules annually depending on how many

dogs have been in competition during the preceding year in each region and how many majors were available. To find out how many points a win carries, consult the catalog of that show, which will include the rating from one through five points (the maximum).

A *major* win consists of from three to five points. Anything lower than this is considered to be *minor* points. So if there are enough bitches competing at a specific show to result in a three-point major win, the WB will receive the major. As a result of excusals or absentees, the number may go below what is required for the major. Under those circumstances the major is said to have *broken,* and the WB receives only two points. Also, as mentioned earlier, if the WB receives only one or two points, but she goes BW and the WD had won a three-point major, then the bitch, too, is so credited. A dog can earn even more points by beating any champions present for BB or BOS. It is even possible for a dog to win points on the Group or BIS level. Suppose the BB Great Dane is not yet a champion and has won three points by winning BB. If he goes on to win First in the Working Group and there was a four-point entry present in Newfoundlands, the Dane would come away with four points. If the same Dane went BIS and there was a five-point entry in Longhaired Dachshunds, the Dane would finish the day with a wonderful *five-point major,* and it doesn't get better than that!

Once a dog has won fifteen points, including both majors under at least three judges, he has earned his AKC championship. Perhaps it sounds easy on paper, but acquiring a championship can be both time-consuming and very expensive. This is even more applicable in a popular breed.

How Do You Enter a Dog Show?

Dog shows are held by both Specialty and all-breed clubs. Most of the physical arrangements for modern shows are handled by a professional show Superintendent, are hired by the club or are taken care of by a show secretary. You can locate the superintendents servicing the shows in your area in the Events Calendar of the *AKC Gazette*. Ask to be included in their mailings for premium lists (see appendix). Once on the mailing list, you'll receive premium lists for all the shows they manage that offer classes for Great Danes.

The premium list provides everything you'll need to know about the show—show name, date, location, judge's name, prizes, entry fee, driving directions and much more. Fill out the entries completely, include the required fee and return them to the designated address in advance of the closing date.

The first item to fill out on the form is the amount of the entry fee enclosed. Next is *Breed*, and of course you'll enter *Great Dane*. The *Variety* box can be ignored, as it does not apply to Great Danes. For *Sex*, enter *Male*, *Female*, *Dog* or *Bitch*. For the *Dog Show Class*, enter the class your dog will be competing in. If you enter the *Open* class, simply write *Open* in the space provided; then in *Class Division*, enter the applicable color division.

Additional Classes is rarely used. Although you *may* enter your dog in any or all of the classes he is eligible for, he must then *win* every one of these classes in order to be eligible to compete in the Winners class. Best to play it safe and enter just one class. The only exception to this would be at a Specialty, where you might want to enter *Sweepstakes* as an extra class or *Parade of Champions* if your Dane is eligible. If your dog is also entered in *Obedience*, this is where you indicate the appropriate class.

If the dog is to compete in a *Junior Showmanship* class, indicate which class in the space provided. *Name of Junior Handler* and *Junior's AKC number* are self-explanatory.

Next you must give the *Full, Registered Name* of the dog. For the number, check the appropriate box and then enter the *Registration Number*. *Date of Birth* and *Place of Birth* are both self-explanatory.

The space for *Breeder* requires the name(s) of the person(s) named as breeder(s) on the dog's AKC Registration certificate. The spaces for *Sire* and *Dam* require full registered names of both parents.

Actual owner information is self-explanatory. If your dog will be shown by a handler, identify that person in the *Name of Owner's Agent* space. Otherwise, ignore the space.

Very Important: Remember to sign your name and include your phone number. Make out the check to the appropriate party and mail it with the entry to the listed address. Be sure to check closing dates. This is a *very strict rule* and will *not* be changed for anyone. There's nothing more disappointing than missing a show entry.

❏ **MASTER** or ❏ **VISA**   FOR FAX ENTRY ONLY - FEE $4 PER ENTRY   **EXPIRATION DATE**

CARD NO.

**CARD HOLDER
NAME**

SHOW   **DATE**

I ENCLOSE $_____ for entry fees.

IMPORTANT - Read Carefully Instructions on Reverse Side Before Filling Out. Numbers in the boxes indicate sections of the instructions relevant to the information needed in that box. (PLEASE PRINT)

BREED	VARIETY (1)	SEX

	DOG (2) (3) SHOW CLASS	CLASS (3) DIVISION Weight, Color, etc.

| | ADDITIONAL CLASSES | OBEDIENCE TRIAL CLASS | JR. SHOWMANSHIP CLASS |

NAME OF (See Back)
JUNIOR HANDLER (if any)

FULL NAME
OF
DOG

❏ AKC REG. NO.   Enter number here   DATE OF BIRTH
❏ AKC LITTER NO.
❏ ILP NO.   PLACE OF BIRTH   ❏ USA   ❏ CANADA   ❏ FOREIGN
❏ FOREIGN REG NO. & COUNTRY   Do not print the above in catalog

BREEDER

SIRE

DAM

ACTUAL
OWNER(S)_____   Please Check If
   ❏ OWNERSHIP CHANGE
(4)   (Please Print)
OWNER'S   or
ADDRESS   ❏ ADDRESS CHANGE

CITY _____ STATE _____ ZIP _____

NAME OF OWNER'S AGENT
(IF ANY) AT THE SHOW _____ ID # _____

I CERTIFY that I am the actual owner of the dog, or that I am the duly authorized agent of the actual owner whose name I have entered above. In consideration of the acceptance of this entry, I (we) agree to abide by the rules and regulations of The American Kennel Club in effect at the time of this show or obedience trial, and by any additional rules and regulations appearing in the premium list for this show or obedience trial or both, and further agree to be bound by the Agreement printed on the reverse side of this entry form. I (we) certify and represent that the dog entered is not a hazard to persons or other dogs. This entry is submitted for acceptance on the foregoing representation and agreement.

SIGNATURE of owner or his agent
duly authorized to make this entry_____

Telephone _____ Pers. ID Code # _____

Sample entry form used for all AKC conformation shows and obedience trials.

You should receive the entry form back from the Superintendent about a week prior to the show date. It will list the time of judging, the ring number, the total number of dogs entered and other pertinent information.

SHOW EQUIPMENT

For your comfort and your dog's, there are several items you should take to shows with you. How much you carry will depend on whether the show is indoors or outdoors, the weather (for outdoor events) and the length of time you'll be spending at the show. If the entry is small and the weather is pleasant, about all you'll need is a folding chair and a soft blanket/pad for your dog. If it's very sunny, take an umbrella that clamps to the back of a chair to shade your dog. Specialty shows and all-breed shows with large entries require much more equipment, the most important being a portable exercise pen.

Here's a list of items that make showing much more enjoyable and comfortable:

- Folding chair.

- Chair umbrella.

- Beach umbrella that can be anchored in the ground. These are great for you and the dog ringside, as they give lots of shade and protection in case of rain.

- Exercise pen. For a Dane, purchase a four-foot-high model. These pens have eight panels and make up a four-foot square enclosure. On days when you'll be at the show for several hours, the exercise pen gives your dog a safe place to rest, shade/shelter, water and a spot in which to relax. It frees up your hands too!

- Kennel cart. Some people call them *dollies* or *trolleys,* but whatever you call them, they are most handy to move all your gear from your car to your show setup and back.

- Water (bottled or from your home tap).

- Water dish that attaches to the pen.

- Pickup tools or plastic grocery bags to clean up after your dog. Use them!

- Cool coat. These are dog coats made of terry cloth that you can wet down to keep the dog cool.

- Warm dog coat for cold weather.

- Spray bottle filled with water.

- Drool towel.

- Grooming tools.

- Bait, usually cooked liver.

- Six-foot training lead.

- Show lead.

- Lunch, snacks, beverages (for yourself).

YOUR FIRST DOG SHOW

Plan to arrive at the show about an hour prior to judging time. This will give you time to unload and

Three of the author's Danes are warm and comfortable on this cold day in their raincoats. They've learned from puppyhood that they are NOT allowed to jump up on their pens. (Jill Swedlow)

Most experienced exhibitors transport their dogs in crates for the comfort and safety of all concerned. (American Kennel Club)

set up your equipment, place your chair at ringside and generally get you and your dog settled in.

If you have a professional handler, she will usually pick up the armband. If not, this is up to you. You may get your armband from the ring steward, who will be at the judge's table at the ring entrance. Place the armband on your left upper arm. If the band doesn't have notches in the sides to hold the rubber band, make a small tear at each side. This will keep the armband from slipping out from under the elastic.

If you don't have to show in one of the first classes, you'll have time to watch the judge's ring procedure so you have an idea of what to expect once you enter the ring. Be at the ring entrance as the class prior to yours is ending. Know your armband number, as you'll probably be called into the ring in catalog order.

As you enter the ring (especially in a large class) take note of who you're following. If you're first in line, notice who is *last*. This is important at an outdoor show in warm weather, because as the class is being judged, most handlers will bunch up under any available shade. Just as the judge finishes examining the last dog in the class, savvy handlers will have their dogs stacked up in line to be ready for the final decisions. If you are first in line and don't know who was last, you won't know when to get your dog ready. If you don't know who was ahead of you, you won't know your place in line.

As the class is being judged, know when your turn is coming up. When the dog in front of you moves off to gait, bring your dog up and have him stacked and ready for the judge to go over when she finishes with the dog in front of you. *Don't* give your dog any bait just as the judge comes up to examine him. Suffice it to say that the impression this makes on the judge will not be a good one.

The judge will go over your dog, beginning with examination of the head. Be sure your dog is properly stacked and under control at this point. (Carol Tucker)

The judge will do a hands-on examination of your dog, beginning with the head, mouth and body, and will manually check testicles on males. If you prepare in advance with a show-prospect puppy by going to training classes, matches and socializing activities in general, your Dane will grow into an easy dog to show and always a credit to your training and the good manners inherent in the breed.

Next the judge will probably ask you to move your dog in a certain pattern. Most judges use the *triangle*, but some will use an *L* or a *down and back*. You'll learn about these patterns in handling class and by observing the judge's procedure. Move the

Start setting your dog up while the judge is examining the dog in front of you. By doing so, your dog will be in its most attractive position the first time the judge sees it. (Carol Tucker)

When returning to the judge, stop approximately six feet away or as instructed and walk your dog into its most flattering pose. (Carol Tucker)

dog easily and on as loose a lead as possible through the pattern. As you turn to come back to the judge, check to see where she is standing so you can bring the dog back to her in a straight line. Don't run over the judge when you come back. Stop the dog about six feet away and pose him. When the judge tells you, gait the dog again to wherever you've been directed.

When you line up for the final examination, keep an eye on the judge. If she wants your dog in first place, you wouldn't want to be gazing into space and miss her signal! Another handler might take the opportunity to run over to the first-place

marker! No matter what your placement, take your ribbon from the judge with a smile and a thank-you. Don't snatch the unwanted ribbon with a sneer, argue with the judge or storm out of the ring. Also, don't be seen throwing your ribbon away on the showgrounds. If you don't want to keep the ribbon, put it away and discard it later.

If you win the class, remember that you still need to take your dog back into the Winners class to compete for points. If you had a second-place dog, you might have to go back into Winners to compete for Reserve if the winner of your class is Winners on that day. So don't throw your armband away or leave the area until it's all over.

If your dog wins the points, remember that you still have to compete in the Best of Breed class. You'll be in that class behind the entered champions, the Winners Dog first and the Winners Bitch behind him. The judge will instruct you on what to do. Now, if you're *really* having a fantastic day and you take Best of Breed, you'll need to keep that armband on because your dog will then represent Great Danes in the Working Group. And of course (now it's *really* fairy-tale time), if you win the Working Group, you'll go on to compete for Best in Show. (Nothing is impossible, after all.)

HANDLERS AND HANDLING FEES

Showing can be a costly hobby. One of the most expensive aspects of showing is the use of a professional handler. Handling fees will vary at various times and in different areas. What can you expect for this fee? With most handlers, you get to see your dog in the ring for as long as your dog is in

A correctly marked harlequin is not always easy to find. Janey Madl

Brindle consists of a striped pattern over a lighter ground color. There are several shades of this attractive color phase. © The American Kennel Club

Blue is an unusual color and is actually a genetically dilute black. © The American Kennel Club

Fawn is the best-known color phase of the Great Dane. Most fawns will also carry a black mask. © The American Kennel Club

The dog on the left is a harlequin, a striking pattern of irregular black patches over a white ground color, and the dog on the right is a mantle. Considered a disqualification in the American breed Standard as this book goes to press, it is an approved color in other countries and there is support for its acceptance in the United States. Walter J. Perkins

As formidable as a Great Dane can appear, it will always find time to stop and smell the flowers. *Christine Mroz*

When the dog in a "one dog welcoming committee" is a Great Dane, the impression on the caller can be both formidable and unforgettable. *Christine Mroz*

Black is a truly stunning color in the Great Dane as modeled by Ch. G'Dieter's Chance Encounter. *Nancy Gale*

The headstudy of this beautiful blue seems to capture the Great Dane's pensive side. Shari Kathol

The Great Dane is ever watchful over those he loves. Jill Coffey

The ancestors of the Great Dane hunted wild boar and served as guard dogs for German nobility. Today the breed still makes an admirable guard dog as well as a sensible, intelligent companion for those who enjoy the presence of a canine giant in their lives. Heidi Osborne

The competition really turns out for a Great Dane Specialty show. © The American Kennel Club

On the show circuit, Great Danes travel safely and comfortably in their own crates. © The American Kennel Club

In the ring it is the handler's job to make the most of all a dog's assets in a very short time. © The American Kennel Club

In this interesting study, the handsome fawn lends his own grandeur to that of the background. John D. Wood

Great Danes tend to enjoy each other's company as this compatible pair clearly demonstrates. Marta Brock

Great Danes normally demonstrate good aptitude for Obedience work. © The American Kennel Club

Given the opportunity, most Great Danes will relish vigorous outdoor activity with their owners. © The American Kennel Club

There is something special about Great Danes that inspires unshakeable loyalty in people who find the breed all that can be desired in a dog. Pets by Paulette

This beautiful Great Dane puppy represents the promise of happy togetherness with a devoted owner for life. Hadley James

The headstudy of this beautiful blue seems to capture the Great Dane's pensive side. Shari Kathol

The Great Dane is ever watchful over those he loves. Jill Coffey

The ancestors of the Great Dane hunted wild boar and served as guard dogs for German nobility. Today the breed still makes an admirable guard dog as well as a sensible, intelligent companion for those who enjoy the presence of a canine giant in their lives. Heidi Osborne

The competition really turns out for a Great Dane Specialty show. © The American Kennel Club

On the show circuit, Great Danes travel safely and comfortably in their own crates. © The American Kennel Club

In the ring it is the handler's job to make the most of all a dog's assets in a very short time. © The American Kennel Club

In this interesting study, the handsome fawn lends his own grandeur to that of the background. John D. Wood

Great Danes tend to enjoy each other's company as this compatible pair clearly demonstrates. Marta Brock

Great Danes normally demonstrate good aptitude for Obedience work. © The American Kennel Club

Given the opportunity, most Great Danes will relish vigorous outdoor activity with their owners. © The American Kennel Club

There is something special about Great Danes that inspires unshakeable loyalty in people who find the breed all that can be desired in a dog. Pets by Paulette

This beautiful Great Dane puppy represents the promise of happy togetherness with a devoted owner for life. Hadley James

competition. Win, lose or draw, the handling fee was earned and so payable. Some handlers actually board, transport, groom and show a Great Dane, but most today do not. The basic routine is that you, the owner, have the dog trained, groomed, bathed and ready to go into the ring. You hand this dog to the handler, who then shows the dog for you. Most handlers will spend a little time working with a dog that has come to them for the first time.

Some handlers will bring portable pens to the shows and set them up so you can have a place for your dog while at the show. If not, you'll need to bring your own pen or keep the dog on leash for the length of the show.

The author's first champion, Sunnyside Daffodil, finished her title under judge Ron Pock. From this photo, it is hard to tell who was more excited.

outside the ring instead of inside. This is because the dog is usually too comfortable and relaxed with familiar company. If the owner is *outside* the ring, the dog will often become very alert—either watching the owner or looking for the owner if the owner has been instructed to hide from the dog.

Certainly you can handle your own Dane to its championship: Many people do. I've put championship titles on two bitches from the Puppy and Bred by Exhibitor classes and put points on others. It takes longer because owner-handled dogs usually just don't sparkle like the dog shown by the professional. Most professional handlers are very skilled in the art of presenting a dog at its best, getting everything the dog can possibly give.

CHOOSING A HANDLER

Do you *need* to hire a handler? No, you don't. The reason for using a handler is that most professionals do a much better job with the dog than the owner. Even the dog whose owner is a capable handler will usually look better when the owner is

People who swear that showing dogs is all politics are wrong. My owner-handled champions are living proof that this is not so. No one knew me when I first started in Danes. I know I didn't cut any deals with any of the judges who put up my bitches. Most judges really do judge the dogs, not

The wise handler always knows the best speed for gaiting each individual dog. (American Kennel Club)

the handlers. Of course there are some judges who do cater to handlers, but in my opinion, they are not the majority.

Many handlers specialize exclusively in Danes or perhaps one or two other breeds. Before you decide on which handler you'll use, watch them in the ring. Some handlers are very skilled with all dogs. Some do best with a dog that is naturally showy, and others excel in handling dogs that are considered "problem" dogs. Evaluate your dog and then make the decision.

When you first approach a handler, be sure to ask what her policy is regarding priority status. Most handlers will give priority to their longest-standing clients. This matters if the handler wins several classes with her dogs. Although most handlers are very good about backing each other up, it's best if your handler can stay on your dog for the Winners class.[2] If a backup handler cannot be found, you may well find *yourself* back in the ring handling your own dog.

Tell the handler that you want her to handle your dog on a trial basis. Decide how many shows you'll consider as a fair trial period. If the dog does not look good or perform well for the handler, you'll want an easy way to end the relationship.

Many handlers are honest enough to refuse to show a dog (and thus waste the owner's money) who is not a good show specimen. But unfortunately, many are not. Their only bottom line is the money. If your dog has not consistently been in the ribbons, preferably blue ones, for at least half the shows, ask your handler for her opinion of the dog. If you don't feel comfortable with this, ask one or two knowledgeable friends to critique the dog, or better yet, ask the opinion of several of the judges who have judged him. If after twenty shows your dog has not taken any points, you might reconsider showing him.

---

[2]*If a handler has several dogs that are eligible for the Winners class, she'll ask another handler who is free to take one of her dogs back into Winners.*

In dog shows, amateurs and professionals compete on an equal footing. This makes for keen competition all around.

Ch. Dinro Sounda's Good Luck Charm, owned by Louis Bond's and Robert Layne's Dinro/Sounda Great Danes.

Obedience Trials, Performance Activities and Other Fun Things

BY LYN RICHARDS

The Great Dane has, by nature, a generally laid-back personality. The breed can also be stubborn as well as gentle and sensitive. These characteristics must be considered when training a Dane puppy. While there are exceptions, generally speaking, a very gentle yet firm hand is effective with a Great Dane. Bear in mind that Danes grow quickly, so developing respect and admiration for the authority and dominance of the trainer/owner early in puppyhood is vital. Praise and consistency are critical ingredients in the training recipe. The following guidelines will help foster admiration, respect and love in your new pup once you bring him home.

In nature, dogs always look to the pack leader or *alpha* for attention, direction and protection. That's your number one job as a Dane owner and trainer. If you can fill that role, then training will come easily. A secure dog will follow your lead no matter where you go, because he trusts you. Try to learn to think

Whatever your training goals are, start when your Dane is still a puppy and establish your authority as pack leader. With this as your basis, the extent of your achievements is up to you.

like a dog and treat him like a dog. This includes teaching yourself about dominance and respect issues, as confidence in yourself is necessary to build trust with your dog. He won't trust you if you don't trust yourself.

Your Dane must know that you will never let him down. The dog is very forgiving in nature and will trust you even if you make mistakes, as long as you are unfailingly dependable. Since the dog doesn't know what you are teaching him, if you make a mistake he won't know that either. Watch what you do, exude confidence and be consistent. Your dog will love you for it.

What is your purpose for training your Great Dane? Do you want a good solid citizen who won't knock over grandma or the nieces and nephews when they visit, or are you thinking of entering conformation or Obedience competition,

taking the plunge into Agility or doing Therapy work with your Dane? How you train is governed by your goals for that training. Reading this chapter will hopefully help you identify your goals and perhaps guide you successfully toward fulfilling them.

BASIC/PET OBEDIENCE: A SOLID FOUNDATION
Training at Home

Obedience training starts in the whelping box. You must depend on your puppy's breeder to provide these basics. If you are well acquainted with the breeder, you are more likely to be able to positively affect your puppy's early training. You will also be better able to make an educated choice of the puppy you want, based on your knowledge of each individual in that litter. If you have never before owned a Dane, the breeder might be better able to select the correct pup for you.

Studies have shown that puppies up to three weeks (twenty-one days) of age are able to absorb very little in the way of education and are unaware of much except mom, food and sleep. Elimination is done by reflex at this point. This changes between the ages of twenty-one and twenty-eight days of life. Puppies begin to leave their beds to look for a corner in which to eliminate. They become acutely aware of their environment and are extremely sensitive to stimuli. In fact, any experiences at this stage (negative or positive) will more profoundly affect the puppy than at any other point in its life. This is when you and the breeder can help shape your puppy's mind and influence the rest of its life.

Crate training and minor Obedience training can actually begin at this age. A large wire crate (big enough to hold all the puppies) padded with blankets is introduced to the whelping box. Papers are layered on the floor around the crate (as they were around the blankets at the beginning). As the puppies explore and roam, they will choose to sleep in the crate and eliminate on the paper.

Puppies can be handled and stacked in a show pose at four weeks, and it is great for them to be socialized and handled by the breeder starting at this point. When stacking, a puppy is removed from the litter, placed in position, held gently for just a couple of seconds and quietly given the *stay* command. Then the puppy is praised softly and released. The breeder can make it a fun, play kind of thing. Calling the puppies as a group, clapping the hands and using a happy voice is an introduction to the *come* command. This is effective as a pretraining method if the puppies can be induced to come to the caller by a second person gently urging them forward, and if lots of praise is used. Puppies can learn many basic skills at four to six weeks, which will save the owner and handler (and also the pup) the headaches and frustration that might occur if the same teaching is undertaken when the puppy is older.

After bringing your new Great Dane pup home, it is best to begin by making the training process a part of the regular home routine. Obedience training should be a matter of daily practice, done at the drop of a hat and at varied times of the day for just a few minutes. For instance, feeding time is an excellent time for an impromptu training session. When placing the feeding bowl down for your dog, you should expect and receive a *sit* before the dog is allowed to eat. Release with an *okay* command, and let the feast begin.

The same theory applies to trips out-of-doors. Before the door is opened, the dog must *sit* and *wait,* allowing the owner to open and then head out the door first, with the dog following politely. Of course if you have a puppy in extreme need of relief, then by all means pick the pup up and race out the door. But in the normal course of events, this type of politeness training is imperative with a dog the size of a Great Dane. I cannot begin to relate even a part of all the mishaps—broken toes, knees, legs, arms—and other assorted and sundry injuries that have afflicted owners of giant dogs that are untrained or trained but forgetful.

My Internet Great Dane e-mail list is constantly filled with Obedience questions. The most frequently asked question is, "How do I make my dog come when I call him?" The second most common question is, "How do I stop my dog from pulling me when he's on leash?"

The answers to both questions are actually very simple. Never give your dog the option of doing it *wrong* to begin with. This does not mean that mistakes will not happen; they indeed need to happen for learning to take place. But the underlying factor of most obedience issues is that the dog just doesn't understand who's in charge and what's expected. You can control the positive outcome of that process.

For example, if you call your dog with a *come* command and he's off lead busily sniffing some track or another interesting item, his refusal to come to you enforces (in his mind) your inability to make him obey and his ability to be alpha or boss. Worse still, he might interpret your actions as muttering incomprehensible words that he doesn't have to obey.

On the other hand, if you only tell him to come when he is on lead and you can pull or guide him in to you, he learns that the word "Come" is enforceable. That means you always win—therefore, you are boss. Consequently, over a period of time with enforced recalls on lead (ultimately using a Flexi-lead or longe line), he begins to respond off lead in nondistracting situations (meaning there is nothing around that is more interesting than you).

Begin in a small room where the dog is not going to be distracted and cannot walk away. Call him to you and praise him lavishly once he arrives, even if you must walk to his location and take his collar to lead him to the point from which you originally called him. Then add a distraction (it could be a person in the room bouncing a ball or singing) and perfect the recall at that stage.

Once the recall is performed consistently in the small room, graduate to a larger room, with a small distraction, then a large one. Ultimately, in a confined situation, the dog will come reliably.

This is where the student graduates to the outdoors, with the dog on a thirty-foot line. The same routine is used, starting with a place of low distraction and graduating to higher and stronger distractions. Ultimately, the dog will come reliably in almost any situation. It takes time but is worth the effort.

Local School and Club Classes

Group or school training is a must for the Great Dane. If a dog of Great Dane size is allowed to reach the age of six months without encountering and interacting with unfamiliar people and dogs, he develops socialization problems. These problems can manifest themselves as aggression, fear, submissive urination or myriad other distasteful and sometimes dangerous behaviors.

Group training is useful in that it teaches the owner how to handle the dog and what methods of training might work best for the owner/dog team. For the dog, the school atmosphere is a way for him to learn about how other dogs act and how to behave around his peers. In a controlled environment, the dog begins to learn pack behavior and the dos and don'ts of proper eye contact.

Schools are also good places to learn about and try different types of activities, such as Obedience competition, Agility, Therapy work and a variety of other competitive and noncompetitive dog activities.

Later in this chapter, I cover some of the more popular and fun things you can try with your Dane. All have been done with Great Danes successfully, so you can try them with confidence.

OBEDIENCE TRIALS

Obedience trials test a dog's ability to perform certain exercises as laid out by AKC rules. The dog must perform a series of exercises and score at least 170 out of a possible 200 points, earning at least half the points in each exercise. Every time the dog receives a qualifying score of 170, he has achieved one *leg* of the three required to earn an Obedience title. There are three levels of titles, and each is more difficult than the previous one. The ultimate goal for many Obedience trial competitors is to achieve the elusive perfect 200 score. Other competitors are satisfied to simply attain a title at the minimum score required.

Competition levels of each title are divided into A and B segments. A classes are for trainers whose dogs have never received a title, while B classes are for more experienced handlers.

[1]The Four Levels of Obedience Competition

Ch. Chauffeured's Lotus Elan UDX, TD, demonstrates a jump over the bar.

- **Novice:** Completion of Novice level earns your dog a Companion Dog (CD) title. In this level of competition, your dog must heel both on and off leash at slow and fast speeds, complete a successful figure eight, come when called (recall), do automatic sits, stay at a sit for one minute and at a down for three minutes with a group of other dogs (while the handler is across the ring) and stand for examination by the judge.

- **Open:** Competition in the Open classes requires good physical soundness. This level, once successfully completed, earns your dog a Companion Dog Excellent (CDX) title. The exercises are the same as in Novice but are performed off leash and for longer periods. In addition, the dog must retrieve a dumbbell on the flat and over jumps.

- **Utility:** Completion of this level earns your dog a Utility Dog (UD) title. At this point in training

and beyond, physical soundness is imperative; otherwise, the dog will injure itself due to the demanding level of agility and strength. There are not many dogs who achieve this distinctive title. The exercises are more difficult and the dog must perform scent-discrimination tasks. Three sets of articles are used: wood, metal and leather. The articles in each set are lettered so that the judge and handler can tell them apart. One article from each set is marked (scented) by the dog's owner. The dog must then pick this one article out of each set without having seen it placed.

- **UDX:** The successful Utility-titled dog can compete for additional titles. The Utility dog that continues to compete and earns legs at ten shows

---

[1]*Information source—AKC brochure, "Getting Started..." For more information about these or other AKC events, contact the AKC at 919-233-9767 or at www.akc.org.*

Daynanin's Blind Obsession, Am., Can. CDX, TD, owned by Marta Brock and bred by Georgia Hymmen, executes a stylish retrieve over the high jump.

becomes a Utility Dog Excellent (UDX). There *are* several Great Danes with this distinctive title, proving that Danes *can* succeed in Obedience.

- **OTCH:** Utility Dogs that achieve a rank of First or Second in Open B or Utility classes earn points toward an Obedience Trial championship (OTCH) This is not truly considered a training level in Obedience competition.

Training Tools

Tools used in training an Obedience dog start simple and advance as the dog's training level or titles advance.

Leashes and collars are the basic tools. Anyone can use them and everyone with a dog has them. Moving up to more advanced levels requires some jumps and a wooden or plastic dumbbell. The more advanced levels require scent-discrimination articles (leather, metal and wood dumbbells).

THE CANINE GOOD CITIZEN PROGRAM, THERAPY DOG TRAINING, ANIMAL ASSISTED ACTIVITIES (AAA) AND ANIMAL ASSISTED THERAPY (AAT)

The American Kennel Club has a certificate program available to all dogs called the Canine Good Citizen Program. While this is not a "title," it is a very important certificate to hold. Possession of this certificate proclaims your dog is an all-around great companion.

Canine Good Citizen (CGC) Test Requirements

Your dog must be able to perform a series of ten exercises that can be learned as part of basic Obedience. The main thrust of the test is to show that your dog's temperament is even; well-mannered; friendly; and never aggressive, shy or fearful. The tests involve simple sits, stays, downs, loose leash walking exercises and reactions to distractions and strangers.

Ch. Chauffeured's Lotus Elan UDX, TD, selects the correct article in the challenging scent-discrimination exercise.

Basic Requirements of a Therapy Dog

As a member of and evaluator for Therapy Dogs International, I find that there are many wonderful people in the community willing to volunteer their pet dogs in nursing homes, hospitals and community adult care centers. While these services are much needed and welcome, I also find that often many of these dogs are lacking in the social skills and worldly experience necessary to perform well as Therapy dogs. In addition, some of the dog owners are unprepared for the situations they will encounter in elder care facilities.

Training for these dogs is difficult to come by locally for many people, so I try to prepare dogs for the rigors of Therapy work by following the AKC/CGC requirements and then adding the additional skills required for the Therapy dog certification.

One of Henry and Christina Bredenkamp's Danes with a leather scent-discrimination article.

The first items of concern are standards of health and cleanliness. The standards set by Therapy Dogs International for qualification for the TDI-CGC test follow:

- Proof of current inoculations, including rabies, distemper, hepatitis, leptospirosis and parvovirus
- Proof of health, such as a current health certificate from a veterinarian
- Visible cleanliness, no sign of fleas/ticks, clean ears and generally well groomed
- Healthy appearance, alert and not grossly overweight or underweight
- Yearly physical examination and stool check
- Annual heartworm test

Therapy Dog Evaluation Test

The test performed to certify a dog for Therapy Dogs International is an AKC/CGC test to which additional requirements have been added. The point of this test is to determine to the best of the evaluator's judgment that the dog being tested is steady, dependable and passive. Any dog that exhibits signs of aggression, stress or fear will automatically be denied TDI status. The following items are amendments to the CGC test.

Amendments that TDI has made to the above tests to adapt it to therapy needs are as follows:

Can. Ch. Daynakin's Born to Be Bold, owned by Paul and Sheryl Picco, Georgia Hymmen and Jack Henderson, is an experienced Therapy dog making visits to appreciative friends in hospitals and nursing homes. (Courtesy Georgia Hymmen/Jack Henderson)

1. Tell the handler that you are going to touch the dog all over, handling it heavily. Ask if there is any reason that the dog will not allow you to handle it. All handling is done at the dog's level.

2. Add patting the dog on the head and conversing with handler.

3. Make a big deal about the brushing and combing. As you do this, drop your clipboard, make a large motion with your arm or body in an attempt to elicit an unusual reaction. Check the dog's nails for proper length, and comment on long nails to owner.

4. Ask the handler to do an Obedience routine that is familiar to them; you may call it if they are familiar with that method. Otherwise, have them walk, changing directions when you ask, watching them for control and ease of handling.

5. Use the other test takers as a crowd. Use all the dogs and handlers as a group (no more than 6 at a time) to test sociability.

6. Sits and Downs are needed in therapy work, so must be done properly.

7. Join in with the handler in praising the dog.

8. Use another dog and handler from the group as greeter for each other using different dog/handler teams to test each dog.

9. Use a variety of noises, stumble near the dog, exhibit jerky motions near the dog. Do not attempt to scare the dog from behind.

10. A volunteer handler holds the leash while the owner leaves the room.

The Great Dane's love of people and inherent gentleness make him an ideal candidate for Therapy dog work. (Pets by Paulette)

Therapy Dog Organizations

The Chenny Troupe
Laura Mensching
Phone: 312-280-0266

Delta Society Pet Partners Programs
321 Burnett Ave. S., 3rd Floor
Renton, WA 98055-2569
Phone: 206-226-7357

Love on a Leash
Liz Palika
3809 Plaza Drive
#107-309

Oceanside, CA 92056
Phone: 619-630-4824

PAWS—Pets are Wonderful Support
P.O. Box 460489
San Francisco, CA 94146-0489
Phone: 415-824-4040

Pet Assisted Therapy Facilitation
Certificate Program
Pearl Salotto
State University of New York
Phone: 401-463-5809

Pets and People Foundation
Sally Jean Alexander, Volunteer Coordinator
11 Apple Crest Road
Weston, MA 02193
Phone: 617-899-5029

Therapy Dogs Inc.
Ann Butrick
2416 E. Fox Farm Road
Cheyenne, WY 82007
Phone: 307-638-3222

Therapy Dogs International
Ursula Kempe, Treasurer
260 Fox Chase Road
Chester, NJ 07930
Phone: 518-377-3559
E-mail: tdi@gti.net

Therapy Pet Pals of Texas
Kathryn Lashmit
807 Brazos Street
Suite 312
Austin, TX 78701

Therapy Dog Associations in Canada

BC Pets and Friends
#250, 167 West 2nd Avenue
Vancouver, BC V5Y 1B8
Phone: 604-879-5991
Fax: 604-879-2992

Pet Therapy Society of Northern Alberta
Edmonton, Alberta, Canada
Phone: 403-413-4682
Fax: 403-413 8805
E-mail: paws@connect.ab.ca
Web site: http://www.shopalberta.com/paws/

St. John Ambulance Therapy Dog Program
Jim Newell
1199 Deyell 3rd Line
Milbrook, Ontario L0A 1G0

Animal Assisted Therapy (AAT) Animal Assisted Activities (AAA)

Animal Assisted Therapy (AAT) is a program where the dogs actually work with therapists to accomplish specific goals with patients or nursing home residents. Tasks such as improving motor coordination by getting a patient to throw a ball for a dog to fetch, caring for a dog's coat with a brush or simply performing the act of petting. When speech therapists use dogs, tasks are given to the patient such as giving commands to a dog in order to recover speech. Psychotherapists use dogs to draw a patient out; many times an abused or psychologically damaged person, especially a child, will talk to a dog even if they will not open up to a person.

Animal Assisted Activities (AAA) is intended to provide opportunities for human-animal interaction, promoting educational and motivational benefits while reinforcing the bond between people and animals. A perfect example of this is a group home that keeps a cat or small dog as a means to elicit responses, soothe emotions and permit contact among its residents. The mere act of touching and petting many times fills a gap that is very wide in those who might go for long periods of time without human-to-human contact such as hugs and caresses.

TRACKING
Description

Having origins in actual service work, AKC Tracking trials test a dog's ability to find and follow a human scent trail, and show enthusiasm and competence while doing his job. This energetic outdoor sport is designed for athletic dogs with good physical constitutions. Unlike Obedience events, which require a dog to qualify three times, a dog must successfully complete only one track to earn a title; it is a noncompetitive outdoor sport. Dogs are required to successfully complete a qualifying track before being allowed to run in a licensed Tracking trial.

Any handler who wants to compete in Tracking must have the commitment to train for at least three days a week. Tracking involves being outdoors for long periods and considerable walking in open spaces and parks. Besides a dog, you will also need bait, a forty- to sixty-foot line, a field or park in which to work, and a good tracking guide or lesson book.

Titles

- **Tracking Dog (TD):** A 440- to 500-yard track over grass and vegetation is laid thirty minutes to two hours prior to a test. The dog earns a TD title by following this track successfully. The rules require specific turns in a 440- to 500-yard track.

- **Tracking Dog Excellent (TDX):** An "older" (three to five hours) and longer (800 to 1,000 yards) track with more turns than the TD track. The challenge is increased by adding physical and scenting obstacles. A dog earns the TDX title with the successful completion of this track.

- **Variable Surface Tracking (VST):** In the real world, dogs track through urban settings, as well as through wilderness areas. A dog that has earned a VST title has proved this ability by following a three- to five-hour-old track that may take him on city streets, into buildings and other areas not necessarily composed of natural terrain.

FLYBALL
Description

Fun and challenging, Flyball consists of teams of four dogs that run a relay race of sorts. The course consists of a start and finish line, and four hurdles spaced ten feet apart, with the first six feet from the start/finish line. The Flyball box itself is fifteen feet away from the fourth hurdle. The overall course length is fifty-one feet.

The dogs leave the start line, leap the hurdles and stomp a spring-loaded pedal on the box, which releases a tennis ball. They catch the ball, reverse and run back, leaping over the hurdles once more.

Ch. Chauffeured's Lotus Elan UDX, TD, concentrating deeply during a tracking exercise.

Once the first dog crosses the finish line, the next dog begins his run. The object is to have all four dogs complete the entire course with no errors.

Tournaments are run usually in a round robin or elimination rounds. The height of the jumps is dependent on the height of the dogs. The height is four inches below the shoulder height of the smallest dog. The maximum height is sixteen inches. This height differential is to encourage a mixture of larger and smaller dogs, as the height of the smallest dog on the team sets the jump height for the runs.

Danes in Flyball

Danes do well competing in their own size group but fare poorly when pitted against breeds such as Border Collies, who are *very* fast. It is best to set up competitions of like-sized dogs when dealing with giants. This increases the fun and makes for a fairer handicap.

Equipment

Flyball boxes, tennis balls and hurdles are all essential items. The safest Flyball boxes have a sloping front, and the ball is delivered to the dog horizontally rather than vertically (popping up in the air) as in the old design. The pedal should have an impact-absorbing rubber cover. The safety of the dog is paramount in the design of all Flyball equipment. If you are interested in learning more about Flyball, contact the *North American Flyball Association* (NAFA) at the NAFA Homepage: http://www.muskie.fishnet.com/~flyball/flyball.html.

AGILITY

The *American Kennel Club* (AKC), *North American Dog Agility Council* (NADAC) and *United States Dog Agility Association,* Inc. (USDAA) all sponsor and sanction Agility events. Whereas the AKC will only allow AKC-registered dogs to participate in its events, USDAA allows all dogs to participate. This to me is preferable, as I believe that participation in Agility should be open to all dogs, just as CGC certification. The AKC and USDAA differ somewhat in a few of the event requirements as well. USDAA requires the weave poles at the Novice level, but AKC does not; AKC has lower jump heights as well.

Activity/Competition Description

The basic Agility competition consists of a series of obstacles and jumps that must be negotiated safely and within a time limit.

Equipment Requirements

The equipment list is both lengthy and specific. Here is a *general* idea of the equipment required:

- Jumps (wing jump, tire jump, long jumps, hurdles)
- Tunnels (a chute or collapsed tunnel and a rigid, curved tunnel)
- Weave poles (closely spaced vertical poles through which a dog must run in a weaving action)
- Contact obstacles (A-frames, tables, dog walks and teeter-totters)

FREESTYLE HEELING
Canine Freestyle

The point of Canine Freestyle is to display a dog performing at its creative and artistic best. There is always a musical selection accompanying the presentation.

In Freestyle heeling, emphasis is placed on the dog being in the heel position and the dog's execution of heeling patterns to music. Heel and front positions are the base for all the technical scoring of the routine, while the artistic scoring is based on movement, direction and rhythm. Emphasis is placed on the correctness and flexibility of the dog, while the role of the handler is of less importance.

A Freestyle routine should not resemble the heeling seen in Obedience competition. Instead it should be a balance of movements between the dog and handler, smooth and harmonious, complementing each other. There should be freedom of movement, an emphasis on the dog's flexibility and athleticism, as well as a unity of motion between the handler and dog.

MUSICAL FREESTYLE (DOG DANCING)

Description of Musical Canine Sports International (MCSI)

MCSI is the only title bestowing body in the sport of Musical Freestyle. In the early 1990s, a group of individuals interested in combining the arts of music, dance and dog Obedience developed the rules of Musical Freestyle. Those rules were tested in various competitions during the mid-1990s, and by 1994, the MCSI rules and guidelines were adopted by the Illini Obedience Association in the United States.

Exposing young puppies to Agility obstacles will familiarize them with the equipment and facilitate later training. (Jill Swedlow)

Sports Requirements

Musical Freestyle is not heeling with music in the background. MCSI rules encourage the dog to move out of the heel position to perform a variety of movements and tricks not found in a traditional Obedience performance. To interpret the music, the handler may use the body, arms and legs in a free, rhythmic manner. A mixture of dance-related steps completes the footwork portion of a routine. Musical Freestyle performances unite creativity and contrast of movement, and a range of actions not available to the more limited Freestyle routines. Emphasis is placed on the teamwork between handler and dog—neither partner is spotlighted, since both are judged equally.

Can Ch. Daynakin's Xactly Rolling Thunder, CGC, TT, NA, N-NA, owned by Marta Brock and bred by Georgia Hymmen and Jack Henderson, clears the Agility high jump.

*Rolling Thunder showing his control on the teeter-totter...
(Ellice)*

Musical Freestyle routines are judged for their technique and artistic impression. In judging technical execution, the judges consider a number of details of the routine:

- Difficulty of the maneuvers

- The dog's demeanor and excitement

- Meticulous movements by dog and handler

The judging of artistic impression centers on

- Choreography

- Interpretation of the music by the handler

- Matching of the handler's and dog's movements with each other and the music

...and his style over the Agility oxer. (Barb Davis)

FRISBEE COMPETITION (FLYING DISC)

Generally speaking, Flying Disc is a complicated game of fetch. Basically good Frisbee skills offer wonderful challenges for the mind and body of the dog and human, as well as strengthens the bond between the dog and owner through fun and skill.

Frisbee competitions may be enjoyed by Great Danes and their owners as long as the dogs are in good physical condition. Caution must be used with a larger dog to be sure the dog does not injure itself attempting to leap too high. The

Ch. Chauffeured's Lotus Elan UDX, TD, does herself proud through the weave poles... (Tien Tran)

...and negotiates the dog walk with ease.

The IDDHA has designed a rating process called a *Retrieval Proficiency Test* (RPT) and has developed a titling process for competition dogs as well.

Frisbee Event Types

- **Toss & Fetch:** Teams have sixty seconds to complete as many throws and catches as possible. Longer throws result in higher scores.

- **Accuracy:** Similar to Toss & Fetch, but dogs must make catches in marked circles.

- **Freestyle:** Introductory division teams (a team is one dog, one handler) have sixty to ninety seconds, and Advanced divisions have ninety seconds, to perform a Freestyle routine. These routines consist of timed throws of the Frisbee.

possibility of bloat or heat stress also presents itself in the case of overexertion or excessive heat.

Recently an organization to unite Frisbee clubs all over the United States was formed. This group, the *International Disc Dog Handlers' Association* (IDDHA), acts to the world of Frisbee as the AKC does to the world of Obedience and conformation competition.

Music, costumes and tricks may be included as part of the performance.

You can contact IDDHA at http://www.iddha.com/
or
1690 Julius Bridge Road
Ball Ground, GA 30107.

SEARCH AND RESCUE (SAR)

THE FOLLOWING IS AN EXCERPT FROM AN ARTICLE BY DANA PERRY, GREAT DANE OWNER AND SAR VOLUNTEER.

Although using Danes is not recommended by most SAR groups, I have found it to be very rewarding. It takes intelligence, drive and a mutual bond of trust to do SAR work and Danes certainly possess these qualities.

I chose to focus on urban and wilderness SAR work for several reasons. In my opinion Great Danes are too large to do disaster SAR work because one of the requirements is to be able to lift your dog. Another concern was that for the victims possibly buried under rubble, another 150 pounds (on the rubble) could mean the difference between life and death. Area search dogs are all off lead and I was hesitant to do this because of my dog's size—he might frighten the subjects when finding them. Trailing dogs are always on lead and are usually activated to search for missing children or Alzheimer patients. By the dog being on lead you are relatively close to your dog at all times and can calm someone rapidly if they are frightened. Keeping up with a Dane in this field of work requires the handler to be in good mental and physical condition. The closer or hotter the trail becomes, a Dane can move swiftly covering a lot of ground, regardless of the terrain. This can include going through heavy underbrush or over large, downed trees, all of which you must get through or over without interfering with the working dog.

Your dog must be physically fit as well. Agility training is a fun way to give your dog confidence and to help him learn where his back feet are. Great Danes are large but they can be agile at the same time. Keeping their weight in check is also important. Obviously an overweight Dane is going to have a harder time if a track ends up being a long one.

Because your dog may become sick or injured on the trail it is vital that you have a good knowledge of canine first aid, including what to do if your dog bloats. No one may be around that can assist you, so your dog's life will depend on your knowledge and your ability to keep calm in an emergency situation. You must be physically and mentally prepared to make a litter and pull your dog back to base camp if necessary.

There is no better feeling than to watch a Great Dane develop confidence and learn the skills to do this type of work. Danes enjoy having a job to do, and who knows—someday they may even save someone's life.

Pacific Trail K-9 Search and Rescue, Inc.
Dana Perry
26735 Wonderly Road
Rainier, OR 97048
Phone/Fax: 503-556-8765
E-mail: stevep@blkdane.com

TRICK TRAINING AND MY DOG CAN DO THAT (MDCDT) TOURNAMENT TRAINING

Trick training is a wonderful, fun way of doing informal Obedience training with classes of students. I used to invent tricks and write out the step-by-step method of accomplishing three or four tricks, and ask my students to have one of them ready to perform on the final night of a six-week course of Obedience classes.

I now use the My Dog Can Do That™ game to teach the students for at least two classes of my six class weeks of training, and we always play the game for our final class. My standard after-session reviews went from "Yes, we learned from and enjoyed your classes" to "Wow! Can you start another class with just your game?"

My Dog Can Do That is a new game designed for the average pet owner. The object of the game is to teach your dog tricks and to advance around a game board. The tricks are written on separate cards, which are divided into levels of Beginner, Intermediate and Advanced, so players of mixed abilities can play together. The best part of this is that the "tricks" are actually a stepped method of Obedience training. For instance, to teach a dog to *beg,* first you must master *sit.* There are seventy-two tricks to master, and every one can be performed easily with some training!

The training manual, included with the game, is written by Terry Ryan and Dr. Ian Dunbar; both are well-known, experienced trainers. Competition or wanting to win is the motivation for students to teach these tricks to their dogs. In turn, as the dog becomes more proficient at the basic commands, layers are added on for the more difficult tricks. All of this is done with an emphasis on *positive* reinforcement and *fun,* which are the keys to any good training program.

An added benefit to playing this game is *family* focus on training and obedience, as well as togetherness and just plain old fun. Great Danes seem to excel at this game. It's amazing to me that the minute we pull this game out, the dogs all troop to the table and SIT!

The company (The ID Store) that manufactures this game has begun to organize nationwide My Dog Can Do That tournaments as fundraisers for local animal shelters and other animal-related charities. At this writing, I am helping organize one for the Manchester, New Hampshire area to benefit the New Hampshire Animal Rescue League, and it promises to be fun *and* educational.

Dan Sherry, the inventor of My Dog Can Do That, points out that the number one reason for more than 25,000 pets being euthanized each *day* is behavioral problems due to lack of good training. So, if for no other reason than that, I think this is an excellent reason to get this game and play it with your family, friends and other dog lovers you meet at training school.

Courtesy Marta Brock

CHAPTER 11

A Photo Gallery of Great Dane Headliners

The dogs included on the following pages are either top show winners or have made a significant contribution to the breed in some other way within the last ten years. Several other dogs could also have been included here, but no photographs were available.

Ch. Amherst-Harlwood Bubba Rondo (Ch. Riverwood's Rondo ex Dan-Mar's Jazmin Potpourri), owners/breeders Don & Betty Lou Wood, is the winner of one all-breed Best in Show, 10 Specialty Bests in Show. He was #1 Great Dane for 1996 and was in the Top Twenty for three years. A top producer in 1995 and 1996, he was the first harlequin to have this distinction. Sire of seventeen champions to date. (Nutting)

Am., Can. Ch. BMW Bull Lea (Ch. BMW Ruffian ex Ch. BMW Fantasia), bred and owned by Laura Kiaulenas with Mary Ann Zanetos. Bull Lea had three all-breed Bests In Show and 24 Specialty Bests, including the GDCA National in 1985 and the GDCA Southwest Regional in 1986. He has produced more than 12 champions. (Ashbey)

Ch. Bridane's Dizzy Ms. Lizzy (Ch. Rika-Brier Indian Uprising ex Ch. Rickdane's Dandelion v. Bridane), owned and bred by Jim & Lora Thill, was shown for less than a year and was the #11 Great Dane in the United States, with a total of 22 Best of Breed wins and five Specialty Bests. She was the dam of at least four champions when this book went to press.

Ch. Dundane's Whistles At Sharcon (Ch. Dundane's Bacarat At Brookside ex Sharcon's Dana v. Diller), owned and bred by Anita Dunne and Suzanne Jedynak, has produced 28 champion get. He was #1 producing sire in the United States for 1995 and #2 for 1996. Among his get have been a Top Twenty competitor, plus the Winners Dog, Winners Bitch and Best in Futurity at the GDCA National Speacialty.

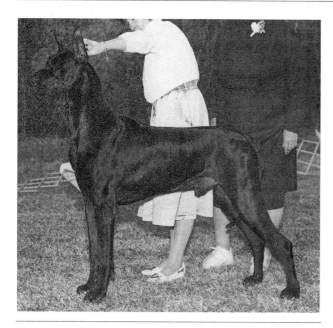

Ch. Longo's Primo d'Aquino (Ch. Longo's Chief Joseph ex Ch. Aquino's Oso Perla Negra), owned by Joe and Tootie Longo and bred by Mario, Rosie and Delia Aquino. Primo was the third black Great Dane in history to win an all-breed Best in Show, his sire being the second and the first in 22 years. He had 11 Specialty Bests, including the National and 3 Awards of Merit. A winner in the Top Twenty Competition in 1995. He had 191 Bests of Breed, 23 Group Firsts and 97 Group Placings.

Ch. Longo's Sweetalk v. Michael Dane (Ch. Longo's Primo d'Aquino ex Michaeldane's Put'n on the Ritz), owned by Joe and Tootie Longo, and bred by Tootie Longo and Michael Chiles. In 1994, Lou-Lou became the first black bitch to be #1 Great Dane, All Systems, after only one year of campaigning. The first black Dane bitch in history to win an all-breed BIS, her record also includes seven Specialty Bests, two GDCA Specialty Bests of Opposite Sex, two Awards of Merit and a winner in the Top Twenty in 1995.

Ch. Michaeldane's Dagon Clorox N'Co (Michaeldane Dagon's Lull's I ex Replica N'Co), owned by Jodie and Bud Kiem, and bred by Pam Litz, Michael Chiles and Trudy Muller. An Award of Merit recipient at the 1993 National Specialty, he was ranked in the Top Twenty until his show career was ended by an injury in May 1994. He is the sire of several champions.

Ch. Patchwork's Ashley Wilkes (Ch Heritage's Beta Von Riverwood ex Ch. Suschen's Spirit Of Christmas), owned by Jack E. Godwin and bred by Jack E. Godwin, Cheryl M. Godwin and Susan Woodward Hitchcock. Ashley's record includes 34 BBs and BIS at the 1990 Great Dane Club of America National Specialty and an Award of Merit at the 1991 National. He finished in the Top Twenty in 1990. (Missy Yuhl)

Ch. Petadane Taly (Ch. Honey Lane's Casablanca ex Petadane Sicilia), bred and owned by Diane and Tom Cerqua, is the first and only Dane (at this writing) to win two National Specialties and 31 regional Specialty Bests. He won a total of 237 BBs, was #1 Great Dane in 1994 and 1995, #2 Great Dane in 1993 and won the Best of Breed Pedigree Award in 1994.

Ch. Mr. Rhett Butler of VZTop, owned by Bill Banks and bred by Lorraine Rainwater. As of April 1998, his show record consists of 54 BBs, eight Working Group Firsts and 18 Group placements. He is the sire of eight champions at the time of this writing with others expected to complete their title requirements. (Kitten Rodwell)

Ch. Riverwood's Rondo, owned and bred by Eva Robinson, accumulated in his very short show career 19 BBs, two Group Firsts and four other Group placements. He has two champion get to date. (Rich Bergman)

Ch. Sandale's What A Guy, ROM, GDCA Hall of Fame (Ch. Sheenwater Georgia Pacific ex Murlo Sybil of Sandale), bred and owned by Dale Suzanne Tarbox. He was #8 Great Dane in 1987, the winner of six Specialty Bests and multiple Stud Dog class wins at GDCA Nationals. He sired 35 American Champions, 8 Canadian Champions, 8 international Champions and 4 Top Twenty Danes. Besides this, Guy also sired 3 all-breed Best in Show winners, a Best in Futurity winner and multiple top producers from a total of 135 puppies. (Bernard Kernan)

Ch. Sheenwater Gamble On Me (Ch. Reann's French Aristocrat ex Ch. Stone River's Delta Dawn), owned and bred by Sally Chandler and Chris O'Connell. Among the top-winning Great Danes of recent date, Gamble won 15 all-breed Bests in Show, 30 Specialty Bests and won the GDCA Top Twenty. He produced well over 30 champion get. (Ashbey)

Ch. Von Raseac's French Dandy, ROM (Von Raseac's French Gigolo ex Hillview's Chantilly), owned by Gene and Brucie Mitchell and bred by Don and Chris Salyers, sired 25 champions from very limited breedings and was the winner of several BBs.

Ch. Von Shrado's I'm A Knock Out (Ch. Sandale's What A Guy ex Ch. Von Shrado's Easter Bonnet), owned and bred by Jim and Sandy Hann. Fridge began his career with a Best in Futurity win as a puppy. He was the #1 Great Dane in 1990 and 1992 and holds the all-time Best of Breed record with 404 wins, in addition to 57 Group Firsts, 163 Group placements, and 10 all-breed Bests in Show. He was the only Dane to be #1 as a Veteran and to place in the Top Twenty for six years. He qualified for the Hall of Fame, having produced 39 champions, including Best in Show winners and Top Twenty competitors. (Chuck Tatham)

Ch. Dinro McKenna's Against All Odds, owned by Louis Bond's and Robert Layne's Dinro/Sounda Great Danes, was a headliner in every sense. An American, Puerto Rican, South American Champion and Champion of the Americas, Brother was the #1 Great Dane for 1991 with a career win record that included 310 BBs, 286 Group placements and 23 independent Specialty wins. He was a Westminster BB winner, a Top Twenty contender for three years and a top producer. At the same time, he served as a nursing home companion/visitation dog. (Chuck Tatham)

The Art of Breeding Great Danes—or, To Breed or Not to Breed. . .

. . . That is the question, to paraphrase *Hamlet* (who was also a Dane).

Breeding dogs is a true art and the artist's medium is living flesh. When you plan a breeding, the only purpose should be breed improvement. Obviously you must be extremely knowledgeable to have a chance of attaining this goal. Breeders must be willing to thoroughly health check both parents, to make sure their temperaments and that of their ancestors is typical of the breed, and to take full responsibility—both practical and financial—for every dog they cause to be born until the day it dies. Breeders must also have a thorough knowledge of pedigrees, conformation and the breed Standard. This knowledge does not come overnight and is one reason a novice should not breed a bitch without guidance from an experienced mentor or extensive prior study. Everyone who breeds a litter should be prepared to spend a *lot* of money in the process and to know in advance that they will *not* make money!

If you have or will purchase a Dane as a companion only, you don't even need to read this chapter because your dog should *never* be bred. Your dog was purchased as a pet because he or she lacked that exceptional conformation that made him/her worthy of breeding. Now I know this sounds a bit elitist, but there are good reasons why the breeder considers your dog a pet. Not every dog must be bred, and that in no way demeans the wonderful attributes of your much-loved pet. Dedicated breeders strive (or *should* strive) to breed only from the very best Great Danes in order to, hopefully, constantly improve overall breed quality from litter to litter. If the breeder of your pet-quality Dane *did not* sell you the dog on limited registration or specify that your dog should not be bred and you're actually thinking of breeding it, please give serious attention to the following. These points appear elsewhere in this book, but they're so important they're included here for added emphasis.

THESE ARE NOT GOOD REASONS TO BREED A BITCH

1. **So the kids can see the miracle of birth.** Children can learn about birth from books and videos. This does not justify causing a litter of perhaps ten puppies to come into the world in need of loving homes. Take a trip to the local animal shelter and see the sad results of many litters born for just this misguided reason.

2. **She should have one litter before she is spayed/he is altered.** Wrong! There is absolutely *no* medical, physical or emotional reason that a dog or bitch needs to reproduce itself except to continue the species. In the case of a pet-quality dog (or even some show dogs), this does not apply.

3. **You want to recoup your investment.** Especially with breeding Great Danes, this reason makes veterans laugh. I doubt there are many breeds *more* expensive to breed than Great Danes. Even if you don't count the expense of showing your bitch and just start with the medical health screenings, it's expensive. All Danes that are even being considered for breeding should, at the very least, have their hips x-rayed to rule out hip dysplasia. More and more breeders are now screening for cataracts, *von Willebrand's disease* (VWD), cardiac health, normal thyroid and even elbow dysplasia. The cost of these tests may vary depending on location, but they will still be high—probably somewhere around $450. A routine check for any uterine or vaginal infections will help ensure a live litter. Add $100. The stud fee to a quality stud who complements your bitch and has passed all his health screenings will run about $500. Now we're at $1,050. If a cesarean section becomes necessary, add at least $350 and probably more. Assuming that there is no need for a section (rare in Danes), you now have a nice healthy litter of, oh, say eight puppies. At six to seven weeks, they are likely going through at least fifty pounds of dog food a week. Add in the first vaccines (likely $20 each from your vet), that's about another $160. Next it's time to crop. Oh, joy. Add $150 per puppy. And, if you've bred a

bitch and have no market for her puppies, you might end up supporting several of them until they're four or five months old or older. Do you have any idea how expensive this is getting? And if you have no ready market for your pups, you cannot get the $1,000 that is about average for a show-potential puppy from top stock. You'll be lucky to get $200 or $300 a puppy. Still think you're going to recoup your investment? Better think again!

4. **She's just so nice, all my friends want one of her babies, and I want one just like her.** Refer to reason three. Those friends who just have to have one of her pups have a strange way of backpedaling when the time comes to actually purchase the puppy with their hard-earned money. And there's no guarantee that you'll have a puppy even remotely like your dog or bitch. So is it worth all the expense to take the chance? It's a lot smarter to just go to a reputable breeder and buy another Dane!

5. **She's a champion! She deserves to be bred!** Not necessarily. True, a championship is a good indication that she is from quality breeding, and many champions *are* of breeding quality. However, there are some really lovely champions that should *never* be bred because of health or temperament problems or many of those problems in their pedigrees. If a dog isn't sound in mind and health, it should not be bred. Conversely, dogs who couldn't finish their championships due to conformation faults can be top producers. The point here is

To the trained eye, the members of this litter are very different from each other and none grew up to exactly resemble either parent. From left to right are Sunnyside Narcissus, Sunnyside Jonquilla, Ch. Sunnyside Peeping Tom and Sunnyside King Alfred. (Jill Swedlow)

that the whole dog along with its pedigree and health screenings must be considered before making the decision to breed or not to breed.

THESE ARE GOOD REASONS TO BREED A BITCH

1. Your bitch has a good pedigree with many champions who are also sound of mind, body, health and longevity. She has tested clear of all indigenous inherited problems and is herself sound of mind, body and health. She has correct conformation with no major or disqualifying faults and is outstanding in at least some conformation traits.

2. You want to improve the breed and select a stud that is your bitch's equal or better in all of the earlier listed traits and who does not share any common temperament or conformation faults with your bitch.

3. You have a better-than-good chance to place each pup in the home that is right for it.

4. You have the funds to properly care for and raise the litter and to handle any unforeseen emergencies that may arise.

5. You have the facilities and finances to properly house and care for a bitch and a large litter, even if the puppies are still residents at six months of age.

6. You have the knowledge and integrity to properly evaluate your litter and will stand behind every sale with some type of health and temperament guarantee.

7. You are not only willing, but insist in writing in the contract, that if for any reason the pup cannot be kept (at whatever age), you will take it back or assist in finding it an appropriate home.

If you can honestly say that all these reasons apply to you, read on. Great Danes need breeders like you.

BREEDING A MALE

It takes two to tango, and males are as responsible for litters as are the bitches. Pet male Danes should be neutered. Period. This is an issue that more commonly is a problem for male owners. Many men have this "thing" that causes them to think that their dog will be somehow "less macho" if he's been neutered. For some reason that I do not understand, this is a real problem for them. I'm here to tell you, gentlemen, that this truly is *your* problem, not your dog's!

First, as with a pet bitch, a pet male should not be bred and for all the same reasons. If he is not to be bred, he should be altered for several good reasons. Altering reduces a dog's chance for contracting testicular or prostate cancer. Altering prevents him from being upset and stressed by a bitch in season that he can smell from some distance. He should be altered so that he will never be responsible for a litter due to someone's carelessness in leaving a door open, allowing him to take off after an in-season bitch. He won't care that he's been altered; he'll be much happier and more content without the stress of overactive hormones that should never be satisfied.

When Should a Male Be Bred?

1. He is superior in conformation, temperament and health compared to most other male Danes. Whether this fact is established by showing him to his championship or by having him evaluated by others knowledgeable in the breed is of no consequence.

2. He has passed all the required health screenings.

3. You've decided you can live with a male who, once he's been used at stud, may suddenly forget his housetraining and start scent marking in the house.

4. You are knowledgeable enough about pedigrees, conformation, health and temperament to know if the bitch being presented to him is a good match, or you have a knowledgeable mentor who will know.

5. You have the fortitude and tact to turn down a bitch if you don't feel it would be a good breeding or if you don't feel she is of breeding quality.

6. You could sincerely suggest a stud that you feel would be a better match for a bitch brought to your dog.

When Shouldn't a Male Be Bred?

1. A breeding male should be *exceptional* in all physical and temperamental qualities. If he is not, alter him. (Occasionally a very average male consistently produces above-average get. Although the exception, these dogs are treasures and should be used as long as it seems that their offspring also produce high quality.)

2. A male (or any Dane) must have a steady, reliably good, typical temperament. No matter how beautiful a Dane is, if he lacks good temperament, he should be neutered—or at least never bred.

3. Some males, no matter how beautiful or how they are bred, simply do not pass their lovely traits on to their get. If, after you've bred a good dog to several bitches from different pedigrees, the puppies are not themselves exceptional, neuter him. The best male Great

Dane I've ever seen was one of the poorest producers. It was a tragedy!

4. Unhealthy dogs or dogs who cannot seem to keep weight on should not be bred.

SELECTING AND EVALUATING A BROOD BITCH

Becoming a dog breeder is a serious responsibility. The puppies you will cause to be born have no choice in the matter, nor do they have any control over their futures. You, and only you, are fully responsible for this, so you'd better make some informed decisions.

Selecting and evaluating a brood bitch begins with the decision to breed your bitch or to purchase a bitch for this purpose. If you are already an established breeder, chances are that you already have considerable knowledge about what breeding combinations should produce the best results. The operative word here is *should*. There are many well-known breeders who will breed bitches without health checks, or who will overlook the fact that the bitch or stud has a poor temperament. Please, before you decide to breed, be honest in your evaluation of your bitch. A championship title is no guarantee that a bitch should be bred. If you have doubts, consult a fellow breeder whom you respect. Sometimes we become so involved with our dogs that we can't see the faults that may be obvious to others. This is called *kennel blindness,* and no one should breed if they're afflicted with it. Unfortunately, those afflicted with it usually never realize it. These are the breeders who consistently

Ch. Sunnyside California Poppy is the kind of brood bitch every breeder loves. She has a wonderful temperament to match her conformation, passed all her health checks and produced two exceptional litters. In the first litter, three of the four puppies became champions, and the second has yielded one champion to date with a couple of others that may also make the grade. She passes her quality and personalities on to her puppies. (Kohler)

produce inferior animals, year after year, litter after litter. Their activity is a vicious cycle resistant to breaking.

If you want to be known as the breeder of a litter, you must own the bitch, not the dog, on the day she is bred. AKC identifies the bitch's owner as the breeder. Any AKC-registered Great Dane bitch can produce a litter of Great Danes when she is mated to an AKC registered Great Dane dog. However, we want to improve on our bitch and hopefully produce a litter of outstanding, healthy, good-tempered, long-lived Great Danes—dogs that will grow into companions that bring happiness to their new owners.

If your bitch *is* of breeding quality, there is still a great deal to consider prior to making the decision to breed.

Whelping a bitch and raising a litter is a full-time responsibility. You cannot expect your bitch to take care of the puppies on her own during the day while you're at work. You need to be with her for at least the first three to four weeks of the babies' lives. A new litter will definitely turn your household upside down.

Consider that the pups usually wait until you've fallen soundly asleep to start arriving in the wee hours. You can usually count on at least one sleepless night, and probably several if you sleep by the whelping box so you can be sure that none of the puppies get crushed by mom. Even the most careful dam can unintentionally hurt a puppy this way.

You must be close by for at least four weeks so that blankets can be washed and changed and messes cleaned up. Yes, mom *does* clean up after the puppies, but her housekeeping will not always be perfect. Once the puppies are being weaned, you must provide from four to five meals a day. And

These innocent puppies never asked to be born. They depend entirely on their breeder to place them in qualified, loving homes where they will live long, happy lives. The breeder must be willing to take them back at any time if they can no longer remain in their homes. (Jill Swedlow)

oh, what a *mess* they make in their first meals. Puppies love to swim in the food pan. This is, of course, a wonderful treat for mom, as she licks her little "pupcakes" clean, but what a mess for *you!* It can often take a half-hour to clean up the food and papers on the floor, wash the food off the pups that mom missed and then police the area.

As the pups become older and leave the whelping box, your work *really* begins. Ten or fifteen cleanups a day is at least average. You'll need to keep fresh newspapers down, provide lots of attention and socialization, mop up the spills around the water dish when the pups begin to learn how to swim (and, incidentally, drink water)

and generally be nearby in case someone gets into trouble, such as becoming stuck between mom and the wall.

When your pups are older, you need to begin lead breaking and socializing outside the property as soon as they have enough vaccines in them, at about eight to ten weeks of age. I will drive mine to a little shopping area where, one at a time, they go on walks around the shops meeting new friends.

All these scenarios are just for a normal, uneventful puppy-raising experience. What if your bitch dies, as my friend Wendy's did, when her litter was four days old? Wendy had to hand-raise a litter of seven, which is a huge task. All pups were bottle-fed rather than tube-fed, as puppies need the time sucking to become well adjusted. Wendy got little sleep for the next five weeks. The puppies also had several problems needing emergency care. (Talk about making huge profits from breeding dogs—the final vet bill came to around $5,000!)

Just be sure that you are willing to give up having a life of any kind other than being a gofer for your bitch and her litter until the puppies go to their new homes. If you've decided that this is what you want to do, read on.

My First Litter

My foundation bitch was named Homewood Country Sunshine. I called her Sunnie. She was a big girl with a lot of bone and substance.

Not long after I bred her to Ch. Von Raseac's Tybo O'Lorcain, she began increasing in width just as a pregnant bitch should. Then I noticed that she seemed to be shrinking! My vet and my friends assured me that this was nothing to worry about. When she first started whelping, I was sound asleep. What came out of her were black, tarry objects that looked like crow skulls with some black material attached. I first became aware of them upon rising and stepping barefooted on one. So at 7 a.m., this was my introduction to whelping. I later found about four more of these strange objects around the house. Once Sunnie actually began producing whole puppies, most were dead. I ended with a live litter of three—one bitch and two dogs. One puppy had to be revived with CPR. He didn't want to nurse, either, so that meant tube-feeding him for a few days until he was strong enough to compete with his siblings. This litter was born on my birthday, and I hope I *never* have another birthday like this one. I was so emotionally exhausted and so disappointed to only have three live pups. (The litter must have been

Although most bitches make wonderful, loving mothers, they cannot do this without your help. If you cannot devote at least four weeks of full-time attention to the project and designate someone to look after mother and puppies at regular intervals during the day after that, breeding a litter is not for you. (Jill Swedlow)

huge, as there were also five fully formed stillborns and the peculiar black objects mentioned earlier.) I didn't know then how lucky I was. A litter of three or four is really fun. Many more than that is pure work. (Fun work, but work nonetheless.)

Because I didn't get the bitch I wanted in this first litter, the breeding was repeated. It consisted of three bitches and four dogs. One of those bitches turned out to be Ch. Sunnyside Daffodil, my first champion.

From the time I began exhibiting her, many of the handlers were hinting around about handling her. She was a gorgeous puppy. Handling fees being what they are, I decided to handle her myself, at least through the puppy classes. I'll tell you, I was one inept handler, too. The first time the judge pointed at us for Winners Bitch, I stopped dead in the center of the ring, stupidly pointed to myself and asked, "Who—*me*?" The second time she took points from the puppy class, I did the same thing. After that I decided that she obviously didn't need a handler, but I'd have to remind myself not to ask "Who—*me*?" when we won.

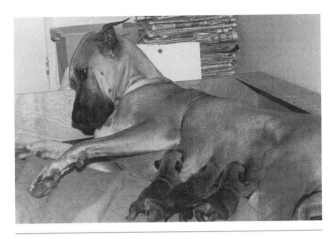

Sunnie and her first litter. (Jill Swedlow)

The point of all this is to show that breeding is time-consuming, hard work and can often be heartbreaking.

Evaluating a Bitch for Breeding

Although the earlier sections on good and bad reasons to breed cover much of this subject, there is still more to it. If you do not yet have your foundation bitch and are about to begin your search, start by researching the families of bitches under consideration.

The first thing that will probably attract you is the general type that certain lines and families produce. Once you've decided on this, start asking about any health and temperament evaluations the dogs in the pedigrees have had. It's unlikely that you'll be able to trace these traits for every dog, but at least try to get an idea. It isn't too much to expect that the dogs for the last two

or three generations or more have at least had their hips evaluated for hip dysplasia. Ask to see the OFA certificates or letters from the veterinarian who did the evaluation.

It's true that many breeders hesitate selling their best puppies to novices. This is why it's a good idea to attend shows, meet breeders and try finding someone who will mentor you as your knowledge of Great Danes grows.

Before you take the first steps toward breeding a bitch, it's a good idea to have at least a working knowledge of genetics.

GENETICS— THE BREEDER'S BLUEPRINT

I am not a geneticist, nor do I claim to be an expert on the subject of genetics. I have, however, done a great deal of reading on the subject and used and studied it in many years of breeding Great Danes, birds and horses. Once you learn and understand the basic principles, they become an invaluable tool to breed improvement. Genetics helps explain why certain traits unseen in the parents' conformation can surface in the conformation of the offspring. With even a modicum of knowledge, you no longer need to feel as if you are groping blindly in the dark in your quest for better dogs.

I do not intend to delve too deeply into how the sperm and ovum carry the genes, or the mechanics of microscopic reproduction. This subject can be learned from many good texts written for the layperson. If you have little or no knowledge of these facts, learn the basics to get a better understanding of the information contained in this section. I have included my own basic descriptions because, without *some* knowledge of reproduction, you will not understand the following concepts. Mainly I intend to explain how you can use genetic understanding to accomplish your breeding goals and how I use it.

THE IMPORTANCE OF A PEDIGREE

When planning a breeding, the more information you have about each parent's relatives, the more accurately you can predict what traits that particular animal is likely to pass on to its offspring. The ancestral names, which appear on a pedigree, have no value unless you have specific information about as many individuals as possible. Try to actually *see* as many of the ancestors as you can. Evaluate each one in terms of conformation, health and temperament and what they have produced if applicable. Keep a file on each dog, either on your computer (my method) or on hard copies so you can refer back as needed. Photographs or videos are also extremely helpful.

If you cannot see the animal in person, interview those who have. Ask them as many questions as you can think of about each dog. The more information you accumulate, the more accurately you can predict what to expect in the litter.

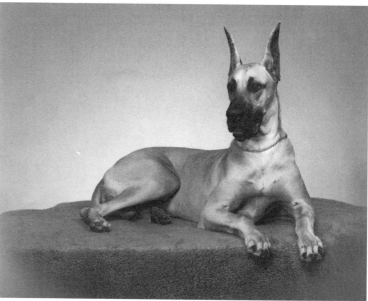

Sanlodane's Lady Chloe, owned by Bob and Mary Brownell. (Olan Mills)

THE MECHANICS OF INHERITANCE

Some elementary genetic principles must be illustrated here so that you will understand what follows.

The new pup inherits half its genes from its sire and half from its dam. The *genes* make up the chemical blueprint that determines every inherited physical characteristic each pup in the litter will have. Genes determine the pup's size, color, whether his back is long or short, whether his head is pretty or common and on and on for every part of his body—inside and out.

Italian Ch. Honky Tonk Woman di Tor Lupara, owned and bred by Salvatore Facella.

Daynakin's Devil in Disguise at six weeks, owned and bred by Georgia Hymmen and Jack Henderson.

There are two types of cells in the dog, as in other living organisms. The body cells, known as *somatic* cells, are found in all body tissue. The somatic cells differ from the sex cells in that they carry a full complement of the animal's genetic material—seventy-eight *chromosomes* in the case of the dog. The genes reside on the chromosomes. The sex cells, called *gametes*, are the sperm cells in the dog and the egg cells, or ova, in the bitch. The gametes carry only half the chromosomes of the

somatic cells. Since the genes are contained within the chromosomes, this means that the gametes only have half the genes of the body cells. This seems to be the most difficult concept for the beginning student of genetic inheritance to grasp, so Figure 12.1 and Figure 12.2 are included to help clarify this point.

DOMINANT AND RECESSIVE GENES

Without going into deep technical detail, it is important to understand the basic concept of dominant and recessive genes. This is probably

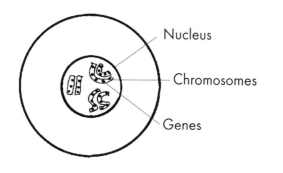

Figure 12.1   A somatic cell (body cell). It contains the nucleus, which carries seventy-eight pairs of chromosomes, which contain the genes. (Only three pairs are shown for clarity.)

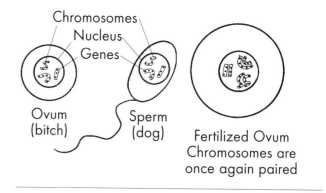

Figure 12.2   The gametes (sex cells) when manufactured within the sperm and ovaries have only thirty-nine pairs of chromosomes for a total of seventy-eight. These will split upon conception, each half carrying its own respective genes.

one of the greatest areas of confusion among those who breed animals but have little knowledge of genetics. Because of these traits, a phenomenon occurs whereby an individual may carry genes to express a specific trait (genotype), but the trait is not expressed physically (phenotype). Let me be more specific. The *genotype* simply refers to the actual genetic makeup of the individual; it's the sum total of a particular genetic makeup. You may or *may not* actually see the physical trait controlled by a certain gene(s). The *phenotype* is the visible physical entity you can actually see, touch and measure, such as a fawn coat color or a bad bite. It is the *proof* that an animal really does carry a gene to control the trait. Again, a trait controlled by recessive genes can often be hidden by a dominant gene, but a dominant gene *always is expressed physically* (phenotypically).

It is worth mentioning here that, unfortunately, very few inherited traits are attributable to only one gene. Most traits are made up from the combined interaction of several genes. In order to understand these principles, though, it is necessary to use the simple dominant and simple recessive traits.

The fawn and brindle coat color genes make a good example, since coat color is an easy trait to see and understand. It is also inherited in a

For the sake of clarity, I have left out a discussion of modifiers, complete and incomplete dominance, masking genes and so on. Not only would they tend to muddy the waters when trying to understand the basics, which is difficult enough, but these topics are always handy scapegoats to use if the unexpected occurs in a breeding. "Oh well, the stud must have carried masking genes and modifiers," you can state wisely.

At seven-and-a-half weeks, these Daynakin puppies have just been cropped and their ears are in forms.

straightforward way and is controlled by one gene. The gene that produces the brindle pattern in Great Danes is a *dominant* gene. The gene that produces a fawn-colored coat is *recessive* to the brindle gene. Since brindle is the dominant gene, a Dane showing this pattern as his phenotype can still carry the fawn-color gene recessively as part of his genotype. Remember, each parent carries two sets of genes and chromosomes but gives its offspring only half its chromosomes, thus half its genes.

Suppose that a fawn bitch who carries *only* fawn genes donates one of her two recessive fawn genes; the brindle dog (who is a *homozygous* brindle, which means that he carries *only* brindle genes and is himself a brindle) donates one of his dominant brindle genes. Their offspring carries

one gene for each color as his genotype, but his phenotype can *never* be fawn because the brindle gene is the *dominant* one of the pair. Now we have a whole new set of genes. What happens if this new individual, who carries both a fawn and brindle gene (making him genetically *heterozygous*, which means he carries a gene for each color), is mated to a bitch who is genotypically identical to him? This means that she carries the same genetic makeup for fawn and brindle, being phenotypically brindle.

There is no certain way to predict exactly how the genes will combine unless the animals being mated are homozygous for the pure dominant or recessive trait. In other words, a mating between a brindle dog and a brindle bitch—both who are homozygous for the brindle gene—can only produce brindle offspring that are genotypically homozygous for brindle, and all will be phenotypically brindle. A dog that is homozygous for such a trait is said to *breed true* for that trait. (If you are getting confused here, refer back to the definitions for homozygous, heterozygous, genotype and phenotype.)

The following chart, called a *Punnett square,* is a shorthand method of calculating the probability of any two genes finding each other at the moment of conception. Here, B represents the dominant brindle gene, and f represents the recessive fawn gene. (The geneticists do it a bit differently, but this will be clearer for our purposes.)

Sunnyside Sassafrass and Sunnyside Autumn display some of the variations found in the brindle pattern. These traits are very probably caused by genetic modifiers. (Gayle Nelson)

Square and pup #1—This brindle puppy's genotype (BB) contains two genes for brindle. He can pass on only brindle genes to his offspring, since he is homozygous for the brindle gene and does not carry a recessive gene for fawn.

Squares and pups #2 & #3—These brindle puppies' genotypes (Bf) each contain one gene for brindle and one for fawn. They can pass on either the brindle or the fawn gene to their offspring, since they are heterozygous for brindle and fawn. Since the fawn gene is recessive to brindle, it is not able to express itself in these puppies' phenotypes.

Square & pup #4—This puppy is our example of two recessive genes finding each other and expressing a genetic trait of its parents, which the parents did not show in their own phenotypes. This pup's genotype (ff) contains two genes for fawn color. His coat color pattern is fawn. He can pass on only fawn genes to his offspring, since he is homozygous for fawn. If he carried a brindle gene, he would *appear* brindle, since brindle is dominant over fawn.

Half of the sperms from a heterozygous male carry a fawn gene and half carry a brindle gene.

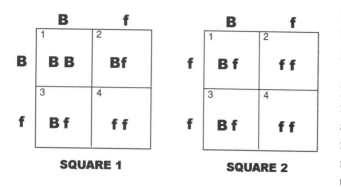

Square #1 shows the color expectancy from the earlier proposed mating of the heterozygous brindle dog and bitch. This average is based on 100 offspring. We will now take each square of the graph individually. Each square represents a pup's genotype and phenotype for the fawn and brindle genes.

The heterozygous bitch has ova with the same makeup—half carry the fawn gene and half carry the brindle. It is pure chance as to which sperm finds which egg. The laws of probability tell us, however, that in a sampling of 100 offspring, approximately 25 percent will be BB (homozygous for the dominant brindle gene with a brindle phenotype), 25 percent will be ff (homozygous for the recessive gene for fawn coat color, with a fawn phenotype), and 50 percent will be Bf (heterozygous for fawn and brindle with a brindle phenotype).

If you grasp this concept, please bear with me through one more example. It is imperative that you understand these principles, since they are the very foundation of genetics. Square #2 mates a brindle dog (with a heterozygous genotype for fawn and brindle, Bf) to a fawn bitch (homozygous for fawn ff).

Squares and pups #1 & #3—Both pups have brindle phenotypes and heterozygous genotypes for fawn and brindle. Both can pass on either fawn or brindle genes to their offspring.

Squares and pups #2 & #4—These puppies have fawn phenotypes and genotypes, since a double dose of a recessive gene is necessary to find expression. If they are bred to a fawn mate, they will produce only fawn pups.

This review should more clearly explain the behavior of simple dominant and recessive gene pairs. Since the chromosomes occur in pairs in the somatic cells, so do genes. Let's continue with the

example of the fawn gene versus the brindle gene. As previously stated, these traits are controlled by single genes, and brindle is dominant to fawn.

When gametes are formed, they contain only half the genetic makeup of each parent. One gamete might end up with the gene causing brindle stripes, and the other gamete might carry the other gene for fawn body color. The same is true of the male's sperm cells. It is pure chance which of the bitch's ova ripens first and ovulates into the fallopian tubes to await the dog's sperm. It could be an ovum with the fawn gene or with the brindle gene. Since there is an equal number of each, there is an equal chance of it being either. Again, the same holds true of the dog's sperm. Approximately half of the millions of sperm contained in each ejaculate carry his fawn gene, and half carry the brindle gene. If the sperm that fertilizes the ovum carries a gene for fawn, and the ovum has the gene for brindle, the pup will be born brindle since brindle is dominant to fawn. The resulting pup will carry one gene for brindle and one for fawn and is genetically capable of producing get of either color depending on the genetic makeup of its mate. If both the bitch's ovum and the dog's sperm happen to carry the gene for fawn, the pup will be fawn and carry two genes for fawn. If the bitch's ovum and the dog's sperm both carry the brindle gene, the pup will not only be brindle but will carry brindle in a double dose and can produce only brindle, since brindle is dominant to fawn.

The laws of probability tell us that with animals carrying simple recessive and simple dominants, the chances are always 50-50 as to which gene is inherited by the puppy. The calculations are over the expectancy of 100 offspring, so if a brindle dog bred to three fawn bitches has produced fifteen brindle pups, there is *still* a 50-50 chance that his next litter could contain fawns. From this you know that he carries a recessive gene for fawn, because he has produced fawn pups even though he is himself brindle. And because he is brindle, he obviously carries the dominant brindle gene.

Semantics can be responsible for misunderstandings at times. One breeder once wondered why her brindle dog sometimes produced fawns instead of always producing brindles if the brindle gene was dominant. She didn't understand that the gene had to be passed along to the pup in order for it to be able to exert its dominance. The chances of the brindle gene being passed along when the dog also carries a recessive gene for fawn is 50-50. Again, only dogs that are homozygous for the brindle gene will produce 100 percent brindle.

Admittedly these examples are greatly simplified compared to polygenic traits. Other types of genes are expressed differently. To accurately predict the expectancy of certain traits, it is necessary to understand the modes of inheritance.

The example of canine coat color is also true of many traits in Great Danes. While brindle is dominant to fawn, there are other colors (and patterns) in the breed that, from a genetic perspective, are not quite so simple to understand and predict. The relationship among genes—which is dominant to which, and which are recessive—can be likened to a pecking order among a flock of chickens. The rooster (or most dominant gene) is at the top of the heap and bosses everyone around. Next is the bossiest hen, who only takes orders from the rooster. Below her are the rank and file of her subordinates, all of whom obey their betters and in turn control their underlings. Finally, you come to the bottom of the heap and find the little hen (or most recessive gene) whom everyone picks on. She never gets to eat or express herself until she is the only one in the barnyard.

You might now be wondering how any of this can be helpful since little is known of the mode of inheritance of many canine traits. Also, few traits are controlled by a single gene. Most traits, such as head shape, are polygenic. There are probably thousands of genes and their modifiers that make up the blueprint that determines the shape of a dog's head. Although it would be very difficult, not to mention impractical, to try isolating each gene and how it behaves in creating the overall blueprint, these controlling groups of genes often tend to act in recessive or dominant ways as a group. Suppose that a dog with a beautiful head is mated to ten bitches whose head type ranges from ugly to plain, but none are gorgeous. If 75 percent of the offspring have beautiful heads like their sire, it is fairly accurate to conclude that the dog is dominant for head type. This conclusion can be applied to any conformation trait or group of traits that tend to occur in the same manner. But what about traits that, as a group, behave in a recessive manner? Since recessives are masked by dominants, they can be difficult to isolate.

We will use an *undershot jaw* (lower teeth protruding over the upper) as our example. Assume that a dog and bitch, both possessing a correct bite, are mated. Some of their puppies are undershot. What does this tell us? It is highly probable that *both* parents carry the recessive gene(s) that produced the bad bite. Remember the brindle dog and bitch who both carried fawn in recessive and produced a fawn pup? The same principle applies here. What makes such a trait difficult to breed out is its recessive nature. These puppies could just as easily have had correct bites and still carried the recessive genes for undershot bite. These recessives can be masked by their dominant *alleles* (genes that appear on a common location on the chromosomes) for generation after generation until they pair with another like recessive and express themselves in the puppy's phenotype. Refer back to the Punnett square, and you will see that there is a 50 percent probability that an offspring of recessive carriers will itself be a carrier.

This is a rather sobering thought, especially when you realize that such recessives can skip generations and the individual must be test bred in order to ascertain if it is, indeed, a carrier. So what is the logical solution to this problem? Intelligent breeding practices and ruthless culling, which are discussed later in this chapter.

Several different methods of planned breeding are used by knowledgeable breeders. All have their good points and their drawbacks. Sometimes you must simply experiment with the methods to establish which will be most effective. This, then, brings us to a discussion of inbreeding, linebreeding and outcrossing.

Handy Lion di Tor Lupara, owned in Italy by Salvatore Facella, was the 1997 Chamion of Italy, the 1998 Champion of Spain and has qualified as an International Champion.

Inbreeding

Inbreeding is generally considered to be the closest type of breeding possible. These are matings of mother to son, father to daughter and the closest pairing of all—full brother to full sister. Ironically, an occasional sister/brother mating might not be genetically close at all, since the possibility exists for each sibling to have received entirely different sets of genes from each parent. This is, however,

At five months, Miss Southern Bell of VZTop (left) and Mr. Rhett Butler of VZTop (right) both displayed the promise of their quality as adults. They are shown here with owner Lorraine Rainwater.

seldom true and can effectively be considered inbreeding.

Those who do not understand genetic principles often condemn inbreeding, claiming that it weakens the animal produced. In many cases this can be true, but inbreeding itself is not the culprit.

By its very nature, inbreeding gives the greatest probability that recessive genes will be expressed. This is because closely related animals are more likely to carry the same recessives in their genotype than unrelated animals. By breeding these close relatives to each other, the chances are high that two recessive genes, or groups of recessive genes, will meet and produce the trait they control in the animal's phenotype. Inbreeding's poor

reputation is due to the fact that traits controlled by recessive genes are often undesirable, such as light eyes or faulty mouths. If the trait these recessive genes control is *desirable,* inbreeding is considered to be successful, but usually inbreeding produces good and bad traits.

Inbreeding can be a very useful tool for pinpointing an animal's genotype. Inbreeding is most safely employed after linebreeding has set a type and there are related dogs who consistently produce the qualities the breeder has been striving to set in her breeding line. Breeders should have a very clear idea of what the gene pool is capable of producing and then use only animals whose phenotypes are as nearly perfect as possible. Even then it can be risky, but if successful, you'll have a real prize. Inbreeding should be a tool held only in the hands of a knowledgeable breeder—it is definitely not for the novice.

Linebreeding

This practice usually includes pairings such as niece to uncle, grandchild to grandparent, half sister to half brother, or a pairing that includes one animal's name somewhere within the first three generations on both sides of the pedigree. Linebreeding is probably the safest approach when establishing a breeding line. Although recessives can certainly be expressed when using this method, the frequency is not as high as with inbreeding. There is a wider margin for error here because progress is more gradual.

As with inbreeding, you must be sure to use only superior-quality individuals when linebreeding. You must also be certain that the ancestor being linebred on is himself or herself a superior specimen and carries the traits you are trying to set in your line. If you linebreed on faulty animals, you will probably get faulty pups. You must also be sure not to breed two animals together that share common faults.

Outcrossing

Outcrossing is the mating of unrelated animals who do not have any ancestors in common within the first four or five generations. Unlike inbreeding and linebreeding, this method will do nothing to make resulting puppies more genetically homozygous. It is very difficult to predict with any accuracy what results might be obtained from such a mating unless one of the pair being outcrossed is, in fact, linebred. The continued use of this breeding method will never produce a group of animals that breed true for any characteristic. One advantage of outcrossing is a reduced likelihood of any recessive genetic problems unless each of the parents carries such genes.

Outcrossing is best used to introduce a trait—for example, improved head type—into a well-established, linebred gene pool. To make the best use of an outcross, the breeder locates a stud dog from a *linebred* family with beautiful heads and who has consistently produced this trait. Even though the dog is the result of linebreeding, he

is unrelated to the breeder's line and the resultant breeding is considered an outcross. If good heads result, the good-headed offspring of this mating are now bred back to the linebred bitches of the original family. The breeder has now obtained the genes to work with to produce beautiful, improved heads on future puppies.

THE CANINE GENOME PROJECT

Currently there is a worldwide effort to map the canine genome. According to the article *Mapping A Brighter Tomorrow,* by Melissa Goodman, DVM, that appeared in the January 1998 issue of the *AKC Gazette,*

> The goal of the canine genome project is to produce a map of all the chromosomes in dogs. This map can then be used as a framework to identify which genes cause a particular inherited disease, as well as genes for other inherited characteristics, such as behavior and conformation.
>
> The development of a genetic map of the dog has already resulted in several helpful assays, including tests for progressive retinal atrophy and copper toxicosis.

Breeders are already using this information effectively to eliminate this latter malady in affected breeds.

You don't have to be a rocket scientist to realize the potential for such a study. Imagine being able to select dogs that are genetically free of health problems, temperament problems and with conformation closer than ever to the breed Standard!

SELECTING A STUD FOR YOUR BITCH

Your bitch has finished her championship. Her temperament is wonderful and her conformation worthy of passing on. You are fully prepared to be responsible for her puppies all their lives, no matter where they live. Her OFA hip rating came back normal, as did her thyroid and cardiac screening. You're ready to breed her!

Although "fault judging" is considered undesirable in the ring, it has a place as a breeder's tool. When you evaluate a bitch for breeding, you must know the faults that need improvement as well as her assets in order to select the right mate. If your bitch toes in, you do not select a mate that toes out. You select a stud that is *correct* for this trait. Otherwise you'll get puppies that toe in and puppies that toe out. Do not overcompensate for your bitch's faults.

When you think you've found the future sire of your litter, one who is correct where your bitch is faulty but also has most of her desirable traits, you next need to find out about his family. What about *his* sire and dam? Were *they* also correct for the traits you're trying to improve? What about siblings? Aunts and uncles? Check them all to get a much broader picture of the stud's genotype. Of course, one of the most important things to look at are any puppies he has sired, along with their dams. If the dams have some similar faults to your bitch and the puppies are correct for those traits, this dog can probably help you accomplish your goals.

When you're evaluating potential studs, *please* make temperament a priority. Great Danes are far too large to excuse dangerous temperaments. Unfortunately, some breeders who should know better are cavalier in this respect. In my opinion this is both irresponsible and indefensible.

This is not meant to condemn the breeder who produces an occasional shy or aggressive dog. This can happen no matter how cautious breeders are. When you consider the original temperament of the first Great Danes imported from Germany, it's amazing that the breed has as good a temperament as it does.

You've selected the best stud you can find for your bitch and you've signed the stud contract and fully understand what it does and does not guarantee. As your bitch's season nears, several things must be done.

PREBREEDING ESSENTIALS

Brucellosis Testing

Most stud owners have, as a minimum requirement, brucellosis testing for all bitches. Brucellosis renders both bitch and stud sterile, and there is no cure. Request proof of this test from the stud owner as well as a copy of the test, and produce a copy of your bitch's test as well.

Additional Testing

Provide the owner of the stud with copies of the OFA papers and all other health tests that have been performed on your bitch, and the stud owner should provide you with the same. If the dogs are microchipped or tattooed, it is desirable to have the vet who performs these tests verify that he is, indeed, testing the dog that is represented.

It isn't uncommon for dogs that are clear for certain health traits to be substituted for others that aren't. Without permanent identification, there is no way the veterinarian who performs the tests can verify that the dog is as represented. If the dog's ID is shown on the test papers, you can be assured that the dog is really clear.

Cultures

I routinely have my bitches cultured shortly after they come into season if they are to be bred. I have my vet perform a vaginal culture and sensitivity test. In this way, if an unusual growth of anything turns up, we know immediately which antibiotic it will be sensitive to. Vaginal flora normally occur in the genital area. However, if one of these organisms is present in unusually large numbers, it's wise to control it.

If you should be unlucky enough to have a growth of mycoplasma show up, it would be a good idea to forget breeding on this season. Mycoplasma almost always results in either no pregnancy or dead/dying puppies. It's best to treat the infection and try for the next season.

Rather than use a systemic antibiotic, I prefer to use an antibiotic douche. Most often these organisms are sensitive to Gentocin, which your vet can make into a douche solution for you.

Douching your bitch is easy. A 500 cc dose syringe and a stallion catheter is all you need. The bitch, being in season, usually is quite receptive to having the catheter inserted. It will usually go up into the vagina about eight inches. You then depress the plunger and you're done. I douche my bitches for two days, morning and night, prior to breeding. *Do not* douche within forty-eight hours of the breeding, as this might kill the sperm.

Owners of stud dogs are wise to occasionally culture the sheath that covers the dog's penis. Any potential problems detected can be treated as required.

Progesterone Testing

Depending on the breeding method used, progesterone testing may be necessary. I use progesterone tests even for natural breedings, especially for virgin animals. If artificial insemination or shipping chilled fresh or frozen semen is involved, progesterone testing should be considered mandatory. All progesterone testing is *not* equally accurate, so talk to those who have used these methods, and use the vets and laboratories that have had the highest rate of success with this.

Semen Evaluation

For a virgin stud, or a proven dog whose last bitch failed to conceive, it's wise to have a specialist do a semen evaluation. Even though it only takes one sperm to fertilize one egg, a very high number of active, normal sperm is necessary to impregnate a bitch. Ask the stud owner for a recommendation, or contact one of the cryobanks that collect and store sperm about semen evaluation.

The Bitch's Estrus Cycle

Most bitches will come into season every six months beginning at about nine months old. For some bitches, it is normal to cycle every four months. For others, every five months or even only once a year can be the norm.

The first noticeable sign of a bitch coming into heat is a bloody discharge from the vulva. If you have a really bad case of "litter fever" and you've been watching your bitch like a hawk, you'll notice that the vulva swells prior to the first discharge. Every book I've ever read on this subject tells us that the discharge will change to a "straw color" as the bitch ovulates. I've *never* seen this in my bitches. They continue to bleed right through the breeding dates. The only change I've ever seen is that the discharge becomes slightly more dilute as the season progresses.

For a natural breeding, you might want to skip progesterone testing and be guided by the dogs. If so, you might want to present the bitch to the dog on her tenth day for a first attempt. The most common breeding dates are day eleven and day thirteen if only two breedings are planned. These are the most usual optimum days for the bitch, but remember that bitches can fluctuate. If you've followed this rule on a virgin bitch and she failed to conceive, consider progesterone testing prior to breeding on her next season. Some bitches are

fertile on day eight and some not until day eighteen. (Days are counted from the first time the bloody discharge is observed.)

NATURAL BREEDING

When I take my bitches to be bred, I ask the stud owners about their procedure. I much prefer to begin with both dog and bitch on lead and the bitch unmuzzled. I like them to be able to greet each other first and play a little, which is what nature intended. Even if a bitch isn't ready and snaps, it's highly unlikely she's going to harm the male. She's just warning him away; he understands this and will defer. Sometimes he can convince her into standing while he mounts, and other times, it just is not going to happen right then.

However, if a bitch will not stand and tries to savage the dog, she should not be bred at all. One of the most important traits you should select for is fertility and dogs who breed readily. It's interesting to note that the dam of the litter mentioned earlier had temperament and health problems and was a very reluctant breeder. She had to be muzzled and held up in order for the stud to breed her. I remember, too, that her *sire growled* during a tie. The resultant litter was full of problems, both temperamentally and healthwise. I guess she knew more than I did about her fitness as a brood matron!

Natural breeding is the most usual and most successful breeding method. Even with all the scientific advancements, I still believe that the dog and the bitch know best when the moment is right.

I like the dogs to meet for the first time while held on six-foot leads. Some dogs will greet the bitch and invite her to play. If the bitch seems so inclined, it's to everyone's benefit to let them both off lead in a small enclosure and let them frolic. The dog will usually try to mount right away. If the bitch is receptive, she'll brace her hind legs apart and flag her tail to the side. Often the tie can be allowed to occur before steadying the bitch's head and helping the male to turn.

The tie occurs when the bitch's vaginal muscles contract and hold the bulb that forms at the base of the penis. The natural impulse of the male is to dismount with both forelegs on one side of the bitch. He will then lift a hind leg and try to turn so that the dogs are standing tail to tail with only the tie holding them together. It is during the tie that the bulk of the sperm is ejaculated. The first fluid is usually clear seminal fluid. When the fluid becomes milky, it's full of sperm.

Be sure to have a good hold on the bitch's head when the tie occurs. This is often painful for her and she might try to turn and bite.

If the dog is interested and trying to breed, and the bitch is standing well but they're just not connecting, don't panic. The chances are that you're a day or two early. Commonly, when you try on the following day, it's a case of instant tie.

Often the handlers want to constantly interfere with the dogs in an attempt to facilitate the breeding. It's been my experience that the dogs are far more adept than we are and if left to their own instincts will accomplish the breeding when the time is right.

ARTIFICIAL INSEMINATION

Artificial insemination is used in dog breeding under several circumstances—when a stud won't or can't breed properly, when the stud is many miles away and shipping the bitch is impractical or when the stud has died and his semen has been stored.

Whether frozen or cooled semen is used, you and your bitch will have to put yourselves in the hands of the experts. The bitch is inseminated in one of two ways—*surgically* or *transcervically.*

Surgical insemination requires that the bitch be anesthetized and the semen introduced directly into the uterus through an incision through her side.

The procedure with transcervical insemination introduces the semen directly through the cervix into the uterus, and the bitch does not need to be sedated. Until recently the pregnancy rate was higher with the surgical procedure, but it is now said to be equal using the transcervical route.

In either case, the bitch's hormone levels must be closely monitored prior to breeding. The bitch is fertile only for a very short period of time, and it's just prior to this that the insemination must occur. Obviously, the vet performing this procedure must have a great deal of experience and past successes.

Sometimes it becomes necessary to use artificial insemination even though the stud is present and willing but cannot achieve a breeding. In such cases, knowledgeable people are still needed. It's not enough to simply collect the semen and get it into the bitch. There's a reason for the tie. It's during the tie that the vaginal and uterine muscles are contracting and helping to move the semen to the uterus. Because of this, the vet or technician must *feather* the bitch. This involves digital manipulation to create the stimulation she would get from a tie. It's also a good idea to gently pull against the vulva as would happen during a real tie.

PREGNANCY—IS SHE OR ISN'T SHE?

You'll never know how long sixty-three days can be until you're waiting for your first litter! Such an exciting time, and there's much to be done while nature takes its course.

First you'll want to verify that she is, indeed, pregnant. There are three methods of doing this. The first, oldest and least accurate, is *palpation*. The vet will check the bitch at approximately twenty-eight days postbreeding. He will feel the uterus through the abdominal wall in an attempt to palpate the walnut-sized fetuses. In smaller breeds this is probably much more accurate, but in Great Danes and other giant breeds, the technique is a very difficult way to determine pregnancy.

The next and most accurate method of early pregnancy detection is an *ultrasound*. This test is performed at about thirty-two days postbreeding. The bitch is laid on her side and the vet applies some contact jelly to her abdomen to facilitate the reading. To an untrained eye, the fetuses are difficult to see; they basically look like black holes. It's hard to do an accurate count, and if your vet counts four puppies, you can almost always count on twice that number.

The most accurate method of determining pregnancy is when a live puppy emerges from your bitch. While this removes all doubt regarding the bitch's condition, this obviously cannot qualify as early detection.

Do *not* x-ray your bitch early in her pregnancy to check for puppies. This could be very harmful to the fetuses at this early stage. Only agree to x-ray during the last few days of a pregnancy if for some reason you simply *have* to know how many puppies there are. The other good use of an x-ray is to verify that all the puppies have been whelped. Most vets can easily palpate to verify this, making an x-ray unnecessary.

When my Skylark had her litter, she and all her eight babies were fine. I had no idea or reason to suspect that there was still one puppy remaining unborn. I just packed her and her babies up and off we went to the vet's for the routine postwhelping check and pit (synthetic oxytocin) shot to clean the uterus. The vet said she could feel another puppy and wanted an x-ray to see how it was positioned. She wasn't sure if it was dead or alive. In view of the time elapsed, I assumed the puppy must have been dead for some time at this point. Whelping began around 8 p.m. the previous evening, and it was now about 9 a.m. I was quite concerned, as I didn't want Skylark to go through a C-section for one last, possibly dead, puppy.

She was given IV calcium and a pit shot to stimulate contractions, and she and I awaited developments. About twenty minutes later, after a couple of half-hearted contractions, our vet checked her and gave her another pit shot.

Suddenly the contractions began in earnest and here was puppy number nine! And he was alive! If we hadn't checked Skylark, she could have died from infection caused by that last puppy had it not been passed.

WHAT TO EXPECT DURING GESTATION

So your bitch has been verified to be in whelp and it's time to get everything ready. What will you need? What should you expect?

Obviously you'll expect your bitch to become much larger as her pregnancy progresses. Depending on the number of puppies she's carrying, this is a reasonable expectation. But it doesn't always happen! Great Danes are *big* dogs, and there's a lot of room inside their mother for puppies to hide. A bitch carrying a very small litter might not show at all, while a bitch carrying nine puppies might appear to be carrying only two or three. My Narcissus was a good example of this. Small compared to most Dane bitches, she stood only about thirty-and-a-half inches tall. At only a few days before whelping, I thought she might have four puppies at the most. No one was more surprised than I was when she presented me with nine puppies!

Be prepared for the possibility of a personality change. Bred bitches normally become quieter and more loving during their pregnancies. This is, of course, a nice change, but it is possible for a bitch to go the other way and become a mass of hormones gone mad. When I bred Skylark, I got an education in the power of female hormones. Lark, who was the baby in the family and had always been the omega bitch (bottom of the heap) suddenly became Super Bitch! She'd strut around the house as if it had been built for her and her alone. She'd pull herself to her full height (in her case, that's *tall*) and give threat signals freely. It got so bad that I would kennel her when I had to leave the house even for short periods. After she whelped and the puppies were four or five weeks old, she began to return to the old Lark we all knew and loved.

While on this subject, I should mention a couple of other things that happened to Skylark during her pregnancy. One morning about a week prior to her due date, I awoke to find Lark standing by my bed with her back kind of hunched up and her neck stretched out ahead of her. When she'd move her neck side to side, she'd cry out. All I could think of was that she'd slipped a disk or done something similar. She'd move around and eat, but it was obvious that certain positions were painful.

My vet examined her and asked me if I believed in chiropractors. After expressing my skepticism, I agreed to take Lark to the recommended chiropractor. Dr. Eaton said Lark's neck felt like it was "out." When we arrived at the chiropractor's office, she examined Lark thoroughly and had me place my hands on a spot in her neck where there was an obvious "hole." After very gently adjusting Lark, she warned me that she might be worse the next day but should improve by day three. She had me feel her neck where the "hole" had been, and it was gone. Sure enough, day two found her really gimpy, but by the next day she was almost back to her old self!

Following instructions, I returned with Lark for one more adjustment prior to her whelping date. Lark's improvement was truly impressive, and I had become a believer.

What caused Lark's problem? Dr. Eaton explained to me that during pregnancy, hormonal activity can cause ligaments and soft tissue to relax to facilitate the whelping process. This affects the tissues throughout the body. Lark has a tendency to stand in one place and leap three or four feet straight into the air. She is also *extremely* active, so the combination of hormonal changes and excess movement caused her spine more flexion than it should have and it moved out of alignment.

PUPPY ROOM ESSENTIALS

Whelping box: Ideally, your bitch will bear the litter in this enclosure, and this is where the puppies will remain until they are about three or four weeks old or until they start piling out onto the floor. A ready-to-use whelping box can be purchased from dog supply catalogs, or you can make your own. Some breeders use and swear by children's plastic wading pools. Their round shape is a more natural shape for a whelping area than the usual square or rectangular models.

I think my first whelping box would have held a litter of elephants—it was so strong! It was on a base made of two-by-fours and had a heavy plywood floor, with sides that came up about nine inches and a shelf running along each long side to keep the bitch from crushing a puppy against the side. Incidentally, this did not work—I had to extract puppies from between the wall and their mom on more than one occasion. Some square and rectangular whelping boxes use *pig rails*—heavy dowels about the circumference of a closet clothes pole—running the length of the box about six inches up from the floor and about four inches from the wall. Frankly, I question their effectiveness, as a puppy could still become stuck between the rail and mom.

After the first litter was born and I tried to find a place to store this 300-pound thing, I decided that there must be a better way. I removed the sides of the box and fastened each short end to the long side with hinges. This allowed the short sides to fold in against the long one, and the whole thing weighed about twenty pounds! The hinges that fastened the other long side to the two short sides used hinges with removable pins. All I do now is pull the pins, and the entire box is collapsed and easily stored.

In actual use, this four-sided box sits directly on the floor over a three-inch foam pad completely covered in Naugahyde. Over this, old blankets and sheets are sewn together—blanket on one side, sheet on the other—to fit over the pad like a pillowcase. There's enough left over at the open end to tuck securely underneath the pad. The beauty of this cover is that it's easily removed and washed, and the puppies can't become hidden under folds of a wrinkled blanket to be stepped on or crushed by their dam.

When a litter is due, locate the whelping box in a private area away from other dogs, cats, people and the general flow of household traffic. After the puppies arrive, mom and her new family will definitely benefit from their seclusion.

Tons of Newspaper: You'll go through lots of this stuff during the actual whelping. I use the whelping pad and cover and then spread a very thick layer of newspapers down. After each puppy is born, I get the bitch up, remove the soiled papers and replace them with fresh papers. I also use newspapers for the floor at the far end of the box once the pups are actively moving around at about two-and-a-half weeks and starting to look for a place outside the nest to relieve themselves.

Baby Scale: Each puppy is weighed at birth, then daily until about the age of ten days. Although a small loss of weight isn't unusual during the first twenty-four hours, you want to see a steady gain every day after that.

Terry-Cloth Hand Towels, Washcloths and Rags: Lay in a generous supply and use these for helping to get a grip on a puppy as it is being born and for drying off newborns. A vigorous rubdown helps get the puppy crying, which brings air into its lungs and helps stimulate it to move around.

Garbage Can and Many Garbage Bags: Self explanatory!

Mosquito Clamps: You will need at least two of these during a whelping, and having more is a good idea. Use one to clamp the umbilical cord about one inch from the belly and the other to clamp about one inch past the first clamp against

the placenta; then cut the cord with dull scissors in the space between the clamps. You can leave the clamp on the pup for a few seconds while you dry it and then remove it.

Dull Children's Scissors: When the bitch bites the cord off, it is never a clean cut, which means that it bleeds very little. Children's dull craft scissors imitate this cut.

Small Cardboard Box: A sturdy box about eighteen inches by twenty-four inches, with eighteen-inch-high sides is about right. It makes a handy place to keep puppies during a whelping while new arrivals are being born, while putting down fresh bedding and as a puppy carrier.

Heating Pad: Use this with the small cardboard box. Place the heating pad over only half the floor of the box and cover it with a towel. In this way, any puppies that become too hot can move off. As each puppy is born, it is put to nurse, which helps stimulate contractions. As another puppy is about to be born, put all the previous puppies in the box to keep them out of the way. Once the puppy is safely delivered, he and all his siblings are returned to their dam until the next puppy arrives. The heating pad is also used in the box when puppies visit the vet for their postwhelping exam and for dewclaw removal at two days of age.

Rectal Thermometer: Use an ordinary human rectal thermometer to monitor your bitch's temperature beginning several days to a week prior to the expected whelping date. When the temperature drops to below 99° F (sometimes as low as 97° F), you can be pretty sure that labor will commence within twenty-four hours. It is also wise to monitor her temperature for a couple of weeks postwhelping to be sure all is well.

Clock: Keep track of the delivery time of each puppy and write it down. You might be too nervous to remember it later.

If the bitch goes much more than three hours between puppies, call your vet. There might be nothing amiss, but it's best not to take chances if you can help it.

Pen and Notepad: Obvious!

Rickrack in Different Colors: Use *rickrack* (flat, narrow braids woven in zigzag forms) to make an identification collar for each puppy. If you have a litter of all fawns, or if you have several puppies of the same color and same sex, this type of ID really helps. Be sure to check the collars daily to make sure they are not too tight. Great Dane babies grow really fast.

Puppy Charts: Keep a chart with the following information to be filled out as each puppy is born.

- Rickrack color

- Time whelped

- Color of puppy

- Sex

- Weight

- A drawing of a puppy on its back indicating any white markings (other markings for harlequins). This helps with ID if the collar comes off.

Lots of Sleep Prior to Whelping: Like so many breeders, I sleep within earshot of a new litter so I can hear if anything is amiss and bears investigation. Some breeders sleep right next to the whelping box.

WHEN BIRTH IS IMMINENT

As mentioned earlier, once the bitch's temperature has dropped, whelping will commence usually within twenty-four hours. She'll probably do a *lot* of panting. She might even strain or appear to be having contractions. She might then decide to go back to sleep now that she's got you all nervous and upset!

Digging is very popular with most in-whelp bitches, sometimes beginning soon after being bred. However, once contractions start, digging begins in earnest. If you have access to a secure outdoor area where the bitch can't sneak off in the dark and have the puppies unobserved, it's helpful to allow her outside to dig—under supervision, of course. This seems to help the contractions along. Otherwise, she will be content to just dig up the newspapers you've so neatly spread in the whelping box.

As a puppy enters the birth canal, most bitches have several strong contractions, often accompanied by grunts. The vulva enlarges as the sac is presented, and then out will come a puppy. If the bitch shows interest, allow her to clean off the sac and lick the puppy. If she doesn't do this immediately, you must burst the sac and clear it away from the puppy's face. If the placenta is present, clamp the cord about one inch from the puppy's body with one mosquito clamp and again next to the placenta. Then, using scissors, cut between the clamps and leave both in place. Keep the clamp on the placenta until you can discard it. If you don't, you will have an extra mess to clean up. The clamp on the puppy can stay in place until you have dried the newborn. Be careful not to pull on the clamp and risk a hernia in the puppy.

If the newborn's breathing sounds very wet, hold the puppy upside down and support its head. Then extend your arms straight out from your body and quickly swing the puppy downward between your legs. The centrifugal force will help to clear fluid from the puppy's airways.

Next weigh the puppy and record all the information on the chart. Don't forget its rickrack. Puppy can now go on to mom and nurse until the next one starts to come. This will continue until the entire litter is born.

You can usually assume that the bitch is finished when she contentedly (and *wearily*) stretches out on her side for some well-deserved sleep. Regardless of how certain you are that she's finished, you should still take her and the litter to the vet to be checked. Having your vet give a pituitrin shot to the bitch is always a good idea, as it helps to clean out the uterine debris. Don't do as some breeders do and keep pituitrin on hand to give at home. If a malpositioned puppy is still inside the bitch, her uterus could rupture with the administration of this shot. As you can see, making absolutely certain that the bitch is completely finished is critically important.

As mentioned earlier, it's a good idea to continue monitoring the bitch's temperature for a week or two postwhelping. Any rise above normal is a signal to get her to your vet. She could be getting an infection or going into eclampsia (milk fever), either of which could kill both her and the puppies.

Keep a close eye on the litter also. A quiet litter is a content litter. Constant fussing and the inability to settle down can indicate a problem. It isn't uncommon for the puppies to go through a period of yellowish diarrhea sometime in the first week. A little is nothing to worry about and will usually clear up on its own as the puppies' systems grow accustomed to digesting milk. But if the stools are green or very smelly, call the vet.

RAISING THE LITTER

The first two weeks of life are a breeze for you and constant work for the bitch. She cleans the puppies, feeds them and keeps them warm. Her licking stimulates the pups and is even necessary for the first week or more in order for them to eliminate. Once most Great Dane bitches have had a day or two with their puppies, they are fantastic mothers, careful and loving of their puppies. They can also be very protective. Don't be surprised if your once easygoing sweetheart becomes a tiger where her babies are concerned. Certainly she must allow *you* to handle them, but if she refuses other family members early on, don't push it. Once the puppies are two to three weeks old, most bitches will become more relaxed about leaving them and allowing other people to touch them. Strangers are still forbidden access. If people come over to see the litter, either remove the bitch to a place where she's contained and cannot see what's going on, or only allow your visitors to stand outside the room and look in.

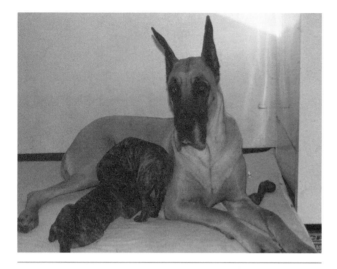

Don't be surprised if your bitch becomes very protective of her puppies with strangers and perhaps even some household members, including other pets. Be sure that she has a private place for the litter. (Jill Swedlow)

Provided she is healthy and has been prepared for having a litter, a bitch of good temperament will usually be an excellent mother. (Jill Swedlow)

Be careful about allowing other dogs in with the bitch and her litter. Some bitches might really resent this. However, I've had some really cute mother/daughter teams raise a litter together. Daffodil did this when her daughter, Kiwi, had her litter. I'd find them both in the whelping box together, Daffi trying to roll the puppies around and play with them while Kiwi was nursing them.

I base my decision to begin supplementing the puppies on their body condition and the mother's milk supply. Cricket had so much milk ten days prior to whelping that when she'd lay down, milk would spurt from her breasts! Her babies were rolling fat balls! When they were four-and-a-half weeks old, I decided to start them on solid food more so I could get some weight *off* them.

Then there was Skylark's litter. Besides all the other problems Lark had that I mentioned earlier in this chapter, her uterine cramping continued for so long and so severely that she was seldom comfortable enough to lie still and let her puppies nurse. Even when they did nurse, she had very little milk. This resulted in very thin babies that began supplemental feedings at two weeks old. (Trying to get eight two-week-olds who had barely begun to wobble on their legs to *drink* from a bowl was a mess, to put it mildly.) But drink they did, and they turned out just fine.

In normal litters, supplementation usually begins when the puppies are about three weeks old. Start them on a bitch's milk replacer mixed with some baby rice cereal to the consistency of uncongealed pudding at first. Gradually add kibble ground in a food processor and canned Eagle™

Weaning puppies is always an experience for dogs and people. Be pre-pared for the mess this creates and remember to keep your sense of humor. Puppies catch on fast. (Courtesy of Bryan and Jennifer Saulsbury)

By age four weeks, puppies should be eating whole, soaked kibble, and by six weeks, the kibble is no longer soaked before feeding. I, like many other breeders, feed a litter together out of several bowls. While it encourages good eating habits, it's difficult to tell exactly how much each puppy is eating. A six-week-old Dane puppy will probably be eating one-and-a-half to two cups of food three times a day. By age seven weeks, most of my litters were only picking at their lunch meal. When that occurs, they're shifted over to two meals a day.

The best way to judge if your puppy is eating enough (or too much) is by his body condition. Dane puppies should be kept lean on a top-quality food. You should *barely* be able to see the ribs but feel them easily. Most Dane fans are anxious for their dogs to become huge. But don't get hung up on the weight/height issue as your puppy grows. Early size and weight are *not* indicative of adult size and weight. Some of the smallest puppies have ended up as the biggest adults. And size isn't everything. For a show dog, overall quality is far more important.

AKC RECORD-KEEPING REQUIREMENTS

The American Kennel Club has several requirements for those who breed dogs. Breeders must

Brand Beef, Liver or Chicken and Rice or a similar product. I start my puppies right out on what I feed the adults, which is Innova™ kibble and Eagle Brand canned meat. You might not be able to find these brands in your area, or you might have been directed to try other brands. As long as you are feeding quality foods and your puppies and adults are doing well, you should be all right.

provide the new owner of a puppy they have bred with an Application for Registration (blue slip) and a contract that contains the following information:

- Names and registration numbers of the sire and dam

- Registered name of puppy/adult (if applicable) and registration number of puppy/adult

- Any permanent ID information, such as a tattoo or a microchip

- Date of birth

- Color

- Sex

- Breeder(s)

If you contemplate becoming a breeder, request information from AKC about these requirements. AKC also will not accept records on computer disk. The breeder must have hard copies available on file.

Although the AKC requires that the blue slip accompany the puppy, it's common practice for breeders to withhold this until a puppy has been paid for in full. In the event that the blue slip is not available when the puppy goes to a new owner, a signed bill of sale properly identifying the puppy should be given.

There is an option for registration called *limited registration*. This is a great tool for the breeder. Any offspring from a dog sold on limited registration cannot be registered with AKC, nor can the dog compete in conformation shows. The breeder, and only the breeder, can remove this stipulation if the dog turns out to be a breeding/show specimen in the future.

SELLING/PLACING GREAT DANE PUPPIES

For reasons both obvious and obscure, Great Danes are *not* for everyone. It is therefore up to you, as the breeder, to do all you can to ensure that your puppies go to homes where they will happily remain for life. You can accomplish this by thoroughly screening your potential puppy buyers.

But first, people need to know that you have a litter available. If this is your first litter, you will probably have a little more trouble finding buyers than breeders with an established reputation. It's best, of course, to have a list of people waiting for your puppies. But how do you reach these people? *Do not* advertise in the local paper. Although you can certainly find occasional good homes this way, they'll most likely be pet homes. This is also fine, but you've bred this litter to produce show puppies. The best show prospect in the world will never earn its championship in someone's back yard!

Start with an advertisement in *Great Dane Reporter* magazine. This magazine has a very wide distribution, and people all over the world will see your ad. Include a good picture of both parents and the pedigree. You might also want to include an appealing picture of the puppies themselves. It's hard to resist a great puppy picture. Don't forget to include your phone number and an e-mail address if you have one.

MacIntosh struts his stuff as he proclaims that today, he's the boss of his litter! He is in perfect body condition for a six-week-old puppy and shows early promise of future quality. (Jill Swedlow)

The Internet is a fantastic tool for advertising a litter. I have received many more inquiries than I have puppies, and then I simply refer to other breeders. I've found that the people who see my Web site and then contact me about a puppy are very sincere and extremely interested in obtaining a Great Dane puppy. They've done considerable research and realize how important health and temperament are in this breed. A number of my puppies have gone to live with people who first contacted me via the Internet. All these people have also become good friends and are wonderful homes for my puppies. I am confident there will be more in the future.

Start an interview by frankly telling the prospective purchaser everything that can go wrong with a Great Dane. This includes the short life span, health problems, temperament problems in some lines, food requirements, destructive ability and whatever else you can think of. I always do this, and if the person is still interested, it is at that point that I start asking the questions.

Ask all the questions you were asked by the breeder from whom you purchased your first puppy. Do you have a fenced-in yard? Will he be a house dog? Can you afford an emergency bloat surgery that could cost up to $3,000, and would you have it done if necessary? Will you have a heart attack if the dog eats your couch/trees/shoes/fill in the blank? Are you willing to spend a lot of time properly socializing and training the dog? Do you have a setup so the dog isn't spending most of the day in his crate? Basically put the potential new owner through the same third degree outlined in chapter 4, "Finding the Right Great Dane for You."

If you're selling a puppy to a show home, you should realize that by having one of your best show puppies in a good show home, you're getting the best advertising possible. Nothing upsets me more than having a new owner come to me with a show hopeful that just doesn't make the grade. Once again some unscrupulous breeder has sold an inferior specimen as a show prospect. As long as you're reasonably certain that this is a good show

A family group of Marta Brock's Rolling Thunder Great Danes. The quality and consistency of breed type in all three dogs is both admirable and obvious.

Ask callers for references from other breeders they have purchased from. Even if this is a breeder you've known casually for years, ask questions and request references. Unfortunately, some of my worst homes have been long-time breeders. I've made the mistake of referring people looking for puppies to breeders whom I thought had a good reputation only to find out later that they did no health checks at all! Don't rely on reputation, find out for yourself.

home, you have nothing to lose and everything to gain by placing your superior pups in great show homes.

You can tell a lot about a person's attitude toward dogs by how they interact with them. I'm always wary of those who stand away from the dogs, arms folded over their chests. Much better is someone who gets down on the floor with the litter and lets the puppies crawl all over them. These are the true dog people. You must like the people who buy your puppies. The buyer of a Sunnyside puppy also becomes a member of my extended family. Whether they buy a pet or show puppy, I want close contact with them until the day that puppy dies of old age and beyond. I require them to contact me if they have any questions or problems at any time. My contract also stipulates that if they ever need to place the dog, it either comes back to me or I have final approval of its new home.

"Pick of the Litter" and What Price for a New Friend?

No one can tell you what to charge for your puppies. The fact is, you will not make up all you've put into them. But at the same time, it's nice to recoup some of the expenses as well as give your dogs value in the eyes of their future owners. Prices will vary at various times and areas and will be affected by whether or not a puppy is to be

Breeders take special pride in the breeding achievements of their dogs and get to showcase them in the Stud Dog and Brood Bitch classes at Specialty shows. Here Robert Layne's Ch. Sounda's Marathon Man is joined by his sons Ch. Z Dane Rolling Roc Rambling Man, Ch. Z Dane's Sounda Music and Ch. Salem Runs Harl-E-Quin v. Ard Ri. (Ashbey)

cropped. It is wisest to ask some fellow local breeders about their asking prices and then make up your own mind.

If I know a home to be a great one, I simply place a puppy there and take much less for it. Placement in a good home should always be the most important consideration for any caring breeder. Sometimes a puppy will be placed on a co-ownership basis or for one or two puppies back. These are arrangements you must decide on at the time. Co-ownerships can be tricky, and many friendships have been ruined over these issues. This is one reason a sales contract is imperative. On the rare occasions I have run into problems with co-ownerships, I always opted in favor of the friendship. Losing a friendship isn't worth the decision of which stud to breed to. I consider

every co-owned bitch the sole property of her owner, and the owner always has the final word.

Packing Puppy's Suitcase

Hopefully you have already given the owner-to-be a lot of information about the puppy and the breed. When the time comes for the puppy to go to his new home, an information packet including the following is very helpful:

- **Registration application:** This is the blue slip the new owner will send into the AKC to register the puppy. If you want your kennel name to appear as part of the puppy's name, or you have a certain name you want to give the puppy, you should agree on this prior to giving the owner this document. Some breeders preregister an entire litter so there is no discussion about a name. AKC's position is that the person who registers the dog owner has the right to name the dog.

- **Five-generation pedigree**

- **Written care and feeding instructions:** This is a written regimen you want the new owner to follow in the care of the puppy. See example on the following page.

- **Contract:** Includes a record of all vaccines and wormings the puppy has had and when the next ones are due. My standard sales contract appears in its entirety in chapter 4.

CARE AND FEEDING OF GREAT DANES

Feeding Your Puppy

The Great Dane is classified as a giant breed. Danes reach their ultimate height usually by two years of age but are very close to it at one year. Because of this extremely rapid growth rate, Great Danes are prone to many skeletal problems related to growth. Recent studies show that if the growth rate could be slowed, especially through the two- to eight-month-old period when it is the fastest, such problems as hip dysplasia, wobblers syndrome, *hypertrophic osteodystrophy* (HOD) and related disorders might be preventable.

To slow the growth rate, feed a premium dog food containing 24 percent or less protein. Meat—usually lamb chicken or beef—is the protein source in premium dog foods. It is also wise to be aware of the terms used on dog-food labels. *Whole meal* (chicken, lamb and so on) means that the entire animal is used. *By-product meal* is the least desirable, as it usually means it is composed of those parts deemed unfit for human consumption (beaks, feathers and feet, in the case of chicken—entirely unusable protein sources for dogs). The first product listed on the ingredients label makes up the highest percentage of the food. The methods used in processing, packaging and storing foods are also very important. One preservative to avoid is ethoxyquin, as it has been proven to cause cancer. Avoid artificial colorings and tomato pomace. *Tomato pomace* is the end product (mostly skin) after all the best parts of a tomato are used. This also contains the highest levels of pesticides of almost any dog-food ingredient. For Danes, it's also nice to have a food that contains *probiotics.* These are natural digestive enzymes that may help prevent bloat, one of the common killers of Great Danes.

Do not feed supplements such as calcium, cottage cheese, high-protein meat or any additive that will throw off the balance of the food you're offering. Next to lower protein, a calcium/phosphorus/vitamin D balance is essential. Throw the balance off (already contained in the food), and your puppy is on its way to bone problems. You *can* add canned foods that are also complete and balanced. You can safely add just about anything as long as it constitutes no more than 15 percent of the dry food.

Vitamin C is one supplement that should definitely be given. It is one of the few supplements that is not harmful and is thought to be beneficial to growing dogs. Give 500 milligrams in the morning and evening meals for a total of 1,000 mg per day. Your Dane should eat its food in two smaller daily meals rather than one large one. Clean, fresh water should always be available.

General Care

Great Danes are not suited to being backyard watchdogs who get little or no attention and rarely get into the house. They are happiest and thrive as house dogs that are considered members of the family. Canines are, after all, pack (family) animals. Although they are naturally well behaved, they still need discipline and respect for their human "pack leader" as well as *all* people. To this end I highly recommend that you and your puppy attend obedience classes, and yes, there are classes for very young puppies—they're usually called *puppy socialization classes.*

I also recommend that you purchase a crate for your puppy that he or she can use as an adult. This becomes a puppy's own private den, a place where it can be away from the bustle of the family for some rest. It also protects the house from possible damage while you cannot be present. But the best thing it does is assist with housetraining. A Dane is naturally clean and does not want to mess its bed, and this tendency is your prime aid. After puppies are three months old, most can get through the night with a clean crate. After this plateau, they easily get the idea that outside is the place to go. *Do not* use the crate continually, however. Using the crate as an overnight sleeping space or for a few hours during the day is enough.

Outdoors, provide a large, *fully fenced* yard in which your Dane can safely romp and play. Exercise is important for growing puppies. If you have other dogs (larger than the puppy) and children, make sure that the dogs don't knock the puppy down or hurt it. Instruct your children on how to treat the puppy, and make sure they know that a growing puppy needs many hours of sleep to grow properly. Don't let your kids tease the puppy. Ideally, you should never allow the children and puppy to play unsupervised. Young children don't realize that certain actions will be harmful to the pup. Conversely, the pup might get too rough for the kids, and those little needle-sharp milk teeth can do some damage, even in play.

Be sure that from the start you continue to lead break your pup (most breeders will have already begun this) and take it in the car with you. Visit shopping malls and public places so the puppy will become accustomed to different sights and sounds. Encourage strangers to pet and play with the puppy. Don't allow the puppy access to other dogs until he has had at least his first adult vaccine. The same goes for attending puppy matches or shows.

Ear Care—The Cropping Issue

If you purchased your puppy from a reputable breeder, the ears were probably cropped before you took delivery. Most show breeders crop their puppies prior to allowing them to go to their new homes. One reason for this is that the breeder has control of who does the crop. A vet who is not experienced with the proper procedures for ear cropping can really mess things up. The puppies he operates on suffer traumatically and aesthetically! Better uncropped ears than ears cut too short or done improperly. An experienced veterinarian is the key here.

If you do have a pup that is or will be cropped, the actual surgery is not the end of the procedure. For ears to stand properly, they must undergo many tapings, sometimes up until the dog is past a year old, but most ears are up by five to six months, sometimes sooner. If you're inexperienced at aftercare, usually the vet who did the original crop can do the taping for you. If not, contact other Great Dane breeders you have met through your activities within the breed.

If you decide to leave the ears natural, there are two problems you might have to face. Uncropped ears are prone to hematomas. These occur when the head is shaken vigorously and the tips of the ears snap. This action of an ear tip snapping back on itself can break the blood vessels within the ear leather, which then bleed and become painfully swollen. The hematoma often must be lanced by your vet, and then the ears are usually taped up on top and across the head until the ear tips have healed. This can take some time. The other problem is that a drop ear is more prone to ear infections. Remember that a drop-eared dog does not occur in nature. Man has created the drop ear, and the crop is his way of correcting the mistake.

Life-Threatening Emergencies: A Word About Bloat and *Hypertrophic Osteodystrophy* (HOD)

HOD is a condition that affects young, rapidly growing dogs usually between three-and-a-half and eight months of age. The symptoms are a very high fever, swelling and inflammation of the joints (usually pasterns) and tremendous pain. Even a lethargic puppy with a slightly elevated fever should be checked by a vet. If caught early enough, this disease will probably subside quickly.

Unfortunately, many vets don't recognize the disease, and the puppy is neither diagnosed nor treated correctly. Immediate diagnosis is made by x-ray. The treatment consists of injectable vitamin C, steroids to combat joint inflammation, Banamine to combat pain (the injectable form is preferred) and antibiotics to combat any secondary infections (pneumonia is the most common) that might take hold when an animal is badly stressed.

Bloat usually occurs in dogs over one year of age but is not unheard of in younger dogs. The symptoms are attempts to vomit that produce only foam. The stomach and/or rib cage appears distended and continues to enlarge. The dog is in obvious distress and is usually panting and restless. *Time is of the essence!* The stomach fills with gasses and begins to rotate. This means that gas cannot leave the stomach and enlargement continues. As the stomach rotates, the blood supplies are cut off and the animal begins to go into shock. The vet will usually try to pass a stomach tube to ascertain if the stomach has already turned and to relieve the gas pressure if it hasn't. (Occasionally a tube can pass into a rotated stomach.) An x-ray will confirm rotation. The only permanent cure is surgery, and the dog must be stabilized before the surgery can be performed. Even then, it is not uncommon for a dog to die of heart complications after a successful surgery.

These are extreme emergency situations, especially bloat. Don't waste any time getting veterinary help. If your veterinarian is not familiar with the special health needs of Great Danes, ask for a referral to a veterinarian who is experienced from the breeder of your dog or your local Great Dane Specialty club.

GRADING YOUR LITTER

Deciding which puppies are show quality and which you'll allow to be placed as pets is your next hurdle. If you've bred many litters and studied the outcomes, you should have a fair idea of what to expect as each puppy matures. As mentioned elsewhere in this book, by the time the litter is six or seven weeks old, there are going to be some standouts, and you'll have begun to rank the puppies in order of merit.

Even the person with a natural "eye for a dog" must gather experience in order to grade a litter.

Notwithstanding, nothing is foolproof; the sensational toddler can grow into a bona fide pet. By the same token, puppies go through stages and some of those stages can be strange looking. Many litters over many years give the veteran breeder an advantage in predicting how a Great Dane puppy will grow. Even then, grading puppies remains the breeder's best-educated guess.

Promising anyone a "pick" puppy is almost always unwise. It is far preferable to match the puppy with its new home in both quality (show versus pet) and personality, as mentioned elsewhere in this book.

© Marta Brock

CHAPTER 13

Caring for the Older Great Dane

Unfortunately, many owners of Great Danes never get to experience life with an aging dog. Those of us lucky enough to have our sweet ones into old age need to keep some hard truths about aging dogs in mind.

Before going further, I must tell you that in order to write this chapter, I have had to lean heavily on my experiences with my own Danes. My experiences will be just like those of so many who have had their lives enriched by these wonderful dogs. With that understanding, please read on.

My oldest Dane to date, Kiwi, made it to a healthy, happy twelve years, and she taught me a lot about our seniors. I can only discuss bitches, as I've not yet owned a male with urinary incontinence and I've never owned a male beyond five years of age. I do know that sometimes older Danes have urinary tract problems. I think this mainly involves the sphincter muscle that controls the urethra. Bitches will dribble urine during the day, urinate in their sleep, or both. A very simple solution is to, after veterinary examination, put them on the hormone *diethylstilbestrol* (DES). Once they start the course, they can usually return to normal control within a week or two. Obviously, your vet should also rule out urinary tract infections or any other causes.

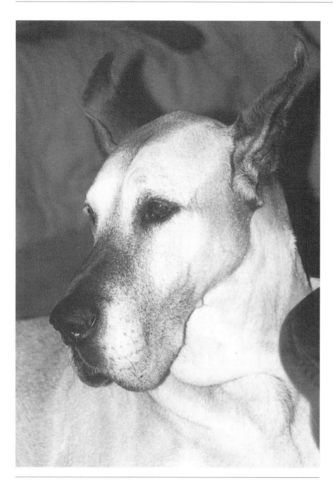

Sunnyside Jonquilla at age nine. At this writing, she's a happy ten-and-a-half and going strong! Hopefully, she will outlive her mother Kiwi. (Jill Swedlow)

Another problem with the sweet oldies is the problem of bowel incontinence. They'll be sleeping or simply ambling along, and several pieces of well-digested dinner will appear with no warning. Luckily, in my experience, this unwanted matter is usually very hard and well formed, thus making cleanup easy. Frankly, when this happens, I feel sorrier for the old ones than I feel personally inconvenienced, as they always seem so embarrassed! My vet tells me that they do this because they lose the feeling that signals them to attend to their needs.

Arthritic changes that cause a physical slowing down are almost always a part of aging. Several of my Danes have formed spinal bone spurs that grow downward from the spine and then fuse the vertebrae together. During the period when these spurs are forming, the spine is extremely painful. Narcissus would yell if she even *thought* my hand was about to touch her back during these times. Once the vertebrae have fused, the pain ceases. The back section of Kiwi's entire spine was fused so that she had no lateral flexion. She had to turn like a battleship. To help them through these painful times, I've used several different remedies (always with a vet's advice). I used MSM with some wonderful results, but that seems to stop working after awhile.

Cosequin™ and Adequan™ were almost like a miracle cure for arthritic problems in the beginning. They help lubricate the joints and areas of cartilage. I think that the injectable Adequan helped the most. However, in my experience, its effectiveness diminished after several months of use.

More recently, a product called Rimadyl™ has come on the market. Its base drug is carprophen. This is a replacement for aspirin for dogs with none of aspirin's side effects. There are some contraindications, but it works like a miracle! I had

Like Danes of all ages, the seniors love their comfort. This photo leaves no doubt that the author's Poppy is queen of the couch.

pretty much decided that it was time to euthanize Narcissus. My vet suggested trying Rimadyl, and it was literally the difference between life and death.

As Danes age, they are more likely to contract a number of serious diseases. Heart disease, cancer and bloat are just a few of the maladies that may affect them. You must be constantly vigilant for warning symptoms.

Bone cancer is common in older Danes. Two of mine have suffered through it. The first, Amber, was affected at the top of her femur. The period from the time of diagnosis to her death was about five months. She was nine years old when diagnosed, and I decided that putting her through the treatments to give her two or three extra months was not in her best interest or mine.

When Pepita was diagnosed with bone cancer, I decided against treatment for the same reasons I had with Amber. She was ten years old, and I was told that it wasn't unusual for spontaneous breakage of the affected bone to occur. She might arise one day and the bone would just snap. Because of this fear, my vet gave me an injectable analgesic to give to her if this should happen. It gave me peace of mind to know that she wouldn't have to suffer if her bone did break. And it gave her extra time that she would not have had if I'd opted to euthanize her immediately.

Poppy, however, has been a different story. Poppy was recently diagnosed with lymphosarcoma—cancer of the lymph glands. One day I noticed that the lymph nodes under her jaw, under her neck and at the backs of her thighs were huge. I immediately took her to the vet, who did a biopsy. I got the results the following Monday, called the clinic where she would go for treatment and was on my way within minutes. Lymphosarcoma is one cancer that reacts well to treatment. Poppy is six years old, so for my Danes, this is young. I wasn't about to just give up on her. I was also told that dogs, unlike people, do not react adversely to chemotherapy. This has been borne out so far in Poppy's treatments. At this writing, Poppy has had ten chemotherapy treatments and was in remission after the first treatment. Veterinarians I have worked with tell me that it isn't unrealistic to hope to add two good quality

Even at eleven years old, Pepita still loved to play and was wonderful with the puppies. Here she's having fun planning to relieve baby Skylark of her toy.

years to her life. From what I'm seeing already, I'd do it again in a heartbeat! Remember that just because your dog is diagnosed with cancer doesn't mean you will lose him or her soon. Learn to take one day at a time and treasure every moment you have together. Having some time to accept that you're going to lose your old one and having that time to say good-bye is truly a gift.

Old age doesn't have to be depressing. When Daffodil and her sister Amber turned eight, I decided to celebrate with a birthday party. This has become a tradition that continues to this day. The last birthday party was for Narcissus and Jonquilla when they turned nine.

Often it's the older ones who make the best baby-sitters for puppies. Amber was a very good grandma, as was Poppy. Because of the pain from her arthritic joints, Narcissus would yell at the puppies if they got too close to her.

Keep up with the oral hygiene of your old dogs. Tartar buildup can lead to all kinds of unpleasant consequences. My Danes let me scale their teeth when needed, but then I don't give them a choice! The *best* remedy I've ever seen for filthy teeth is the Nylabone™ Hercules Dental Device. I've seen this item almost completely clean up the most disgusting mouths. Only a little tartar is left to deal with, and the dogs *love* them.

Also, older dogs seem to need a bit more pampering at mealtimes. Be sure to give an aging Dane very high-quality foods without allowing it to become fat. However, I've always kept my older ladies a little heavier than perhaps I should, because if something *does* go wrong and they quit eating, they'll have a bit of a reserve on them.

Keep an old Dane's nails short so that walking is not painful. Check the mouth for any growths. One of my old ones, Pepita (who lived to age eleven when I had to put her down due to osteosarcoma), began to occasionally gag. I'd look in her mouth but couldn't see anything. I had decided that her cancer had just moved into her lungs, so I didn't pursue it. But on the morning she stopped eating, it was time to put her down.

The greatest disadvantage of living with a Great Dane is the breed's normally short life expectancy. Owners find that the richness Danes contribute to the lives they touch partially makes up for the void left by their early passing. Common sense and good precaution by the owner will make for greater quality of life for the older Great Dane. (Nanette Schlegel)

A postmortem examination revealed a large tumor in her throat. I really felt bad that I hadn't been more thorough. However, she'd really acted normally until her last morning.

Here's the birthday cake I designed for Daffi and Amber's eighth birthday party. (Carol Tucker)

All this brings up the most difficult subject—letting them go when it's time. I used to pray (and still do) that I could find my old ladies dead in the morning, having passed on quietly in their sleep. It hurts *so much* to have to make these decisions and then carry them out. But our dogs deserve this from us, and what I've learned to do is let the dogs tell me when it's time. If you're observant, you'll recognize the signs. The pain will become too great, a glutton will quit eating, there will be a *look* in her eye… if you know your dog well, the signs become unmistakable. Of course, I always hold them in my arms as they leave their sore, old bodies. They were born into my hands because I

Sometimes the old girls are the best baby-sitters. Here Amber indulges an obnoxious puppy.

willed them to be conceived; how could I deny them their final grace?

Through your veterinarian, you can arrange with a pet cemetery or crematorium to have remains buried, cremated and buried or cremated and returned to you. I always have mine cremated, and then I bury the ashes in the planting hole with a memorial tree. If you bury a dog on your own property, be sure you are in compliance with local health laws. Kiwi, who loved to stand with her head buried in plants, or with trees softly touching her back, is under a weeping willow. Narcissus' ashes are under a bed of paper white Narcissus. Amber is at the base of a Liquid Amber tree, Garfield has a Pussy Willow, and so on. For me these little rituals really help to heal the raw emotions brought about by the loss of a well-loved canine friend.

Because it's appropriate to this subject, I have included this lovely tribute by the celebrated writer Eugene O'Neill to his Dalmatian. I hope you will find it as comforting as I did.

THE LAST WILL AND TESTAMENT OF AN EXTREMELY DISTINGUISHED DOG

BY EUGENE O'NEILL
TAO HOUSE, DECEMBER 17, 1940

I, SILVERDENE EMBLEM O'NEILL (familiarly known to my family, friends, and acquaintances as Blemie), because the burden of my years and infirmities is heavy upon me, and I realize the end of my life is near, do hereby bury my last will and testament in the mind of my Master. He will not know it is there until after I am dead. Then, remembering me in his loneliness, he will suddenly know of this testament, and I ask him then to inscribe it as a memorial to me.

I have little in the way of material things to leave. Dogs are wiser than men. They do not set great store upon things. They do not

waste their days hoarding property. They do not ruin their sleep worrying about how to keep the objects they have, and to obtain the objects they have not. There is nothing of value I have to bequeath except my love and my faith. These I leave to all those who have loved me, to my Master and Mistress, who I know will mourn me most, to Freeman who has been so good to me, to Cyn and Roy and Willie and Naomi and—But if I should list all those who have loved me, it would force my Master to write a book. Perhaps it is vain of me to boast when I am so near death, which returns all beasts and vanities to dust, but I have always been an extremely lovable dog.

I ask my Master and Mistress to remember me always, but not to grieve for me too long. In my life I have tried to be a comfort to them in time of sorrow, and a reason for added joy in their happiness. It is painful for me to think that even in death I should cause them pain. Let them remember that while no dog has ever had a happier life (and this I owe to their love and care for me), now that I have grown blind and deaf and lame, and even my sense of smell fails me so that a rabbit could be right under my nose and I might not know, my pride has sunk to a sick, bewildered humiliation. I feel life is taunting me with having over-lingered my welcome. It is time I said good-bye, before I become too sick, a burden on myself and on those who love me. It will be sorrow to leave them, but not a sorrow to die.

Dogs do not fear death as men do. We accept it as part of life, not as something alien and terrible which destroys life. What may come after death, who knows? I would like to believe with those my fellow Dalmatians who are devout Mohammedans, that there is a Paradise where one is always young and full-bladdered; where all the day one dillies and dallies with an amorous multitude of houris [lovely nymphs], beautifully spotted; where jack rabbits that run fast but not too fast (like the houris) are as the sands of the desert; where each blissful hour is mealtime; where in long evenings there are a million fireplaces with logs forever burning, and one curls oneself up and blinks into the flames and nods and dreams, remembering the old brave days on earth, and the love of one's Master and Mistress.

I am afraid this is too much for even such a dog as I am to expect. But peace, at least, is certain. Peace and long rest for weary old heart and head and limbs, and eternal sleep in the earth I have loved so well. Perhaps, after all, this is best.

One last request I earnestly make. I have heard my Mistress say, "When Blemie dies we must never have another dog. I love him so much I could never love another one." Now I would ask her, for love of me, to have another. It would be a poor tribute to my memory never to have a dog again. What I would like to feel is that, having once had me in the family, now she cannot live without a dog! I have never had a narrow jealous

continued

THE LAST WILL AND TESTAMENT OF AN
EXTREMELY DISTINGUISHED DOG

spirit. I have always held that most dogs are good (and one cat, the black one I have permitted to share the living room rug during the evenings, whose affection I have tolerated in a kindly spirit, and in rare sentimental moods, even reciprocated a trifle). Some dogs, of course, are better than others. Dalmatians, naturally, as everyone knows, are best. So I suggest a Dalmatian as my successor. He can hardly be as well bred or as well mannered or as distinguished and handsome as I was in my prime. My Master and Mistress must not ask the impossible. But he will do his best, I am sure, and even his inevitable defects will help by comparison to keep my memory green. To him I bequeath my collar and leash and my overcoat and raincoat, made to order in 1929 at Hermès in Paris. He can never wear them with the distinction I did, walking around the Place Vendome,

or later along Park Avenue, all eyes fixed on me in admiration; but again I am sure he will do his utmost not to appear a mere gauche provincial dog. Here on the ranch, he may prove himself quite worthy of comparison, in some respects. He will, I presume, come closer to jack rabbits than I have been able to in recent years. And for all his faults, I hereby wish him the happiness I know will be his in my old home.

One last word of farewell, Dear Master and Mistress. Whenever you visit my grave, say to yourselves with regret but also with happiness in your hearts at the remembrance of my long happy life with you: "Here lies one who loved us and whom we loved." No matter how deep my sleep I shall hear you, and not all the power of death can keep my spirit from wagging a grateful tail.

Epilog

I hope that you have gained an idea of what it's like to have Great Danes in your life.

Perhaps you have learned something that has enabled you to more accurately evaluate the quality of your Danes. Perhaps I've saved you from making an inadvisable breeding or helped you to locate a stud dog that will be a good cross with your bitch. Maybe you've decided not to breed at all, based on the advice in this book. That, too, is a valuable lesson.

It could be that you recognized the symptoms of bloat in time to save the life of your beloved dog. Or maybe by health testing your bitch, you realized that she should not be bred.

It is possible that you've become involved with showing your Dane and having done so, made many new and close friends who will last throughout your lifetime. Maybe, someday, you will be among the most reputable, concerned breeders of Great Danes and, in your turn, will write your own book full of helpful advice.

Should this be so, then this book has accomplished what I intended.

—JILL SWEDLOW

Resources List

American Kennel Club (AKC)

5580 Centerview Drive

Suite 200

Raleigh, NC 27606-3390

Phone: 919-233-9767

Web site: http://www.akc.org

Great Dane Club of America (GDCA)

Linda Tonnancour, President (1998)

16622 Sanlo Street

Yorba Linda, CA 92886

Phone: 714-961-0590

E-mail: toncorrl@inreach.com

Web site: http://www.users.cts.com/king/g/gdca/

GREAT DANE WEB SITES

Great Dane Foundation (rescue)

Cathy Mitchell

Rescue Coordinator

3919 Westmeadow Drive

Houston, Texas 77082

281-496-5130

E-mail: CathyGDBCS@juno.com

Web site: http://www.geocities.com/

Heartland/Meadows/2235/

Mintie Keltz-Pickel

Education Coordinator

3218 Meadway Drive

Houston, Texas 77082

281-497-2360

MintieGDF@juno.com

The Great Dane Home Page
Web site: http://www.ualberta.ca/~dc8/ dane.htm

The Great Dane Reporter (magazine)
P.O. Box 150
Riverside, CA 92502-0150
Phone: 909-784-5437 (909-784-4GDR)
Fax: 909-369-7056
E-mail: gdr@pe.net
Web site: http://www.gdr.com/

Great Dane Rescue, Inc.
Sandy Suarez Boutin
P.O. Box 5543
Plymouth, Michigan 48170
Phone: 734-454-3683
E-mail: danelair@ismi.net
Web site: http://www.ddc.com/rescue/dane/

**Sunnyside Farm Great Danes &
Miniature Horses**
(Jill Swedlow)
E-mail: sunyside@pe.net
Web site:
http://www.pe.net/~sunyside/index.html

Besides these sites, there are numerous private party sites online. You can access many of these from my Link page on my Web site, which appears on the above list.

HEALTH REGISTRIES AND WEB SITES

Canine Eye Registration Foundation (CERF)
Veterinary Medical Data Program
South Campus Courts, Building C
Purdue University
W. Lafayette, IN 47907
Phone: 317-494-8179
Fax: 317-494-9981
Web site:
http://www.breeders.com/chn/cerf/index.htm

**Canine Genetics and Dog Health
Home Page**
Web site:
http://www.teleport.com/~gback/cghp.html

**Institute for Genetic Disease Control
in Animals**
Web site:
http://mendel.berkeley.edu/dogs/gdc.html

Natura Pet Products (Innova Dog Food)
E-mail: natura@naturapet.com
Web site: http://www.naturapet.com/

NetVet Veterinary Resources
Web site: http://netvet.wustl.edu/vet.htm

Orthopedic Foundation for Animals
2300 E. Nifong Boulevard
Columbia, MO 65201-3856
Phone: 573-442-0418
Fax: 573-875-5073
Web site:
http://www.prodogs.com/chn/ofa/index.htm

Virtual Veterinary Center
E-mail: jmartindale@vmsa.oac.uci.edu
Web site:
http://www-sci.lib.uci.edu/HSG/Vet.html

PERFORMANCE INFORMATION AND WEB SITES

North American Dog Agility Council (NADAC)
HCR 2, Box 277
St. Maries, ID 83861

South Coast Agility Team (SCAT) Home Page
Web site: http://home.earthlink.net/~playk9/

Therapy Dogs International
6 Hilltop Road
Mendham, NJ 07945

Trans-National Dog Agility
410 Bluemont Circle
Manhattan, KS 66502

U.S. Dog Agility Association
P.O. Box 850955
Richardson, TX 75085-0955

Breeders Code of Ethics of the Great Dane Club of America

This Code is established in accordance with the objectives of the GDCA to protect and advance the interests of Great Danes, and to provide guidelines for responsible ownership and ethical breeding practices.

ALL MEMBERS SHALL:

- Maintain the best possible standards of health, cleanliness, safety, and care of their dogs.

- Take all appropriate measures to assist a Dane in distress.

- Display good sportsmanship and conduct, whether at home, at shows, or in hotels, in such a manner as to reflect credit upon themselves and the GDCA.

- Not alter the appearance, physical structure, condition, or natural temperament of a dog by any means other than allowed for in the Official Breed Standard if the dog is to be exhibited.

- Bear the responsibility for the truth and accuracy of any information and/or photographs submitted for publication.

ALL BREEDERS AND OWNERS OF GREAT DANES (BITCHES AND STUD DOGS ALIKE) SHALL:

1. Breed Great Danes which are temperamentally and structurally sound.

2. Be familiar with the Breed Standard and breed only those dogs and bitches which most closely conform to it.

3. Keep well informed in the field of genetics and work to eliminate hereditary defects from the breed.

4. Refrain from further use of a Great Dane for breeding if the dog or bitch has produced any offspring with serious inherited defects detrimental to an animal's well being (physically or mentally), and has produced like results with a different mating partner.

5. Not breed to an unregistered Great Dane.

6. Not wholesale litters of Great Danes, sell to Brokers or Pet Shops, provide any animal for prize or raffle purposes, nor use a Stud Dog in like manner.

7. Keep all puppies with the litter until at least 7 or 8 weeks of age.

8. Adhere to State and local laws regarding the sale of puppies.

9. Sell dogs in good condition, health, and sound temperament at time of delivery. They shall be free of internal parasites to the best knowledge of the seller; will have received the necessary inoculations to date; a record of dates and types of immunizations will be given; and a health certificate provided if required. Written instructions on the feeding, health care, training, and any other information necessary for the dog's well being (e.g., ear crop care), will be made available after the sale to assist the new owner.

10. Provide a four- or more generation color-marked pedigree and the AKC registration at the time of sale of each dog. Any dog sold as a pet and not for breeding should be given a limited registration or a written contract specifying conditions of sale (e.g., spay/neuter agreement, show or pet quality, co-ownership, breeding rights, etc.).

11. Provide the buyer with copies of all pre-screenings done on both parents to assure the buyer that every possible effort has been made to produce puppies free of hereditary problems.

12. Sell or place each Great Dane with the contemplated final owner; therefore the seller should ascertain that the prospective buyer has the knowledge and facilities to properly care for a growing or grown dog. As a condition of sale or placement, the breeder shall retain the right of first refusal should the purchaser ever decide to transfer ownership or resell the dog, therefore giving the seller every opportunity to help

the purchaser find a new home for the dog if necessary.

13. All dogs sold (puppy or adult) shall have a signed agreement between the seller and purchaser that the animal shall be examined by a Veterinarian of the purchaser's choice (and paid for by that party) within 72 hours of purchase or delivery. If the dog is deemed unhealthy or possessing an inherited defect which would impair the use for which it was purchased (pet, show, or breeding program), the seller will refund the full purchase price upon the return of the dog with a Veterinarian-certified documentation of the condition. The dog will be returned at the purchaser's expense.

14. Use only the agreed-upon Stud Dog at a breeding in the absence of the owner of the Bitch.

15. Provide and honor all contracts regarding sales, co-ownerships, breeding rights, agreements, compensation for future puppies, leasing a bitch, stud service, etc.

IT IS STRONGLY RECOMMENDED THAT:

1. All dogs and bitches to be bred be x-rayed prior to breeding and declared free of hip dysplasia by a knowledgeable Veterinarian or the OFA. It is also encouraged that any and all technology available be used to screen all animals to be used for breeding, according to known problems within the breed (e.g., cardiac check, thyroid check, VWD, PRA, etc.).

2. A written Stud Contract be used which specifies all conditions of the breeding, and a color-marked pedigree be provided by both parties.

3. A stud dog should be a year or more of age before breeding, and a bitch not less than 18 months.

4. A bitch not be bred more than once a year.

5. Both parties provide Veterinarian reports certifying that each animal is clear of any transmittable infections.

6. With the agreement of both the seller and the purchaser, any puppy sold as a show prospect which subsequently develops a disqualifying defect shall be:

   (a.) replaced by the breeder with another show prospect puppy and the dog returned to the seller, OR

   (b.) the money refunded and the dog returned to the seller, OR

   (c.) the buyer's money refunded to the extent of the difference between the price paid and the price of the pet puppies sold from the same or similar litters if the buyer retains and spays or neuters the dog.

7. Breeders adhere to the GDCA Breeders Color Code.

Code of Ethics Committee

Co-Chairpeople: Clare Lincoln and Margaret Shappard
Members: Karla Callahan, Anita Dunne, Col. Harry Hutchinson, Marilyn Riggins, Teri Welti

BREEDERS' COLOR CODE

as endorsed by The Great Dane Club of America

There are only five[1] recognized colors; all these basically fall into four color strains:

1. FAWN and BRINDLE

2. HARLEQUIN and HARLEQUIN BRED BLACK

3. BLUE and BLUE BRED BLACK

4. BLACK

Color Classifications being well founded, the Great Dane Club of America, Inc. considers it an inadvisable practice to mix color strains and it is the club's policy to adhere only to the following breedings:

COLOR OF DANE	APPROVED BREEDINGS	DESIRED PEDIGREES
1. FAWN	1. FAWN bred to FAWN or BRINDLE only.	Pedigrees of FAWN or BRINDLE Danes should not carry BLACK, HARLEQUIN or BLUE upon them.
1. BRINDLE	1. BRINDLE bred to BRINDLE or FAWN only.	
2. HARLEQUIN	2. HARLEQUIN bred to HARLEQUIN, BLACK from HARLEQUIN BREEDING or BLACK from BLACK BREEDING only.	
2. BLACK (HARLEQUIN BRED)	2. BLACK from HARLEQUIN BREEDING bred to HARLEQUIN, BLACK from HARLEQUIN BREEDING or BLACK from BLACK BREEDING only.	Pedigrees of HARLEQUIN or HARLEQUIN BRED BLACK Danes should not carry FAWN, BRINDLE or BLUE upon them.

[1] *By the time this book is published, there may well be a sixth color, Mantle, which is a pattern found in the Harlequin color strain.*

COLOR OF DANE	APPROVED BREEDINGS	DESIRED PEDIGREES
3. BLUE	3. BLUE bred to BLUE, BLACK from BLUE BREEDING or BLACK from BLACK BREEDING only.	
3. BLACK (BLUE BRED)	3. BLACK from BLUE BREEDING bred to BLUE, BLACK from BLUE BREEDING or BLACK from BLACK BREEDING ONLY.	Pedigrees of BLUE or BLUE BRED BLACK Danes should not carry FAWN, BRINDLE, or HARLEQUIN upon them.
4. BLACK (BLACK BRED)	4. BLACK from BLACK BREEDING bred to BLACK, BLUE or HARLEQUIN only. *(See note below)*	Pedigrees of BLACK BRED Danes should not carry FAWN, BRINDLE, HARLEQUIN or BLUE upon them.

NOTE: Black-bred Great Danes may be bred to Blacks, Blues or Harlequins only. Puppies resulting from these breedings will become Blacks or Harlequins from Harlequin breeding (category 2 above). Blacks or Blues from Blue breeding (category 3 above) or Blacks from Black breeding (category 4 above).

IT SHALL BE THE GOAL OF ALL TO BREED FORWARD, NEVER BACKWARDS, TO ATTAIN PEDIGREES OF PUPPIES WHICH HAVE THE DESIRED COLOR STRAINS ENDORSED BY THE GREAT DANE CLUB OF AMERICA.

Bibliography

The Great Dane Reporter Magazine
  P.O. Box 150
  Riverside, CA 92502-0150
  909/784-5437
  FAX: 909/369-7056
  Email: GDR@pe.net
  Web site: http://www.pe.net/~gdr/index.html

The New Owner's Guide to the Great Dane,
  by Jill Swedlow
  T.F.H. Publications
  One, TFH Plaza
  Neptune City, NJ 07753

*The Great Dane: An Owner's Guide
  to a Happy, Healthy Pet,*
  by Jill Swedlow
  Howell Book House
  Macmillan Publishing
  1633 Broadway
  New York, NY 10019-6785

The Basic Guide to the Great Dane
  Various Breeders
  P.O. Box 91
  Dace Publishing, Ruckersville, VA 22968
  1997

Great Danes Today by Di Johnson
Howell Book House, NY, NY 1994

The Great Dane: Dogdom's Apollo,
by Nancy Carroll-Draper
Howell Book House, NY, NY 1981

AKC Video series on the Great Dane Standard
American Kennel Club
5580 Centerview Dr., Ste 200
Raleigh, NC 27606

This Is the Great Dane, by Ernest H. Hart
T.F.H. Publications

The New Complete Great Dane, by Noted
Authorities
Howell Book House, NY, NY 1972

Great Danes, by Jean Lanning
John Gifford, Ltd., London, 1966

The Great Dane, by Anna Katherine Nicholas
T.F.H. Publications, Neptune City, NJ 1988

The Great Dane, by Jean Lanning
Arco Publishing, NY, NY 1962

The AKC Gazette
5580 Centerview Dr.
Raleigh, NC 27606–3390
919/233-9767
Web site: http://www.akc.org

Dog Fancy Magazine
P.O. Box 6050
Mission Viejo, CA 92690

Dog World Magazine
29 N. Wacker Dr.
Chicago, IL 60606

NUTRITION
INFORMATION

*Dr. Pitcairn's Complete Guide to Natural Health for
Dogs & Cats,* by Pitcairn and Pitcairn
Published by Rodale Press

The Holistic Guide for a Health Dog,
by Volhard & Brown
Published by Howell Book House

The Collins Guide to Dog Nutrition,
by Donald R. Collins, DVM
Published by Howell Book House

Index

A

B

C

I

T